Signs of the Times

Signs of the Times

Religious Pluralism and Economic Injustice

GREGORY BAUM

NOVALIS

© 2007 Novalis, Saint Paul University, Ottawa, Canada

Cover and layout: Pascale Turmel
Cover image: © Jupiter Images

Business Offices:

Novalis Publishing Inc.
10 Lower Spadina Avenue, Suite 400
Toronto, Ontario, Canada
M5V 2Z2

Novalis Publishing Inc.
4475 Frontenac Street
Montréal, Québec, Canada
H2H 2S2

Phone: 1-800-387-7164
Fax: 1-800-204-4140
E-mail: books@novalis.ca
www.novalis.ca

Library and Archives Canada Cataloguing in Publication

Baum, Gregory
    Signs of the times : religious pluralism and economic injustice / Gregory Baum.

Includes bibliographical references.
ISBN 978-2-89507-907-1

    1. Religious pluralism–Catholic Church. 2. Religious pluralism–Christianity. 3. Economics–Religious aspects–Catholic Church. 4. Economics–Religious aspects–Christianity. 5. Distributive justice–Religious aspects–Catholic Church. 6. Distributive justice–Religious aspects–Christianity. I. Title.

HN31.B39 2007   261.2   C2007-903209-5

Printed in Canada.

We acknowledge the financial support of the Government of Canada through the Book Publishing Industry Development Program (BPIDP) for our publishing activities.

5   4   3   2   1   11   10   09   08   07

Contents

Introduction

A key concept in the documents of Vatican Council II is the discernment of the signs of the times.[1] In the New Testament, the signs of the times have eschatological significance: they refer to occurrences that indicate that the end of history is near (Matthew 16:1-3). The contemporary meaning of the signs of the times is different: it refers to historical events or developments that have a profound impact on human life in society, and thus oblige Christians to interpret the meaning of these events in the light of the Gospel. Historical circumstances are called signs of the times when they challenge the inherited self-understanding of Christians and oblige them to rethink the implications of their faith. Pope John XXIII referred several times to recent historical events that question the Church's received teaching and call for a creative response in fidelity to the Word of God. Because the signs of the times challenge traditional teaching, the Church is tempted to overlook them and continue its teaching as if these events had not taken place. The appeal to the signs of the time made by John XXIII and Vatican Council II was therefore a truly prophetic gesture. Catholics continue to marvel at this boldness.

For John XXIII, the Universal Declaration of Human Rights promulgated by the United Nations in 1948 was a sign of the times. Catholic teaching, in response to the French Revolution and the creation of the liberal state, had repudiated civil liberties, including religious liberty. The popes were afraid that the emphasis on personal freedoms would undermine the truths and values on which society was based, and which assured its cohesion and its moral well-being. The Universal Declaration of Human Rights made John XXIII rethink the Church's traditional teaching. He himself had been deeply moved by the horrors committed during World War II. He was grateful that in response to the widespread contempt for human life and human dignity displayed during that conflict, the United Nations produced a charter, signed by the nations of the world, proclaiming the dignity of human beings and their right to have their freedoms protected by governments. Moved by this sign of the times, John XXIII reread the Scriptures for guidance. He was impressed by two biblical themes in particular: the creation of humans in the image of God, and the redemptive work of Christ that summons every person to become a friend of God.[2] These biblical themes, he argued, reveal the high dignity of the human person, which is the theological foundation of their human rights. By reflecting on a recent historical development in the light of divine revelation, John XXIII changed the Church's official teaching of an earlier period and proclaimed the human rights of men and women as part of the Good News. His teaching was confirmed by Vatican Council II.

A dark sign of the times that provoked serious reflection at Vatican Council II was the Holocaust. Challenged by this sign, Pope John XXIII wanted the Council to redefine the Church's relationship to the Jews. Reflecting on the Holocaust in the light of the Gospel, the Council acknowledged with deep regret that the Church's anti-Jewish religious discourse had created a culture hostile to Jews that produced little resistance to the spread of modern racially based anti-Semitism. Rereading the Scriptures, the Council found in St. Paul's Letter to the Romans the assurance that God has not rejected his first-loved people, despite its refusal to believe in Jesus: the Jewish people remain "most dear to God because of their forefathers, since the gifts and the call of God are irrevocable" (Romans 11:28-29). Interpreting the Scriptures in response to the signs of the times allowed the Church to change its religious discourse, recognize God's blessing on the Synagogue, and foster dialogue and co-operation with the Jewish people.

Reading the signs of the times initiates the Church into a contextual theology, a theology that takes its historical location seriously and responds to the challenges addressed to it. At Vatican Council II, the Catholic Church was seriously challenged by the pluralism of religion. When the Council decided to publish a statement on the Church's relation to Judaism, the bishops of Africa and Asia asked that the Council also define the Church's relationship to the religions on their continent. In the past the Church's overseas mission had often supported the colonizing powers and trained the Christian converts to respect the governing authority of the colonizers. The bishops in these lands now asked themselves how to define the Church's mission after the collapse of colonialism. The new historical context demanded new theological reflection. While Jesus is the only mediator between God and humans, Jesus is also the prince of peace and the great reconciler in whom the walls that divide humanity into hostile camps are overcome. God's Word, incarnate in Jesus, resounds in the whole of history, summoning people to pursue the truth and practise love, justice and peace. In the declaration *Nostra aetate*, the Council recognizes the echo of God's Word in the world religions and asks Catholics to engage in dialogue and co-operation with the followers of these religions to promote peace and justice on this deeply divided globe.

In his encyclical *Pacem in terris*, John XXIII mentions three signs of the times that deserve the Church's attention and call for a creative response. First, there is the labour movement. Workers all over the world want to be treated as responsible agents in industry and in society in general (40). The Church must listen to this quest for co-responsibility. Second, there is the women's movement. "Since women are becoming ever more conscious of their human dignity, they will not tolerate being treated as mere material instruments, but demand rights befitting a human person, both in domestic and public life"(41). The Church must respond to this development. Third, there is the anti-colonial movement. "Since all nations have either achieved or are on the way to achieving independence, there will soon no longer exist a world divided into nations that rule others and nations that are subject to others" (42). While John XXIII was critical of many aspects of modernity, he admired the modern struggles of human emancipation and believed that the Church had to search for their theological significance. The teaching of John Paul II moved in the same direction. He regarded the ecological crisis as a sign of the time that demanded new thinking on the part of the Church.[3] (In the essay in Chapter 7 of this book I contrast the admiration of John Paul II for the emancipatory thrust of modernity with the attitude of Benedict XVI, who sees in modernity only the turn to ethical relativism and the indifference to divine transcendence.)

Some of the problems that challenged the Church at Vatican Council II have, forty years later, become more intense. The essays collected in this book deal in various ways with two of signs of the times – religious pluralism and economic injustice. These challenges demand new theological reflection and summon the Church to respond to them in fidelity to the Gospel.

Tension is growing among the world religions. Political and economic developments have produced increasing inequality of wealth and power in the world, generating conflicts among peoples of various religions and encouraging fundamentalist trends in all of them. Some political leaders are using religious discourse to enhance their power and legitimate aggression. In addition, increasing poverty and authoritarian rule in Asia, Africa and Latin America are producing waves of immigrants that introduce a new religious pluralism in the industrial countries of the West, for which their history has not prepared them. How should Christians respond to this new situation? I am grateful that the official teaching of the major Christian churches, including the Catholic Church, advocates respect for the world religions and fosters interreligious dialogue and co-operation. I am also grateful to Kevin Burns of Novalis for deciding that the papers I wrote over the last few years deserve to be collected and published as a book, and to Nancy Keyes and Anne Louise Mahoney for being competent and generous editors of my texts.

Part I of this book deals with the challenge of religious pluralism. The first essay, on Muslim-Christian dialogue after September 11, 2001, introduces the reader to the progressive thought of a new generation of Muslim intellectuals. The second essay makes use of the sociology of knowledge to explore the dark side of religion: its capacity to generate arrogance, breed contempt for outsiders, and legitimate conquest and violence. The third essay explains why Christians reject the relativism of truth and values characteristic of modernity and at the same time honour the pluralism of religious and philosophical traditions. The fourth essay deals with the shadow the Israeli-Palestinian conflict casts upon Jewish-Christian dialogue and co-operation. The fifth essay compares Jewish and Christian reflection on divine providence after the horror of the Holocaust. The sixth essay reports the recent change in Jürgen Habermas's thinking, recommending that society become post-secular: reacting against the domination of positivism in today's society, Habermas abandons his commitment to secularism and calls upon non-believers, such as himself, to pay attention to the ethical values fostered by the religious traditions. The seventh essay compares the teaching of John Paul II on pluralism and modernity with the theological evaluation of these topics by Cardinal Ratzinger prior to becoming Benedict XVI, and then examines the teaching of the new pope on these topics.

Part II of this book deals with Christians' responses to another sign of the times: the globalization of the unregulated market system. In the 1960s, the decade of Vatican Council II, the universal trend in Western societies supported the welfare state and social democracy, a trend that the Council respected and fostered. Yet since the early 1980s, powerful political and economic actors have produced a counter-movement of deregulation and privatization that has led to the globalization of the free market economy and the inability of governments to protect the economic well-being of their population. The first essay of Part II, essay 8, demonstrates that the present neo-liberal globalization has reproduced a new historical situation, in which Christians must rethink what faith, hope and love mean in today's world. The Catholic Church's recent social teaching demands support for the global common good and calls for universal solidarity, beginning with the poor and oppressed. Essay 9 turns to recent biblical research that recognizes resistance to empire in the preaching of Jesus Christ and the letters of the Apostle Paul. St. Augustine interpreted resistance to empire in his own historical situation; today, Christians committed to justice and peace find themselves increasingly obliged to resist the thrust of Western capitalist and political hegemony. Essay 10 presents John Paul II's critique of neo-liberal capitalism and his amazingly radical ideas on economic justice. Essay 11 finds in the pastoral statement of the Canadian bishops support for community economic development: the joint effort to create an economy from the bottom up. This is followed by essay 12, on the evolution of the Church's teaching on the common good and its economic implications. The final article tells the story of the critical theology – Protestant and Catholic – produced in Canada since the 1960s.

Wrestling with the questions raised by religious pluralism and economic injustice, Christians reread the Scriptures and their tradition to hear anew God's Word addressed to them and search for new ways of incarnating the Gospel in the life of society.

Part I

Religious Pluralism

1

Muslim-Christian Dialogue after 9/11

Since September 11, 2001, North Americans have been preoccupied with Islam. They do not realize that Islam is a cultural and religious continent of great richness, variety and subtlety. Attempting to understand this religious tradition in a perspective derived from September 11 leads inevitably to a caricature. Singling out the passages in the sacred texts that express contempt for outsiders and permit the use of violence creates the impression that Islam is an aggressive religion defined by values incompatible with our own.

This is a prejudice that had already been articulated in Samuel Huntington's book *The Clash of Civilizations,* published in 1996. According to this American author, conflict between the two civilizations, Islamic and Western, is almost inevitable because Islam is inimical to the Western values of human rights and democratic freedom. Because the West has abandoned its Christian roots, Huntington argues, the West lacks the spiritual power to resist Islamic enthusiasm. What is needed for the safety of America, according to him, is for America to return to its Christian roots and affirm its cultural power. This theory has appealed to the new

Christian Right in the US and is not without influence on decision-making at the White House.

Since September 11, prejudice and discrimination against Muslim citizens in the US and even Canada have greatly increased. Antiterrorist legislation in the two countries assigned new powers to the police, permitting them to arrest and detain persons in protective custody on suspicion alone, suspicion that may be raised by language or appearance. Even if the Canadian legislation is milder than its American counterpart, Canada's Bill C-36 effectively suspends the centuries-old common law principle of habeas corpus. If you look like an Arab or are dressed like a 'Muslim,' you could be arrested at any time. Bill C-36 institutionalizes prejudice and assigns it a legitimate place in Canadian culture. Islamophobia differs therefore from anti-Semitism, which is fostered by right-wing currents in society without approval from on high. Bill C-36 has been severely criticized by Canadian human rights organizations and church committees.

Interreligious Dialogue

Against the theory of the clash of civilizations, the UN has promoted 'the dialogue of civilizations.' I am glad to report that the same dialogical approach has been adopted by the federal government in articulating Canada's relationship to countries of the Muslim world. The Report of the Standing Committee on Foreign Affairs and International Trade, published in March 2004, and the Government's Response, published in March 2005,[4] are enlightened documents that deserve to be read. I am grateful to the Christian churches and leaders, especially Pope John Paul II, for supporting the UN in its call for 'the dialogue of civilizations.'

Permit me to quote a number of Catholic texts in support of interreligious dialogue: I am of course well aware that other Christian churches and especially the World Council of Churches fully support interreligious dialogue and co-operation.

The Catholic Church committed itself to dialogue and co-operation at the Second Vatican Council (1962–65). This is what the Council said about Muslims:

> The Church regards with esteem also the Muslims. They adore the one God, living and subsisting in Himself; merciful and all-powerful, the Creator of heaven and earth, who has spoken to men; they take pains to submit wholeheartedly to even His inscrutable decrees, just as Abraham, with whom the faith of Islam takes pleasure in linking itself, submitted to God. Though they do not acknowledge Jesus as God, they revere Him as a prophet.... Finally, they value the moral life and worship God especially through prayer, almsgiving and fasting.

> Since in the course of centuries not a few quarrels and hostilities have arisen between Christians and Muslims, this sacred synod urges all to forget the past and to work sincerely for mutual understanding and to preserve as well as to promote together for the benefit of all humankind social justice and moral welfare, as well as peace and freedom.[5]

I will not discuss here the theology that allows the Church to foster interreligious dialogue. In the past, it is well remembered, the Church thought of itself as sent to convert to Christian faith the followers of other religious traditions. The danger to human well-being created by a world deeply divided by political power, economic inequality and ideological differences has persuaded the churches to see themselves as agents of peace and reconciliation. Let me quote a text from a speech delivered by John Paul II at the Great Omayyad Mosque in Damascus on May 6, 2001.

> Christians and Muslims agree that the encounter with God in prayer is the necessary nourishment of our souls, without

which our hearts wither and our will no longer strives for good but succumbs to evil. Both Muslims and Christians prize their places of prayer, as oases where they meet the All Merciful God on the journey to eternal life, and where they meet their brothers and sisters in the bond of religion.... It is my ardent hope that Muslim and Christian religious leaders and teachers will present our two great religious communities *as communities in respectful dialogue, never more as communities in conflict.*[6]

Here is another pertinent text revealing John Paul II's attitude towards Islam.

We Christians joyfully recognize the religious values we have in common with Islam. Today I would like to repeat what I said to young Muslims some years ago in Casablanca: "We believe in the same God, the one God, the living God, the God who created the world and brings his creatures to their perfection."[7]

Learning about Islam

Because I am deeply disturbed by the prejudice inflicted on Muslims living in North America, I have taken the call to dialogue very seriously and have started to study the Muslim tradition. This has been a great spiritual adventure for me. I discovered the creative reflections of contemporary Muslim intellectuals who want to be faithful to the Qur'an and the Tradition and at the same time respond with openness to the challenges of modern society. Because these thinkers are not well-known in our society, I wish to present some of their ideas in this essay.

Let me first say a few words about the internal pluralism of religious traditions. At one time, scholars believed that it was possible to gain a deep insight into a religion and define its essential characteristics. At the beginning of the 20th century, Adolf von Harnack, the famous Protestant theologian and historian, published *The Essence of Christianity*; Leo Beck, the learned German rabbi, published *The Essence of Judaism*. Today, scholars no longer suppose that religions have an essence. What is recognized today is that religions are produced by communities of interpretation whose faith is based on sacred texts or sacred persons, sources that summon them to worship and guide them in their daily life. Religions are constituted by faith communities that read and reread their sacred texts in the ever-changing circumstances of history. In the search for fidelity to the originating texts or persons, the hermeneutic communities are involved in internal debates and in conversation with the culture in which they dwell. Religions thus have no permanent essence: their identity is created by their effort to remain faithful to the sacred texts. Religions are therefore inevitably marked by an internal pluralism. Each religion has many faces.

This dynamic understanding of a religious tradition obviously applies to Christianity. The biblical texts have been read and reread in various contexts; there have always been ongoing internal debates as well as influences derived from different cultures. Christianity has many faces. This internal pluralism of Christianity not only defines the different confessions and traditions, but it also inhabits each Christian church. In each church we witness a lively debate over what fidelity to the Gospel means at a particular time. Among the many faces of Christianity are also sinister ones: in our long history we have blessed aggressive wars, colonialism, the use of torture and contempt for outsiders. Yet, by returning to the sacred texts and engaging in dialogue with cultural movements, the churches have experienced spiritual renewal.

The same dynamism is operative in the other world religions. The open-ended nature of religious traditions accounts both for their creativity and for their deviations. Religions have the capacity to respond in an original way, faithful to their sacred texts, to new historical challenges. Yet they are also vulnerable to a reading of the sacred texts that supports an alliance with political and cultural domination. Religions have thus many faces: they are ambiguous historical realities.

Like Christianity, Islam has many faces. It is a grave error to approach the study of Islam from the perspective of the religious fanaticism revealed on September 11, 2001. Such an approach, as I said earlier, produces a caricature of Islam. Islamic extremism exists; it is a dangerous phenomenon, like all forms of fanaticism, and it deserves a careful analysis, taking into account the various factors, and not only the religious ones, that have produced it. This is not my task here. Still, I wish to quote a paragraph dealing with this issue, taken from the speech of October 15, 2001, given by Archbishop Rafael Martino, then the Vatican's Permanent Observer at the United Nations.

> We do a disservice to those who died in the tragedy of September 11 if we fail to search out the causes.... Though poverty is not by itself the cause of terrorism, we cannot successfully combat terrorism if we do not address the worsening disparities between the rich and poor. We must recognize that global disparity is fundamentally incompatible with global security.... Poverty along with other situations of marginalization that engulf the lives of so many of the world's people, including the denial of human dignity, the lack of respect for human rights, social exclusion, intolerable refugee situations, internal and external displacement, and physical and psychological oppression are breeding grounds only waiting to be exploited by terrorists. In searching out the root causes of terrorism, we are in no way condoning terrorism. But any serious crime reduction effort cannot be confined only to intensified police work. Any serious campaign against terrorism needs to address the social, economic and political conditions that nurture the emergence of terrorism.[8]

The Renewal Movement

The principal error committed by people who approach Islam from the perspective of September 11 is that they interpret the astounding revitalization of Islam beginning in the 1970s as an expression of fundamentalism. Yet this is not what happened. What took place was an emergence of religious enthusiasm among Muslims in the Middle East and the Maghreb that revealed to people on all levels of society the practical relevance of Islam. I think it is possible to compare this renewal to the eighteenth-century Great Awakening in British North America that produced a common consciousness among people belonging to the different colonies and thus contributed to the eventual revolution against the British Crown.

The Islamic awakening of the last three decades is a phenomenon that has a variety of sources. One of them has been the disappointment of people in Islamic countries that the struggle to improve their collective well-being by nationalism or socialism – both ideologies derived from Western modernity – has not been successful. The political ideas of the elites have not been able to inspire the hearts of the great majority. People were therefore ready to listen to the message that their own inheritance, the Islamic faith, was the spiritual resource that would allow them to create a more just and more humane society. Obedience to divine revelation made known through the Great Prophet Muhammad would generate a social order of justice and peace.

The theological preparation for this awakening was the Islamic renewal movement, with roots in the second part of the nineteenth century.[9] In that century, the Islamic societies encountered modernity in its colonial form. Muslims confronted the contradiction of modernity that advocated democracy at home and imposed colonial domination abroad. Algeria became a colony, then Tunisia, Morocco, Egypt, Libya and faraway India, and eventually – after World War I – colonial mandates were established in Palestine,

Lebanon, Syria and Iraq. It is not surprising that Arabs interpreted the creation of Israel as part of this colonial wave, while we in the West thought of Israel as a house against death, a national home for a persecuted people.

Already in the second part of the nineteenth century, Muslim thinkers, humiliated by the colonial conquests, asked themselves how this defeat could have happened. Why had they been unable to resist the European empires? Religious thinkers among them argued that Islam had become stagnant: it had ceased to inspire people, it had made them complacent, and consequently it offered no resistance to the foreign invasion.

One of the reactions to this stagnation was the effort of certain religious thinkers to interpret the Qur'an as the divine message allowing believers to react creatively in a new situation. The first theologian calling for renewal was the Persian known as al-Afghani (d. 1897). His work was continued by the Egyptian Muhamed Abdou (d. 1905) the Indian Ahmad Khan (d. 1898) and the Lebanese Rashid Rida (d. 1935). These thinkers lamented the spiritual decline that Muslim culture had experienced: Islam had ceased to be a creative force. To revitalize their faith, these authors read the Qur'an in the light of the Islamic tradition that trusted human reason as God's gift to humanity and thus saw no contradiction between reason and faith. Studying modern science was no danger to Muslims' faith. These authors regretted that the elite in Muslim countries often abandoned their faith and turned to secular Western ideas. What was necessary, they argued, was to wrestle against Western colonialism, create greater unity among Muslims of different regions, introduce social reform to overcome the existing inequalities, and give men and women access to education. It is not surprising that these revolutionary thinkers were denounced by the colonial powers, by the ruling sultans, and by conservative representatives of the Islamic tradition.

A second reaction to the stagnation of Islam moved in a different direction. These religious thinkers argued that the domination of the Western empires happened to Muslims because they had adopted a liberal interpretation of religious laws, become lax and made life easy for themselves. What was demanded was not greater openness to reason, but the return to a rigorous fidelity to the divine laws. The conservative leaders retrieved the rigid interpretation of Islam made in the eighteenth century by Muhammad Ibn Abd al-Wahab, who had denounced the dominant form of Islam as false and corrupted. The new voices of radical conservatism rejected the hermeneutic approach to the Qur'an and refused to dialogue with their critics. We have here the beginning of Muslim fundamentalism. It is well-known that Wahabism has been sustained and promoted in the world by the royal house of Saudi Arabia. Still, fundamentalist Muslims did not approve of the arbitrary use of violence.

The Muslims' response to modernity in its contradictory colonial form was therefore twofold: it gave birth to a renewal movement and to a fundamentalist current. The German sociologist Max Weber, a scholar of the world religions, paid special attention to the impact of piety on society. He offered the famous arguments that the genius of Calvinism had been to generate a piety that urged believers to become active in the world. Sociologists argue that every faith or spirituality has a certain impact on society, and refer to this as the coefficient of secular commitment. Using this vocabulary allows us to say that the versions of Islam promoted by the renewal movement and the fundamentalist current greatly increased the coefficient of secular commitment. The two movements made Islam an activist faith.

The New Muslim Intellectuals

What interests me are the contemporary Muslim intellectuals who play a creative role in the renewal of Islam, even though most of them find themselves opposed by governments, by the guardians of orthodoxy, and in many cases by secular Western thinkers. [10] Until recently, these intellectuals were not well known in the West. However, the evolution of e-mail and the Internet has enabled these thinkers from all over the world to be in conversation with one another, and has allowed Western observers to follow their debates.

In 2002, a large conference on the topic of Muslim reactions to modernity was held in Leyden, Holland, which was attended by Muslim scholars from Africa, Asia and Europe.[11] The conference revealed the creativity of these new Muslim intellectuals. They define themselves against conservatives, who respond to modernity by repeating the discourse of the past, and against modernists, who are willing to adopt a secular discourse. They want to be faithful to the Qur'an and at the same time remain in an open dialogue with modernity.

The new intellectuals in Muslim countries repudiate theocratic regimes as contrary to the Qur'an. Sovereign is only God: government and people are both subject to the Islamic law. These thinkers advocate the reform of society from below – that is, the creation of a culture of faith that fosters social involvement and solidarity. The new intellectuals living in Western pluralistic societies argue that the Qur'an calls Muslims to promote justice and social peace and serve the common good of their country and the world.

Further on, I shall discuss two Muslim thinkers, Fethullah Gülen and Tariq Ramadan, who have inspired many people and have a strong following – and whose work I greatly admire. There are, of course, many other scholars whose work deserves to be studied.

The new Muslim intellectuals are often misunderstood by Western secular thinkers. Because these men and women are believers, because they revere the Qur'an as divine revelation and want to be faithful to it, they are often interpreted by secular thinkers as clever apologists for Islam or, worse, disguised fundamentalists. As a Catholic theologian, I find it easy to understand these Muslim thinkers, because I, too, while open to critical thinking, want to remain faithful to the Christian Gospel. Christian theology lives out of a double fidelity: fidelity to divine revelation and fidelity to human intelligence. This double fidelity is shared by the new Muslim intellectuals in their own religious context.

There is another reason why I, as a Catholic theologian, find it easy to understand the present debates in the Muslim community. In the Catholic Church, the encounter with modernity has also produced turmoil, condemnations, debates and new ideas. The papacy repudiated modernity in the nineteenth century; it rejected democracy, the liberal state, human rights, separation of Church and State, as well as the principle of religious liberty. The papacy demanded that government protect the true religion, i.e. Roman Catholicism, by appropriate laws restraining heretics and infidels. In countries where Catholics were a minority, they were permitted to advocate religious liberty because there this freedom served the true religion. Theologians who disagreed with papal teaching, beginning with Lamenais in the 1830s, were censored or even excommunicated. We had to wait for the great thinkers of the 20th century, such as Jacques Maritain, who were able to combine a critical openness to modernity with classical theological orthodoxy. Yet their message was not heard at first. Today, the new Muslim intellectuals, offering a novel interpretation of their tradition, are not widely heard in Muslim countries. Their situation reminds me of the Catholic theologians who rethought their own tradition, were frowned upon by the ecclesiastical authorities, and had relatively little influence on ordinary church-going Catholics, yet whose thought eventually received official recognition. In the 1960s, relying on these thinkers, the Second Vatican Council was able to offer a reading of the Bible and the Catholic tradition that urged the Church to endorse human rights, democracy and religious pluralism.

Today, the worldwide Muslim community is involved in a public debate. I interpret this as a positive phenomenon. Internal debates make people critically aware of what they believe and allow them to discover the practical consequences of their faith. To listen to these debates is an instructive exercise. For example, on the Islam21 website (www.islam21.net), we find a collection of statements, articles and exchanges of ideas offered by reflective Muslims; and if we then click on 'links,' we find a long list of other websites where Muslim believers are in conversation. Let me add as an aside that the recent controversy over the institution of Muslim arbitration courts in Ontario was a painful experience for many of my Muslim friends, yet it served an important function: it brought the entire believing community into critical conversation. By examining this issue, the Internet allows us to follow the changing self-understanding of women in Islam. A starting point is the web site of the Canadian Council of Muslim Women (www.ccmw.com).

Let me now turn to two particular Muslim thinkers.

Fethullah Gülen[12]

Fethullah Gülen is both a mystic and an organizer of the renewal movement in Turkey (www.en.fgulen.com). To understand his bold originality, we must take a look at the situation of Islam in the Turkish state, which has been formally declared secular by its founder, Kemal Atatürk. From the beginning, the governing elites were not only secular, they were in fact suspicious of religion. Islam, which remained the faith of the majority, was strictly controlled by the government. It had to be interpreted as personal piety, its ethical teaching had to support government policies, and it had to refrain from contact with Muslims in other countries. The Turkish government prohibited any Muslim-inspired social movement.

Yet in its struggle against communist influence in the 1970s, the government permitted the political organization of Muslims, opposed as it was to communist atheism. This opened a door for Gülen's social movement.

Fethullah Gülen grew up as a pious Muslim; as a boy he learned the Qur'an by heart. Very early in his life he was influenced by the Sufi tradition that had survived in Turkey and had recently been revived by a gifted spiritual author, Said Nursi. Sufism represented a mystical tradition in Islam. Putting the emphasis on the inner life allowed Gülen to read the Qur'an by giving priority to the passages that proclaim the universal virtues of justice, honesty, respect and compassion, and summoned Muslims to act responsibly in society and foster the education of men and women. With other new Muslim intellectuals, Gülen retrieved an ancient Muslim tradition – the Mutazili School – which regarded intelligence as a divine gift to men and women and promoted education as a religious duty. In fact, he founded many schools that cultivated faith as well as science. He was critically open to Western thought, but strongly resisted Western secular presuppositions. The study of science and technology, he argued, did not have to lead to the domination of instrumental reason and 'the disenchantment of the world,' as it did in the West. Instead, this study could intensify worship of the Creator whose supreme intelligence was embodied in the material world.

Gülen insists that in today's world the Qur'an calls upon true believers to honour religious pluralism. Summarizing passages from the Sunna, he writes, "The Prophet, upon him be peace and blessing, defined a true Muslim as one who harms no one with his or her words and actions, and who is the most trustworthy representative of universal peace."[13] Because he respects the pluralism in God's creation and recognizes the need for freedom to converse about the truth, Gülen admires democratic political institutions and advocates interreligious dialogue. He visited the head of the

Orthodox Church in Istanbul, the Chief Rabbi of Jerusalem, and Pope John Paul II in Rome.

Gülen is a controversial thinker. Because he is an ardent believer and a man of prayer, Turkey's secular elite tends to mistrust him. Some of its members fear that hidden behind the liberal vocabulary is the intention to transform Turkey into a Muslim state ruled by Muslim law. In reality, Gülen envisages the renewal of society from below through education, co-operation and economic creativity. He refuses to join a political movement; he even remains aloof from the democratic Islamic party that has gained some power in Turkey. Islam for Gülen is a social faith, a culture-creating religious movement that should stay away from the ups and downs of political life. What he dreams of is a Turkish modernity sustained by the Muslim faith of the people.

Tariq Ramadan

A Muslim theologian whose work I have studied and whose pastoral engagement I greatly admire is Tariq Ramadan (www.tariqramadan.com). Born in Switzerland of Egyptian parents, he received an education in Western thought and subsequently in Islamic science. Like millions of Muslims living in Europe and North America, Ramadan thinks of himself as a Western Muslim. He wants to be faithful to the Qur'an, but as an active citizen of a Western democracy. His theological approach is revealed in the titles of two of his books that have been translated into English: *To Be a European Muslim* and *Western Muslims and the Future of Islam*.[14] He argues that Western Muslims must do their own theological thinking; they cannot rely on counsels and judgments made by Muslim religious leaders living in the East. In the name of their faith, Western Muslims will want to take an active part in the political life of their country, a role they are deprived of in Muslim countries, ruled as they presently are by authoritarian governments. The call of the Qur'an for equality among humans, the sharing of wealth and concern for the needy has political implications that make Muslims into critical citizens who promote social justice in their country and the world.

With the new Muslim intellectuals from East and West, Ramadan raises a hermeneutical question: How shall we read the Qur'an and the Sunna in a new historical context? What does it mean to be faithful to divine revelation when you live in a Western society? Living in a pluralistic society makes Muslims pay special attention to the passages of the Qur'an that respect differences, call for peaceful conviviality and offer wisdom addressed to all.

With the new Muslim intellectuals, Ramadan emphasizes the universal message of the Great Prophet Muhammad. What are primarily revealed in the Qur'an are transcendent ethical principles such as justice, compassion, human equality, honesty and the love of truth, which apply to all cultural situations, even if their concrete implications must be worked out in each particular culture. By following these principles, people surrender themselves to God's will. Ethics is here divine worship.

In addition to the universal message, Ramadan continues, Muslims have been honoured to receive a detailed set of laws and practices that allow them to surrender themselves to God more intimately and thus find in God the strength to live up to the universal ethical demands. Ramadan does not use the universal message of the Qur'an to render less significant the ritual practices and legal traditions of Islam. He is both modern and boldly conservative.

According to Ramadan, the Muslim tradition urges believers living in a pluralistic society to follow the laws of the country and to rely on Islamic law only in cases where public legislation diverges from Islamic ethical teaching. That is why, on his many visits to Canada, he has expressed himself against the institution of Muslim arbitration courts. He argues that Canadian law offers an adequate protection of the family and the interests of husband and wife. In fact, one of his major pastoral principles is that Western Muslims should stop thinking of themselves as minorities and understand themselves rather as responsible citizens. Transcending the preoccupation with their own communities, Muslims must be concerned with common good of society. Faithful to the divine message, they must promote justice and peace.

Ramadan is quite willing to confront the hard texts of the Qur'an and the Sunna that shock modern ethical sensibilities, such as those concerning corporal punishment and the death penalty by stoning. Since 'the consensus of the learned' has interpretative authority in Islam, Ramadan holds that an agreement among believers could offer a new reading to these texts. In March 2005, he published a declaration calling for a moratorium of all corporal punishments in Muslim countries in order to promote a debate on this topic in the worldwide Muslim community. Ramadan also deals with the position of women in Islam. He respects the scholarly work of Muslim feminists. With them, he argues that Islam favours the education of women and recognizes women as responsible agents in society. The subjugation of women practised by Muslims is a cultural inheritance; it is not grounded in divine revelation and hence should be abolished. He wants women to be free – free also to decide whether or not to wear the veil.

In France, Ramadan is a controversial thinker. The French Republic is committed to a doctrinaire form of secularism that tolerates religion as a private faith, but will not allow religious ideas to be heard in public debates. There is no place for religion in the public discourse. In this cultural climate, many French intellectuals are suspicious of Tariq Ramadan because he wants Muslims to participate in society in the name of their faith, i.e. out of obedience to divine revelation. Ramadan has been accused of being a fundamentalist in disguise.[15] He wants Muslims in France to integrate in society, yet without abandoning their Muslim faith and their Muslim identity. Because he advocates social justice on a universal scale and is critical of neo-liberal globalization, he is often referred to as *un tiersmondiste* [a thirdworldist], a pejorative term in France that refers to someone who blames the problems of developing countries on exploitation by rich capitalist countries. Ramadan has been critical of Israel's expansionist policies, and yet has always denounced the anti-Semitism that is widespread among Arabs. Despite these public denunciations, Ramadan has been accused by some French intellectuals of anti-Semitism. He is also vilified because his grandfather was Hasan al-Banna who, in 1928, founded the Muslim Brotherhood in Egypt. Having carefully studied the controversy in France (there are entire books on the topic), I have come to the conclusion that this great Muslim theologian has been unjustly denigrated.

As a Catholic theologian, I understand the new Muslim intellectuals better than many secular commentators do. Being acquainted with our own debates over the relation between faith and reason and with the tension between the personal and social meaning of religion, I have a certain affinity for the religious thought of contemporary Muslim thinkers. In Montreal I regularly attend the meetings of the Muslim association Présence musulmane, which offers a forum for Muslims to discuss the power and relevance of their faith in contemporary society.

Like Christianity, Islam has many faces. Thanks to the mass media, it is the political Islam of Islamic countries and the rigid Islam of the fundamentalists that are widely publicized. What is often overlooked is that, like all religious traditions, Islam is enlivened by internal debates and conversations with adjacent cultures. I have presented a brief introduction to the renewal movement in Islam and more especially to the new Muslim intellectuals. It is the task of the Christian churches, especially after September 11, to defend Muslims against prejudice and discrimination and to support the humanism implicit in the Muslim tradition.

2

Interreligious Dialogue Attentive
to Western Enlightenment

We are grateful that the world religions have learned to respect one another, engage in dialogue and act jointly in the service of peace. We are grateful for the World Conference of Religions for Peace, the Parliament of the World Religions and other interreligious world organizations that foster mutual understanding and co-operative action. I am personally grateful for the development in my own Church at the Second Vatican Council that acknowledged God's universal mercy, respected religious pluralism and recommended interreligious dialogue.

At the same time, September 11 and the pre-emptive strike against Iraq have made us keenly aware of the dark side of religion: that is to say, the power of religion to encourage arrogance, generate contempt, produce hatred, create conflicts, encourage aggression and even legitimate violence. How do we explain this dark side of religion?

This is a question that greatly troubles me. I cannot forget that the history of my own Christian tradition includes acts of arrogance, aggression and violence. I am unable to forget the Crusades, the Inquisition and use of torture to defend the truth, the religious wars between Catholics and Protestants, and the blessing of empire and colonialism by the Christian churches. At the same time, I believe that Christianity and the other world religions are luminous traditions, bringing light to the world, illuminating the path that leads to love, justice and peace. How, then, do we account for the dark side?

Here is how the Kyoto Declaration of 1970 answers this question: "As men and women of religion, we confess in humility and penitence that we have very often betrayed our religious ideals and our commitment to peace. It is not religion that has failed the cause of peace, but religious people."[16] The religions are here seen as flawless: to be blamed are the acts of religious people. But is this an adequate answer? Are the religions really flawless?

We often hear the argument that people who, in the name of their religion, foster hatred or commit acts of violence use their religion as an instrument to enhance their power. Here again the religions are seen as flawless; responsibility for the evil deeds rests upon the actors who have instrumentalized their religion. But is this analysis sufficient? Is the harm done by religious actors simply their personal choice? Or may it not also be structural, the result of flaws in the religious tradition itself?

This is a disturbing question. Let me give an example from the Christian tradition. For centuries, the churches promoted contempt for Jews and the Jewish religion, resulting in destructive consequences for the Jewish communities in Europe. Who is responsible for this contempt? Should we simply blame individual Christians who violated the divine commandment of neighbourly love? Or did the anti-Jewish bias have a structural cause? Was the flaw in the tradition itself? Today we have answered this question. We recognize that the Church's official liturgy condemned the Jews for their unbelief and depicted them as deserted by God. Contempt for the Jews was thus structurally mediated: it was produced by a flaw in the tradition, a flaw introduced by actors in the past who sinned against the love of neighbour. It was only after the Holocaust that the churches recognized their flawed inheritance, reread the Holy Scriptures and found in them resources for changing their teaching. Today the Church honours Judaism and respects the world religions in the name of Jesus.

Religious traditions are complex historical movements, constituted by diverse currents and engaged in a never-ending debate about the meaning and power of their sacred inheritance in ever-changing cultural contexts. Recent events force us to admit that religious traditions have a dark side, even as we greatly admire these traditions for their capacity to renew themselves and respond creatively to new historical challenges. Often writers deal with the luminous side of religion, promoting love, justice and peace and rendering an indispensable service to the well-being of humanity. Here I wish to do something different: with a heavy heart I wish to explore the dark side of religion. The examples I use shall all be taken from my own tradition. I leave it to members of other religious traditions to test whether my analysis sheds light on their own history.

To gain a better understanding of the dark side of religion, I wish to engage in dialogue with an intellectual current of the Western Enlightenment. I realize, of course, that the Enlightenment was an ambiguous intellectual movement. On the one hand the movement, boasting that its values were universal, generated contempt for traditional societies and in particular for non-Western cultures. This was the imperialist dimension of the Enlightenment. At the same time, the movement also advocated the rescue of people from oppressive institutions. This was the emancipatory dimension of the Enlightenment. The desire for emancipation or rescue from oppressive structures is, in my opinion, truly universal. All colonized peoples want to be free; all hungry people want to live in conditions that allow them to eat and feed their families; all despised people want to live in a culture that honours them.

Dialogue with this emancipatory current of the Enlightenment promises to be helpful in my inquiry into the dark side of religion. I shall pay attention in particular to the sociology of knowledge, which analyzes the capacity of ideas and symbols to affect cultural development and influence people's behaviour.

The Destructive Potential of Religion

Before turning to the sociology of knowledge, I wish to make two more general remarks on the destructive potential of religions.

i) The venerated sacred texts of religion contain certain harsh passages that, if applied literally, cause damage to innocent people. Some passages in our sacred literature praise conquest by the sword, foster contempt for outsiders and even legitimate violence in the name of God. We have to wrestle with these harsh texts, show their location in a particular historical situation, and demonstrate that they have been transcended and therefore invalidated by subsequent currents in the same tradition.

Christians are troubled by passages in the early parts of the Old Testament that depict God as a heavenly warrior, describe the conquest of Palestine as a genocidal military campaign and present the tribes surrounding the people of Israel as steeped in evil. These passages are transcended and invalidated in parts of the Old Testament written at a later period, telling us that God is merciful, that God has made a covenant with the whole of humanity, and that God's mercy and justice are operative in all the nations. Here God is revealed not in the loud clap of the thunder, but in the still, small voice.

Christians are also troubled by the passages in the New Testament according to which all who do not believe in Jesus Christ will be condemned – a verdict that excludes the majority of humankind from God's mercy and creates a division in humanity that can never be healed. These passages are transcended and invalidated by texts in the New Testament, according to which people will be saved by their love of God and neighbour and their solidarity with the poor and the needy. In a parable of Matthew's gospel, Jesus addresses a group of persons who have never met him, yet selflessly offered help to people in trouble. To them he said, "What you have done to the least of them, you have done to me."

Not all believers are willing to transcend and invalidate the harsh texts of their tradition. They prefer to apply the harsh texts literally, even if in doing so they do harm to innocent people. In my opinion, the harsh texts of the sacred literature contribute to the ambiguity of the religious traditions.

ii) The sacred literature we have inherited is to a large extent written in a poetic style, using images, similes and hyperboles. It is thus not surprising that the commandments and counsels we read in them are not always rationally consistent and may even be contradictory. They may reflect different contexts or represent different forms of speech.

Thus in one place in the New Testament we read that all worldly authority comes from God, and to disobey this authority is disobedience to God (Romans 13:1-5), while in another context we read that disobedience to authority may be justified because "it is better to obey God than man" (Acts 4:19). Here is another conundrum: At one point, Jesus says, "Any one who is not with me is against me" (Luke 11:23), while at another point he tells his disciples, "Anyone who is not against you is with you" (Luke 9:50). A simplistic reading of the scriptures, relying on a single text, without qualifying it with reference to other texts, may well inspire extreme and unbalanced behaviour harmful to society.

A Definition of Ideology

Let me now turn to the sociology of knowledge – in particular, to the concept of ideology, which is here defined as the distortion of truth for the sake of collective self-interest. Societies tend to generate ideologies in a largely unconscious process to secure their identity, enhance their power, and legitimate or disguise their oppressive structures. Not only do societies want to look good, they want to hide their unjust practices and look better than they are. The dominant culture of any society is thus affected by an ideological bias: as a result, its members tend to assimilate this distortion as the truth and defend it with passion. By contrast, the carefully disguised institutional injustices are clearly recognized by the victims of society and by persons in solidarity with them.

In the early 1960s, the American author John Howard Griffin decided to colour his skin and travel through the United States as a black man in order to see the world through the eyes of the disadvantaged and despised. In his bestselling book, *Black Like Me*, he told us that moving through the streets as a black man, he was unable to recognize the cities with which he had been familiar. The same experience is recounted by Dorothee Soelle, a German Protestant theologian, who was radicalized in the 1950s when she, a young woman of a comfortable class, accompanied a group of women refugees searching the city for employment and a place to live. As she walked with these women through her own city, she no longer recognized it. These women, she wrote, helped her to discover the truth. She became aware that the dominant culture makes the sinister aspects of society invisible.

Ideological Bias I: The Unreflective Us-and-them Discourse

Can we admit that religious traditions are also affected by ideologies? Every religion has the sacred duty of defining its identity and articulating the faith and practice that distinguish it from other religions and from the surrounding culture. The legitimate discourse distinguishing between 'us' and 'them' is a mechanism that easily generates ideology. We hold the truth, they are in error; we are enlightened, they live in blindness; we live holy lives, they practise vices. The 'us' and 'them' discourse tends to produce an elevated self-understanding and a false sense of superiority of our own community, accompanied by a denigrating perception of other communities seen as inferior. Since in their history most religions have defined themselves against a competing religion or against a culture that resisted them, their sacred literature tends to refer to outsiders in a manner that demeans them and generates conflicts.

Distinguishing between 'us' and 'them' does not have to produce ideological distortions. In every religion, the truth is received in humility as a gift for which one is grateful. We embrace the truth that has been granted to us, yet without boasting about it as if we had achieved it ourselves. To have contempt for religious traditions other than our own sins against humility, reveals false pride and misappropriates the truth entrusted to us. Feeling superior is not the work of faith, but of arrogance. Looking down upon other religions is therefore a self-damaging process. The ideological self-elevation that leads to the contempt of outsiders actually distorts one's own religious inheritance.

In a Christian context, this point was strongly made by St. Paul. He told Christians to remember that despising the Jews for refusing to believe in Jesus was a sign that they – the Christians – looked upon their faith as a personal achievement, not as a free gift, thus endangering their justification before God (Romans 11:17-22). One wishes that the Church had listened to St. Paul.

It was only in the 20th century, largely as a response to the horrors of World War II and the Holocaust, that the Christian Church began a critical examination of its inherited discourse about 'outsiders' – about Jews, members of the world religions, Native peoples, unbelievers, Christians deemed heretical, and homosexuals. Rereading the Scriptures with a new openness, the churches discovered theological foundation for addressing outsiders with respect and engaging in interreligious dialogue. A similar process of self-correction is taking place in other religious traditions.

Respect for outsiders and, more especially, for other religious traditions does not make us into sentimental observers of human history, refusing to recognize the conflictive world in which we live. We are not naive: we do distinguish between good and evil in the world. Yet the distinction between 'good' and 'evil' is quite different from the distinction between 'us' and 'them.' Good and evil are dimensions present in all communities: they pervade 'us,' i.e. our own community, as well as 'them,' i.e. the communities of the others. Standing against injustice, oppression and exploitation is an ethical struggle that focuses first on the faults in our own community before we turn to what is wrong and damaging in others.

I conclude from the preceding remarks that the discourse used by a tradition to distinguish between believers and non-believers easily generates ideologies that damage the purity of the tradition, produce conflict in society and allow themselves to be instrumentalized for the enhancement of political power.

Ideological Bias II: The Language of the Powerless Adopted by the Powerful

Another principle of the sociology of knowledge is that the meaning of a sentence changes as the speaker moves to a different social location. An example I often refer to is the anthem "Germany, Germany above all," which was the song of the failed liberal revolution of 1848 calling for a united Germany over all the divisions produced by the feudal order. Yet after the creation of the German Empire in 1870, the same song acquired a totally different meaning: "Germany, Germany above all" now became an expression of political arrogance. The meaning of a message changes dramatically if it is uttered by a powerful actor.

It is a recognized principle of hermeneutics that to understand the literal meaning of a scriptural passage, one must situate it in its historical context. The sociology of knowledge draws attention to the fact that when this passage is recited in a new historical context, its meaning may change significantly. In particular, the rhetoric of resistance employed by individuals or small communities threatened by an aggressive enemy will acquire a different meaning when repeated by persons or communities in possession of power. When prophets or leaders face strong opposition or suffer persecution, they express their resistance by predicting the ultimate victory of truth and pronouncing God's judgment on their enemies. Yet if the identical sentences are used by persons or institutions possessing great power, they become a discourse of domination, asserting the victory of truth over all dissidents and God's judgment on all who challenge the establishment. The truth uttered by the weak becomes ideology when repeated by the powerful.

To illustrate this point I remind my students of the song "We shall overcome," sung by powerless people in the civil rights struggle to express their trust that in the long run, truth and justice will prevail. Yet if the police department had adopted "We shall overcome" as its theme song, the song's meaning would have been quite different: it would have meant that the police shall use their guns and their armoured cars to quell dissent and establish order.

Let me apply this principle to the Christian discourse about truth. Jesus, we read in Scripture, came to reveal the hidden truth of God. Jesus said to those who believed in him, "If you make my word your home you will indeed be my disciples; you will come to know the truth, and the truth will set you free" (John 8:31-32). The truth he proclaimed would free people – it would "give sight to the blind, set the captives free and liberate the oppressed" (Luke 4:18). Jesus and the first Christian community preached the truth with great courage against the imperial culture of Rome, the worship of the Emperor and the Jewish aristocracy complicit with the Empire. The early witnesses were willing to die for the liberating truth.

Yet in subsequent centuries, when the Christian communities had become powerful churches, commitment to the truth became the source of endless quarrels, the justification for persecuting dissidents and the legitimation of violent conflicts. The truth uttered in resistance to Empire now became an instrument to promote the power of the churches. Truth came to be looked upon increasingly in conceptual terms, separated from the practice of love: it came to be used as an instrument to promote the establishment and suppress alternative interpretations. Today we remember with embarrassment the Inquisition and the use of torture in the name of God's truth and are unable to forget the religious wars between Catholics and Protestants in the sixteenth and seventeenth centuries. The atheism of many Enlightenment thinkers, we now recognize, was a reaction to the endless religious violence. The religious compromise achieved by the Peace of Westphalia in 1648 initiated long centuries of non-communication between Catholics and Protestants, each side using the truth as an instrument to triumph over the other. We are grateful to God that the ecumenical movement of the 20th century has radically changed the religious situation: we have learned to respect ecclesiastical pluralism and hope to move closer to one another.

Ideological Bias III: The Uncritical Support of Religion for the Political and Economic Elites

We now turn to the infamous critique of religion proposed in the nineteenth century by Karl Marx. He argued that religion was an ideology designed to protect the existing social order; to utter blessings on the prince and the royal court; to demand obedience from the people; and to console them in their misery with promises of a higher life in the spirit, as a reward for their virtue. We reject the Marxist critique of religion. As counter-evidence we turn to the message and the actions of the founders of religions and to the lives of the sages, prophets and saints. At the beginning and, later, at its best, religion has always been at odds with political domination. At the same time, the grain of truth in the Marxist critique deserves attention.

When religion is welcomed in society, encouraged by government and supported by public funds, it tends to understand itself as the spiritual guardian of society and a defender of the established order. Religion here becomes the sacred canopy of the secular realm. In this situation, religion may call for social reforms to create a more just society, yet religion may also become a reactionary force, defend the power of the dominant elite and offer ideological support for the status quo.

Taking my examples from the Christian tradition, I recall that the colonial conquest of the European Empires was blessed by the Christian churches. They interpreted the colonial expansion of the European powers as a providential event opening the door to the worldwide Christian mission. With few exceptions, the churches were so deeply identified with European culture and European arrogance that their religious mission acquired a political meaning: they preached obedience to the king and promoted what they regarded as a superior civilization. Here religion clearly assumed the ideological character denounced by the Marxist critique.

There are many other examples where the ecclesiastical establishment wedded itself to the political order or the economic elite. I am thinking, for instance, of the unbelievable spectacle during the First World War when the European churches prayed against one another, each for the victory of its own nation – an experience that contributed to the subsequent secularization of European society.

This leads me to the topic of war, which deserves careful attention but which I cannot treat in detail in this essay. The Christian tradition has, in the past, accepted the so-called just war theory, specifying the conditions under which a defensive war is ethically permissible. Most religions have developed such a theory, even as all of them had – and still have – ardent believers committed to non-violence. Because the American war against Iraq was a pre-emptive strike against a nation that had not been a threat to the United States, the leaders of the major American churches refused to recognize the ethical legitimacy of this war, even if the organized Christian Right in America strongly supported the war.

To illustrate the ideological distortions of religion, I draw upon examples from my own tradition. I am fully aware that similar examples can be drawn from other religious traditions, but I leave this task to their own followers. All over the world, religion has repeatedly legitimated conquest.

In some historical situations, religion has also motivated resistance to domination. In the Christian tradition, the just war theory has been applied to justify revolutionary violence. Most of the American churches approved of the American Revolution against the British Crown in the 1770s, arguing that in the struggle against domination, the rational and disciplined use of violence was ethically acceptable. Yet Christian teachers – and teachers in all religious traditions – have always repudiated the irrational and arbitrary use of violence, even when practised in defence of a just cause. Violence is irrational and arbitrary when it is an expression of rage, directed at innocent people, and devoid of a rational plan for improving the unjust situation. In the face of oppression and exploitation, religion may well produce anger, but if it blesses the practice of random violence it becomes ideologically distorted.

We are grateful to God for people of faith in all the world religions who recognize the ideological taint in their tradition and summon their fellow believers to re-embrace the authentic message and the deepest values of their faith. The religions are sent to offer light to the world.

Ideological Bias IV: The Exclusion of the Feminist Perspective

I must make a brief remark about another ideological bias. According to the sociology of knowledge, the perception of reality depends in part on the social location of the observer. Implied in this principle is that men and women, located as they are on different levels of social power, will have different perceptions of reality. To understand who we are as human beings and what our inherited religion means for human life, we will have to listen to women as well as men. Limiting ourselves to the male perspective produces an ideological distortion of the truth. In my opinion, the stubborn commitment to the male perspective in the world religions is a mental disease.

Blind Idealism

I have offered a brief description of four ideology-producing processes operative in religious traditions: i) the unreflective us-and-them discourse, ii) the language of the powerless adopted by the powerful, iii) the uncritical support of religion for the political or economic elites, and iv) the exclusion of the feminine perspective. I have also briefly mentioned the danger of religion legitimating rage.

Since I am exploring the dark side of religion, I will now turn to another problematic dimension of the role religion has played in human society. Let me return to an idea of Karl Marx, with whom we are in disagreement, but whose proposals demand reflection. In his book *The German Ideology*, Marx made fun of the German intellectuals of his day who, influenced by the philosopher Hegel, would spend all day debating the problems of society. In their discussions, Marx claimed, they analyzed the irrationalities of society and tried to resolve them in theory, and then, when the day was over, they would leave their meeting satisfied, believing that they had changed the world. Marx called this German intellectual approach 'idealism,' i.e. the belief that changing the ideas in the head is sufficient for changing the world. He conceded that new ideas are necessary for restructuring society, yet they are never sufficient: changing the world also demands action.

The question I ask myself is whether religious believers are sometimes inclined to practise this problematic idealism. Responding to the violation of peace and justice, religious leaders often propose that what is needed is a change of mind and heart and a renewed commitment to the love of neighbour. Implied in this proposal is the idea that if people become more loving, more forgiving and more generous, then oppressive practices and violent conflicts will disappear. There is an element of truth in this proposal: a conversion of mind and heart is indeed necessary for the reconstruction of a defective social order. But a change of consciousness is not sufficient; we must also wrestle with the concrete conditions of society.

Let me be more specific. If a religious group wants to promote peace in society, it is not sufficient to call for the spiritual conversion of people: it is also necessary to join the public debate dealing with the causes of the conflict, the policies of the government and the interests of the weapons industries. Canada is an arms-producing country, and its industries make millions of dollars selling arms all over the world. Dedication to peace demands more than a change of heart; it calls for a critique of the arms industries and the participation in political debates. Should we who stand for peace demand that labourers in the arms industries give up their jobs? But then, where will they find a new job at a time when unemployment is on the rise? Advocating peace demands more than a conversion of the heart; it includes a wrestling with the concrete problems of society.

Confronted by issues of grave injustice, religious people of goodwill often think that all we need is love, forgiveness and generosity. This is the message of many religious leaders. A recent encyclical of Benedict XVI, *Deus caritas est,* is an expression of this kind of idealism. A different counsel was given many decades ago by Pope Pius XI, when he said that justice demands "the correction of morals and the reform of institutions" (*Quadragesimo anno*, 77). We who are prompted by our faith to promote justice must not only purge our heart and deal justly with our neighbours, we must also challenge the structures of injustice that exploit and oppress innocent people. Under the apartheid regime in South Africa, many people bravely resisted the government at great risk, including Christians, Jews, Muslims, Hindus, and secular men and women. The Kairos Circle, a group of courageous Christians, criticized the churches in their country: they denounced the Afrikaans-speaking church for legitimating apartheid with arguments drawn from the Bible, and then accused the English-speaking churches of asking their members to reject apartheid in their heart but not demanding that they stand against apartheid in the public sphere. The English-speaking church practised what we have called 'idealism.'

I greatly admire the World Conference of Religions for Peace because it urges religious leaders and religious communities to purify their heart, seek the peace of soul, and at the same time join the public debate, reveal the causes of conflicts and wars, and co-operate with non-religious actors who share their commitment to justice and peace.

Gratitude

Some of us, as believers, are convinced that our faith commits us to engage in dialogue and seek co-operation in the service of humanity. In doing so we participate in a spiritual movement for which there is no precedent prior to the 20th century. We have access to a new spiritual energy. In this essay I have concentrated on the ideologies that have marred religious traditions because I believe we must face the dark inheritance of our own tradition to open ourselves to spiritual renewal. All our traditions have a hidden potential enabling us to become partners in a movement that offers light to the world, illuminating the path that leads to justice and peace.

3

Relativism No, Pluralism Yes

The Christian churches must wrestle with the difficult question of how to oppose the dominant relativism of contemporary culture and at the same time honour cultural and religious pluralism. In his homily of April 18, 2005, during the solemn Mass prior to his election to the papacy, Cardinal Joseph Ratzinger expressed his fear that society was steadily moving towards "a dictatorship of relativism."[17] The true and the good are increasingly defined in utilitarian terms: ideas are true and values valid if they serve people's material interests. In present-day society people no longer believe in abiding truths of universal relevance. For this reason, said the Cardinal, they look upon the articulation of Christian teaching as a form of fundamentalism. Against this present trend, the Church must defend the single great truth of God's self-revelation in Jesus Christ.

At the same time, the Christian churches have anguished over the issue of religious pluralism. They are presently learning to honour non-Christian religions, engage in dialogue with them, and defend their followers against prejudice and discrimination. In our increasingly divided world, marked by political conflicts, economic domination, violent struggles and massive social inequality, the Church's commitment to the one truth of Jesus Christ demands that it foster justice, peace and reconciliation and affirm with other religious communities the realm of the spiritual over against the aggressive materialism of the world. Yet if we no longer accept the old distinction between true and false religions, are we not encouraging the dominant relativism marking contemporary society?

Relativism versus pluralism is an issue that demands a great deal of reflection, raising questions that cannot be dealt with in a single essay. Still, even a fragmentary study of the issue has a pastoral usefulness. The churches must teach their members how to react to the new religious pluralism in Canada. I am grateful to the churches for respecting the religions brought by recent immigrants and making no effort to convert them to the Christian faith, even if the theological ground for this new openness has not been universally clarified.

It is not my intention to deal with the Christological issue here. Instead, after describing the baneful impact of the dominant ethical relativism, I wish to offer an analysis of cultural and religious pluralism that reveals their potential for creativity and offers hope for the future.

Before turning to contemporary relativism, however, I wish to question whether it is really true that relativism is the dominant cultural influence. It is possible to argue that the great threat to contemporary society comes from absolutism. What divides countries, peoples and groups today seems to be the inability to respect the rights of others and the refusal to negotiate a compromise that would grant a living space to all concerned. The violent outbursts in the ghettos of France are not the product of relativism, but the result of public policies and public opinion that render the integration of foreign immigrants almost impossible. The violent conflicts between nations or ethno-religious communities in many parts of the world are products of competing absolute claims that suffer no compromise. This absolutism is symbolized by the famous phrase of President George W. Bush prior to the war in Iraq: "Those who are not with us are against us." There is no middle ground; there is no give-and-take; there is only one truth. In the present historical situation, strong currents have emerged in the world religions that profess their truth in absolute terms, refuse to engage in dialogue, and define dissidents and outsiders as enemies. Absolutism is indeed a great danger.

The Monopoly of Scientific Rationality

At the same time, the relativism of truth and values is also a threatening cultural development. What has characterized modernity are the extraordinary achievements of science and technology that have led to the transformation of nature into an obedient and resourceful servant of human interests. This spectacular success has persuaded mainstream intellectuals and large sections of the population that scientific rationality is the only valid approach to truth. One can say without exaggeration that scientific rationality has become the guide of contemporary society. Yet since the sciences deal only with means and have nothing to say about ends, they are unable to define the good, lay the foundation for values and illuminate the meaning of human life. The domination of instrumental reason has created an ethical void in which people, bereft of substantive rationality, make moral decisions in terms of utility. The good has been redefined as the useful.

We cannot deny that the philosophy of utilitarianism has also had positive consequences. It has been argued, for instance, that if a moral principle has demonstrated its usefulness for society over many centuries, it continues to deserve public support. On this basis, some utilitarians accepted Christianity as having proven its truth by its beneficent impact on civilization. Utilitarian reason was also employed to foster the reform of some ancient practices, such as cruel punishments for criminals, that had damaging consequences for society as a whole. Thoughtful utilitarians argued that the moral norm for public decisions should be the promotion of the greatest good for the greatest number. This principle may offer a useful method for deciding where to construct a bridge or build a highway, but in other contexts it may have devastating consequences. What happens when murder promises to produce advantages for a community? We remember the phrase "It is expedient for us that one man should die for the people so that the whole nation may not perish" (John 11:50). The greatest good for the greatest number persuaded the acting high priest that, to keep the peace in occupied Jerusalem and not provoke the anger of the Roman colonizer, it was morally acceptable to sacrifice Jesus, though he was innocent, to prevent an uprising of his enthusiastic followers. Today utilitarian reason is used in many countries to admit the return of torture, thus assuring the greatest good for the greatest number. The reduction of the good to the useful has deadly consequences.

Sociologists studying the cultural impact of modernity have long lamented the decline of ethics and the domination of instrumental reason. Ferdinand Toennies offered this interpretation in the 1880s. He was followed by Max Weber and Georg Lukacs. They predicted the disenchantment of the world, the decline of ethics and religion, the reification of human existence, and the imprisonment of humanity in the iron cage of techno-scientific rationality.

I have always been impressed by the critical theory of the Frankfurt School, developed before, during and after World War II.[18] The rational Enlightenment, these philosophers argued, has today become the great obstacle to human liberation. The original Enlightenment, they argued, looked upon reason as the organ of human liberation, yet here reason embraced techno-scientific rationality as well as substantive reason dealing with ends, such as liberty, equality and solidarity. Emmanuel Kant, philosopher of the German Enlightenment, recognized two dimensions of reason: 'pure reason,' producing the sciences, and 'practical reason,' laying the foundation for the ethical life. Yet in the course of the nineteenth century, the Frankfurt School argued, Enlightenment reason has been reduced to instrumental reason alone. Because of the collapse of ethical reflection, the Enlightenment has pushed society into the dehumanizing logic of techno-science, betraying the Western humanistic tradition, and thus becoming the great obstacle to human liberation.

According to these social thinkers, values in modern society are thought to have no objective reality: they are simply private choices, and, because they depend entirely on the subject, are hence inevitably relative. According to these thinkers, truth in modern society equals scientific truth. Truth claims referring to the meaning and destiny of human life are seen as subjective proposals, as pure speculations, and hence as inevitably relative – a cultural development that has prompted Benedict XVI to speak of "the dictatorship of relativism."

This interpretation of modernity is perhaps excessively dark. The philosophers of the Frankfurt School advocated the decentring of instrumental reason and the retrieval of ethics, yet they offered little hope. By contrast, I have been greatly impressed by a major event of ethical retrieval, namely the Universal Declaration of Human Rights promulgated by the United Nations in 1948. This magnificent defence of human dignity was based not on a set of rational arguments but on the spontaneous, emotive revulsion over the crimes against humanity committed during World War II. Human rights are built on the recognition that human beings are ends to be honoured, never simply means to be used. Although we will not pursue the topic in this essay, the churches and the world religions have been deeply impressed by this Declaration; it has affected their thinking, and it is helping them learn to see themselves as divinely commissioned to promote justice and peace in the world.

Cultural and Ethical Pluralism

The issue of relativism is also raised by our awareness of cultural pluralism. The problem here is quite different from the previous one. Here ethical relativism is not the result of an epistemology that confines objectivity to the order of the sciences and considers values the product of self-interested choices. The ethical relativism to which we now turn reveals itself first in the history of our own tradition in which ethical values have changed over time, and second, in the diverse values inscribed in different cultures.

A provocative example for the first case is the changed evaluation of torture as part of the judicial process.[19] Torture was recognized under Roman law, its use was denounced by ancient Christian authors, and it ceased to be practised in Europe after the collapse of the Roman Empire. Yet beginning in the eleventh century, ancient Roman law began to be revived, which persuaded canon lawyers in the early thirteenth century to recognize the use of torture in civil law procedures. In 1253, in his instruction *Ad extirpanda*, Pope Innocent IV approved the use of torture and recommended it for the prosecution of heretics, to be performed by the civil authorities. This practice was confirmed by Alexander IV in 1259 and by Clement IV in 1265. According to ecclesiastic teaching, the application of torture was limited: it should not cause the loss of a limb nor the loss of life. Torture was later widely practised during the Inquisition and legitimated with ethical arguments by canonists and moral theologians. A reaction against the use of torture gained strength only in the eighteenth century, and eventually the Catholic Church changed its official teaching. We have here an example of ethical relativism in the history of one religious tradition, but examples of this kind can be found in all cultural and religious traditions.

We also have become keenly aware of ethical pluralism in the world because the economic globalization of the present has brought us into contact with non-Western cultures, and because recent immigration has introduced people into Western societies who have inherited cultural values different from our own. Samuel Huntington's theory of 'the clash of civilizations'[20] – a false and dangerous theory, as we shall see – symbolizes for many people the startling difference in values between traditional non-Western cultures and modern Western society. It seems obvious to us that ethical ideas are related to particular cultures.

The ethical relativism across different societies and within the same religion over time obliges us to reflect on the nature of cultural traditions. Such a reflection prepares us for thinking in a new way about religious pluralism. The cultural traditions of human communities are dynamic historical realities enlivened by an internal debate among their members and an ongoing contact with other cultures. The vitality of cultural traditions allows them to respond creatively to historical challenges by rethinking their ideas and values and reforming their customs and practices. Cultural traditions that suppress internal debate and refuse external dialogue become atrophied. Their fate is insecure. They may be extinguished or absorbed by an empire, or they may dwindle away due to the lack of inner dynamism enabling them to renew themselves. Further on we shall see that the world religions are cultural traditions of a particular kind, founded as they are on sacred texts, to which they continue to refer themselves.

This short remark on cultural traditions is sufficient to convince us that in the course of their history, the ideas and values of these traditions undergo important changes. We have become keenly aware that cultural traditions have been profoundly affected by their encounter with the modernity created by industrial capitalism and the institution of democracy. This encounter has produced vigorous internal debates, debates that continue in Western society and that are at an early stage in the rest of the world. These cultures have to wrestle with the contradiction built into modernity, i.e. the tension between the self-interest generated by the market system and the social solidarity summoned forth by democratic institutions. Modernity is inspired by two conflicting visions: the society of winners and losers produced by the unregulated market and the society of equals envisioned by democratic practices. Cultures and religions wrestle with the impact of the institutions in different ways.

There is, then, no reason to be surprised that cultural traditions have changed their ethical ideas and practices over time, and that the arrival of modernity is a particular challenge that prompts internal controversies and demands rethinking inherited attitudes. Yet while these traditions change their values, they may well be committed to underlying, abiding principles that guide them in rethinking their values in response to new challenges. As we shall see, this observation applies especially to religious traditions: change may go hand in hand with fidelity in principle.

Because of the dynamic character of cultures, dialogue and cooperation across boundaries have a creative impact on these cultures. Cultures that first seem foreign to one another discover that dialogue and joint action in moments of historical urgency generate shared values, which allow each culture to remain true to itself without compromise.

The dynamic character of cultures allows us to refute 'the clash of civilizations' theory proposed by Samuel Huntington. According to this American scholar, civilizations are characterized by different and, in fact, incompatible values, and for this reason the clash between them is almost inevitable. He warns Americans of the Muslim threat in particular. Democratic freedom valued in the West, he argues, is not respected in the Muslim world. What Huntington overlooks is that cultures, especially religious cultures, are dynamic historical phenomena capable of responding creatively to new conditions.

Prior to Vatican Council II, some American political thinkers detected a cultural clash between Catholicism and American society.[21] Since Catholicism had officially repudiated the principle of religious liberty, they argued, Catholics could not be trusted as reliable citizens. If they became the majority, they would force the government to declare the Protestant churches illegal. Yet, wrestling with the institutions of modernity, the Catholic Church experienced internal debates that eventually allowed it to reread its tradition and discover there theological resources for respecting religious pluralism and supporting democratic practices. At the present time, a lively debate is taking place among Muslim intellectuals over the rereading of the Qur'an that would support democratic pluralism and human rights.[22] Progressive Muslim thinkers in traditionally Islamic societies envisage a Muslim version of modernity, sustained by faith in divine revelation – and therefore different from the secular modernity of the West. Progressive Muslim thinkers in the West ask themselves how the practice of Islam can foster the common good of society.

After the violent protests in the suburbs of France in the fall of 2005, we hear French intellectuals – among them Alain Finkielkraut – using the rhetoric of cultural incompatibility. The young immigrants did not revolt, we are told, because they are unemployed, locked into their ghettos, and despised for reasons of race and religion; they revolted, it is said, because they are Muslims and thus hold social values at odds with French republicanism. Fortunately, progressive French citizens as well as the French churches have refuted this interpretation.

The incompatibility of ideas and values across cultural boundaries is asserted for rather different reasons by postmodern thinkers. Postmodern thought is non-political, yet in fact it undermines movements of universal solidarity and thus always protects the existing power structures. Philosophers who call themselves postmodern argue that radical differences exist between cultures.[23] Since they have no common values and share no common ratio, conversation between them is impossible. The arrogant illusion of the Enlightenment, the postmoderns argue, was that its truth and its values were universally valid and could thus be imposed upon others. The call for dialogue across boundaries is still inspired by the illusion of modernity: it presupposes a common ratio in all human cultures that makes conversation possible. Yet this common ratio, the postmoderns argue, does not exist.

This provocative idea has been generated in an armchair. The postmodern authors underestimate the creativity of culture, its internal debates and its communication with outsiders. This creativity comes to life most readily in moments of historical urgency. We have witnessed the entry into conversation and the eventual reconciliation between Germany and France after World War II that overcame a century-old hostility and laid the foundation for a united Europe. Harold Wells and I published a book many years ago that documented several Christian efforts at reconciliation between nations or groups after a history of hostility.[24] My contribution was a study of the slow process of reconciliation between Germany and Poland after World War II, which involved cross-cultural dialogue, called forth gestures of repentance and forgiveness, and produced a certain cultural affinity between the two countries.

The issue of ethical pluralism leads us to the important political question of whether there exists a common set of values acceptable in all cultures. We have to admit that the claim of the Enlightenment authors that the values of the emerging modernity had universal validity was excessive. They felt no need to listen to non-Western cultures, since they regarded modern values as true and liberating, destined to overcome the attachment to traditional values. The claim to universality thus became – consciously or unconsciously – a strategy for world domination. Even the Universal Declaration of Human Rights – a major historical event, to my mind – is largely formulated in liberal, Western terms, with the emphasis on the political rights of individuals. People's cultural and collective rights were recognized by the United Nations in Covenants only as of the 1960s.

Some critical voices in Asia and Africa reject the human rights as formulated by the UN as inapplicable in their cultures. They claim that Western individualism undermines their own collectivist traditions. These voices receive support from postmodern thinkers in the West who, for quite different reasons, consider the claim to universality as incipient totalitarianism. I disagree with this proposal. I believe that considering cultural creativity will help us to arrive at a different conclusion.

Cultures are alive by an internal debate and an ongoing conversation with outsiders. Co-operation on matters of great urgency enables members of different cultures to engage in fruitful dialogue, discover certain common values, and initiate renewed thinking within their own tradition. In moments of great need, people belonging to different cultures are straining after unity of action. Here is a significant example.

The fear of a nuclear exchange during the Cold War persuaded religious leaders to found the World Conference of Religions for Peace,[25] where members of the world religions came together to discuss how they could prevent the outbreak of war and foster the non-violent resolution of conflicts. At their meeting, members of the different religions confessed that in the past, their tradition had at times supported unjust rulers and blessed the use of violence, but that the most authentic values of their tradition actually supported justice and peace in human relations. Given the urgency of the situation, the members promised to engage in the renewal of their religious tradition, making them guardians of peace and justice.

This historical example suggests that the formulation of universal values cannot be achieved simply by philosophical thought. The effort of Hans Küng and other religious thinkers committed to universal peace to formulate a universal ethics acceptable to all civilizations and world religions[26] is praiseworthy, but in my opinion it remains too abstract. I believe that it is co-operation in emergency conditions that prompts people of different cultures and religions to work together, engage in dialogue and discover that, despite their different backgrounds, they share certain ethical convictions.

The argument that oriental cultures have a collectivist tradition and hence are unable to acknowledge the rights of individuals is usually proposed by governments or people close to them who want to protect authoritarian rule. Studies of ancient civilizations reveal that there were classical religious texts from the beginning that expressed respect for the dignity of persons.[27] While it is too early to say that a common set of values acknowledged by all cultures and religions exists, there is evidence that there are people all over the world who are straining for unity in truth and values.

The ethical pluralism described in these pages is very different from the ethical relativism produced by the domination of the techno-scientific mindset. To emphasize this difference, the German sociologist Karl Mannheim introduced the distinction between 'relativism' and 'relationism,' the latter recognizing the relatedness of truth to a particular context.[28] The historical context defined by a common commitment to peace in a dangerously divided world will give rise to thinking that promotes the convergence of truth and values. Agreement of ideas is achieved in a process that involves joint action.

The Church and Religious Pluralism

These reflections on cultural pluralism will help us in dealing with the difficult theological question of how to combine faith in the Christian Creed with glad acceptance of religious pluralism. In this essay I want to introduce thoughts on these matters offered by David Tracy who, more than any other theologian, has been interested in philosophical and theological pluralism. Tracy is fully aware that pluralism can be an ideology harmful to truth: it can encourage lazy thinking or satisfaction with mere opinions or indifference to evidence and consistency; ideological pluralism can bless the multiplication of arbitrary judgments to avoid debate on significant issues, or it can replicate in the realm of the spirit the many offers made by the supermarket. Yet David Tracy has the greatest respect for the pluralism of ideas among people committed to depth and wholeness.

Here I can give only a brief account of Tracy's theory of the pluralism-of-traditions.[29] The American Catholic theologian regards religions as cultural traditions marked by a specific difference. Religious traditions are grounded in sacred texts or sacred persons to which they constantly refer and which provide them with a perpetual vitality. Religions are created by hermeneutic communities that read and reread their sacred texts in ever-changing historical circumstances. They seek fidelity to their sacred source through an internal debate involving differing interpretations and through a careful listening to the wisdom they find in their cultural context. This process is by no means smooth. Religious traditions are also drawn into power games, used by governments to control the population and transmuted into ideologies of conquest. Religions are thus ever in need of renewal: they depend on their faithful members who are willing to recommit themselves to the sacred text or the sacred person and boldly propose new patterns of living in the present.

The contemporary age is a time of special favour. Tracy argues that the collapse of colonialism after World War II has revealed to the churches the danger of absolutism. Not only did they bless the colonial enterprise, but also the arrogant claim of possessing the whole truth rendered them incapable of respecting the cultures and religions of the conquered peoples. Today the churches recognize that they are called to be open to other religious traditions. Their task is not to alter or water down their creed, but simply to be open: to listen to others and try to understand them. A second new event is the process of globalization, which brings followers of the world religions together around issues of common concern. The threat to peace, to the environment and to human life itself demands that religious people co-operate, talk to one another, and discover the values that unite them in defence of the global common good. These two changes, Tracy concludes, have created the conditions for interreligious dialogue.

Interreligious dialogue summons forth renewal in all the participant religions. First, this dialogue reveals to us how others see us; it makes us aware of how we have distorted our original inspiration; it reveals to us that our discourse about others is uninformed, prejudiced and causes harm. Second, interreligious dialogue makes us discover the wisdom in other religious traditions. We learn to appreciate their efforts to renew themselves and respond to the challenges of the present. The spiritual insights we find in other traditions make us reread our own sacred texts and, in many cases, find that these insights have an affinity with our religious inheritance and can thus be integrated into our own ever-developing tradition. Interreligious dialogue, according to Tracy, stimulates the creativity of religious traditions. The religions become here keenly aware that they have not reached their full potential and that, due to cultural or political pressures, they have overlooked aspects of their inheritance, lost their balance or even become gravely one-sided. The encounter with other religions urges them to retrieve forgotten elements of their tradition, regain their equilibrium and recover their spiritual depth.

This proposal of the pluralism-of-traditions, Tracy writes, is conservative in the best sense of the word. It summons the participants, including the Church, to remain faithful to their vocation and explore the richness of their inheritance. No one asks the Church to abandon its faith in God's self-revelation in Jesus Christ. All that is demanded of the Church – and of other traditions – is to be open: to listen, to understand, to enlarge the common ground and to hope for a reconciliation of religions that serves the well-being of humanity. As a Christian theologian, Tracy believes that a joint effort to arrive at such a unity-in-pluralism is sustained by divine grace. He thinks of the God revealed in the Gospel as the transcendent Rescuer and Reconciler of a humanity grievously at odds with itself, yet destined to celebrate its plurality.

Tracy describes four 'sins' that damage the pluralism-of-traditions: the sin against openness, i.e. the refusal to listen; the sin against depth, i.e. the trend to reduce the ideas of the others to one's own categories or to accept reductionist interpretations; the sin against justice, i.e. the unwillingness to recognize the ideological role played by one's own religious tradition; and the sin against compassion, i.e. the indifference to the suffering caused by religious conflicts.

A Concluding Thought

I think we can safely conclude that relativism and pluralism refer to quite different historical phenomena. The contemporary relativism of truth and values is produced by the dominant presence of techno-scientific reason, while cultural and religious pluralism is produced by people deeply committed to rich and creative traditions. While contemporary relativism threatens the well-being of humanity, cultural and religious pluralism provides resources for the renewal of human well-being. For reasons of political self-interest, cultural and religious pluralism can create tensions, hostilities and even violent conflict. Yet sin does not have to rule: the divine summons to co-operation and dialogue can lead the many cultures and religions of the world to a dialogical existence, a divinely sponsored unity-in-plurality.

4

Jewish-Christian Dialogue under the Shadow of the Israeli-Palestinian Conflict

Prior to World War II, Jewish religious thinkers who moved beyond the tradition of Orthodoxy were in dialogue with modern culture, including dialogue with Christian thinkers who were also searching for new religious responses to the challenge of modernity. Paul Tillich's Circle of Religious Socialists, founded after World War I, included Christians and Jews, Martin Buber among them. Yet even after World War II, the young German-Canadian philosopher Emil Fackenheim, a Jew, saw himself as an ally of Christian theologians in a joint effort to communicate the word of God to a society that had become secular. He gladly acknowledged an affinity of his theological approach with neo-orthodox Christian thought. Yet in 1967, gripped by the fear that Israel might be destroyed, he assigned the Holocaust a central position in his thinking. He heard God's commanding voice speaking out of the Shoah giving Jewish men and women a new commandment: to struggle for their collective survival so that Hitler would not be granted a posthumous victory. "Never again shall the Jewish people be humiliated and destroyed!" he declared. Fackenheim now took up dialogue with

Christian thinkers in a new key, demanding not only repentance over the Church's ancient anti-Jewish discourse, but also whole-hearted support for the state of Israel, the concrete symbol of Jewish survival and security in the world.[30]

I first met Emil Fackenheim in the 1940s in Hamilton, Ontario, where he worked as a rabbi and I was a student at McMaster University, and in time we became friends. But I was ill at ease with his mature theology. It seemed to me that in 1967 my friend responded to the Holocaust by focusing on the struggle for Jewish survival and the security of the Jewish state, while turning his back on the oppression and the violence inflicted upon other peoples. I was more impressed by the American scholar and rabbi Irving Greenberg, who responded to the Holocaust by saying "Never again!" – meaning that never again shall the Jewish people *or any other people* be humiliated and destroyed. On this basis, Greenberg supported the Jewish state and, at the same time, opposed the war in Vietnam and criticized the American Orthodox Rabbinate for its silence on that conflict. Greenberg also argued that with the foundation of the state of Israel, Jews find themselves in a new his-torical situation. Since they are now able to exercise power, which they were unable to do in the past, they are presently obliged to engage in ethical reflection on the right use of power.[31] I preferred Greenberg's theology to Fackenheim's.

Learning from Jewish-Christian Dialogue

Dialogue between Jews and Christians has made an important contribution to the self-understanding of Christianity. By dialogue I refer not only to round-table discussions between Jews and Christians, but also and more especially to literary exchanges be-tween them. Jews and Christians have begun to read one another's religious reflections. Jews helped the Church to enter the painful process of becoming aware of its ancient anti-Jewish rhetoric. I am thinking especially of Jules Isaac, who participated at the

Seelisberg Conference that recognized the anti-Jewish discourse in the New Testament, produced a set of guidelines for correcting this baneful inheritance, and started a movement in the Christian Church to redefine its relationship to the Synagogue and the Jewish people.[32] In the Catholic Church, this movement had an impact on the Second Vatican Council. The conciliar declaration *Nostra aetate* introduced a new discourse on the Jews and their religion, recognized the ongoing validity of God's ancient covenant with the Jewish people, and called upon Catholics to engage in dialogue, co-operation and friendship with Jews. Similar processes occurred in other Christian churches. A remarkable statement on Christian respect for Jews and Jewish religion has recently been produced by the United Church of Canada.[33]

Dialogue with Jews had a multiple impact on Christian theology. We, who spoke so confidently of redemption, became aware of the unredemption dwelling among us and retrieved the eschatological yearning. We, who focused on the salvation and sanctification of souls, recovered the social message inscribed in the Scriptures and linked faith in Jesus Christ to commitment to social justice. We, who desired to bracket the body and live for the soul, became reconciled to ourselves as bodies unashamedly, in awe of the physical universe around us. In this evolution of Christian self-understanding, dialogue with Jewish religious thought played a considerable part. Even going further, some Christian thinkers who had seen in the order of the universe a sign of God's existence had their vision shattered by the Holocaust and agreed with Rabbi Greenberg that this event had spelled the end of 'untroubled theism.' Christian theologians anguished with Jewish religious thinkers, wondering in what sense it is still possible to think of God's omnipotence and believe in divine Providence.[34]

Our changed relationship to Jews and the awareness of our inherited anti-Judaism have had a profound effect on our study of the Scriptures, our theology of redemption, our catechetical instructions and the preaching on Sunday morning. I was not surprised that several churches, reacting to Mel Gibson's film *The Passion of the Christ*, reminded their members that the story of Christ's suffering had been used over the centuries to stir up hatred for the Jews, and that it was shameful and irrational to put the blame for the passion of Christ on an entire people. The United Church of Canada published an excellent theological statement on this issue as well.[35]

Christian Reactions to the State of Israel

What has been the reaction of Christians to the state of Israel? It is my impression that in Europe and North America the great majority of Christians, repenting of Christianity's anti-Jewish heritage, became strong supporters of the new Republic. Yet there were also conservative Christians, especially at the Vatican, who believed that the expulsion of the Jews from Jerusalem after the Roman conquest in 70 CE was God's judgment on Israel after her refusal to receive Jesus as their Messiah. These Christians held that the Jewish people may not return to Jerusalem and, therefore, that the foundation of the state of Israel was contrary to the divine will. Christians in the Middle East and some Western Christians in solidarity with them regarded the foundation of the Jewish state as the continuation of previous colonial oppression preventing the local population from political self-determination.

The most ardent defenders of the Jewish state were theologians and activists in the churches who loved their Jewish dialogue partners and passionately wrestled against Christian anti-Semitism. The literature they produced affected the American and Canadian Catholic bishops and shaped the public statements the bishops made in support of Israel. The North American bishops urged the Vatican to give official recognition to the Jewish state, an event that happened very late, in 1993.

In the early '70s I gave a talk in Toronto, later published in the American review *The Christian Century*, in which I scolded a Christian journalist for depicting the Jewish state as oppressor of the Palestinian nation.[36] I argued that because of their vilification of the Jews over the centuries, Christians had lost the right to teach ethics to the Jewish people. At that time, Johann Baptist Metz, the important German Catholic theologian, insisted that "Christian theology may never turn its back upon Auschwitz," and defended the state of Israel as "a house against death" in response to accusations uttered from within the German political Left.[37]

After the start of the first Intifada in 1988, the mood in the churches began to change. This is how I started an article written at that time:

> The North American churches have on the whole been relatively silent on the plight of the Palestinian people. Church groups in Canada and the US have hesitated to give strong expression of their solidarity with the Palestinians in their quest for a homeland. Thus churches find themselves in a dilemma. The topic is so delicate because it is situated in the intersection of two major trends in contemporary church life, both which spring from the same theological root.[38]

What are these two major trends? The Christian Church in the West has been wrestling with a twofold guilt: first, the guilt over its ancient anti-Jewish discourse, the contribution it made to modern anti-Semitism and its cowardly silence during the Holocaust; and second, the guilt over its past identification with European empires and their colonial conquests. Not only did the churches regard these conquests as providential, opening the door to the spread of the Gospel, they also assumed the superiority of European civilization and tended, with some remarkable exceptions, to see their mission as the promotion of the white man's culture. In Canada, the churches have made the painful discovery of the ambiguity of the missionary efforts among the Native peoples. The Church's remorse over its anti-Jewish rhetoric and its contempt for Jewish religion is therefore accompanied by the Church's remorse over its identification with empire and its spread of the white man's religion. As a consequence, the Church is deeply committed to the Third World, i.e. to the efforts of the colonized nations to free themselves from foreign domination and create social conditions of greater justice. To express this new solidarity, some authors have begun to speak of the Third Church.[39]

The churches of the West have become aware that the frontiers of the new nations in Africa and Asia were drawn by the colonial powers indifferent to the natural cohesion produced by a common ethnic and linguistic inheritance. Iraq, for instance, was created by the British Empire out of a group of communities, formerly part of the Ottoman Empire, that had nothing in common with one another. The divisions and conflicts in many parts of Asia and Africa are derived from their colonial past. Since the Third Church, troubled by its former loyalties, supports the self-determination of the formerly colonized peoples, it has spontaneous sympathy for the Palestinians.

Jews suffered discrimination in the European empires and thus were not in any way associated with military conquest and colonization. There is no reason for Jews to share the remorse of the churches over their past loyalties, nor their deep concern for the liberation of the Third World and the Native peoples. Many Jews support the struggle for greater justice in these parts, yet they don't do this – as do the churches – as acts of reparation.

After the first Intifada in 1988, the churches began to speak of a twofold solidarity binding them to the state of Israel and the Palestinian people. They supported the security of the Jewish state in safe borders and the creation of a Palestinian state on a contiguous territory. Some American Evangelical churches lobbied in favour of the Jewish state, and a council called The Churches for Middle East Peace lobbied in favour of Palestinian self-determination, yet most of the churches pleaded more even-handedly for a political, non-violent solution to the present conflict.

After the Second Intifada

The second wave of the Intifada after Ariel Sharon's visit on the Temple Mount on September 28, 2000, and the military reaction to it by the state of Israel caused renewed anguish among the Western churches. The leaders of the Canadian churches felt they had to speak to this new situation. Relying on the research done over the years by ecumenical church groups, these leaders composed a draft statement destined for publication in Advent 2000, addressed to the churches in the Middle East as well as to Christians in Canada. For the sake of 'transparency,' the church leaders decided to send the draft to the Canadian Jewish Congress (CJC). Little did they expect to get a reply pleading with them not to publish the statement as drafted. The church leaders complied with these wishes, postponed publication of the statement, and published it in a modified form in January 2001.[40]

What were the objections raised by the CJC? The draft statement was accused of being one-sided, looking at the Middle East conflict only from the side of the Palestinians and being silent about Israel's internationally recognized right to a peaceful existence within safe borders. "We deeply regret your decision not to walk even one inch in the Jewish people's shoes, especially when in Canada you have sought positive Christian-Jewish relations," the CJC wrote. According to the CJC, the Christian draft statement did not adequately acknowledge the violence committed by the Palestinians and simply assumed that the origin of the conflict was the fault of Israel. The CJC regretted that the draft spoke of Israeli settlement on Palestinian territory as "built on confiscated land" and insisted that a just peace treaty required the removal of these settlements from the West Bank and Gaza. The CJC was also offended that the draft statement gave explicit support to UN Security Council Resolution 1322 of October 7, 2000, criticizing Israel for the use of excessive violence and calling for the withdrawal of Israel from the occupied territories.

The Canadian church leaders accepted the CJC's demands. They could have argued that the position adopted in their draft statement corresponded in several points with the Canadian government's policy on the Middle East at that time. The Canadian government supported the security, well-being and rights of Israel as a legitimate, independent state, but did not recognize permanent Israeli control over the territories occupied in 1967 (the Golan Heights, the West Bank, East Jerusalem and the Gaza Strip). Canada opposed all unilateral actions intended to predetermine the outcome of negotiations, including the establishment of settlements in the territories and unilateral moves to annex East Jerusalem and the Golan Heights. Moreover, Canada supported the UN Security Council Resolution 1322.

Yet the Canadian church leaders, deeply attached to Jewish-Christian friendship, altered their draft and produced an even-handed statement that recognized the right of Palestine and Israel to exist in peace and security and demanded that the spiral of violent protest and violent repression give way to non-violence and negotiations. The final statement still demands, even in less specific terms, "the speedy implementation of the relevant United Nations Security Council resolutions, the withdrawal of Israel from settlements in Gaza and the West Bank and the provision of territorial integrity for a Palestinian state."[41]

Jews in North America are, on the whole, deeply offended by the demand that Israel end the occupation, withdraw to the Green Line and order the settlers to return to the Jewish state. This demand, they argue with the Canadian Jewish Congress, puts the entire blame for the present conflict on Israel, without recognizing the threats to its very existence. Authors or speakers who call for the end of the occupation and the return of the settlers can find themselves designated as anti-Semites. It is, of course, quite true that people prejudiced against Jews may criticize Israel to express their personal bias in an acceptable form. Anti-Zionism may be a cover for anti-Semitism. But there are people, church people among them, who have proven their loyalty to Jews and who now express their opposition to the occupation and the settlements. To designate them as anti-Semitic is not only unjust but also unfair, since there is no way a person accused of this prejudice can demonstrate his or her innocence. Such is the mood in society at this time that people hesitate to reveal their critical reflections on the Israeli-Palestinian conflict. They prefer to remain silent, yet they feel frustrated and wonder if they are not being cowardly or dishonest.

The shadow of the Israeli-Palestinian conflict also falls on Jewish-Christian dialogue in North America. On both sides, the dialogue partners feel safer if there is no mention of the Middle East. Since Jewish public opinion in North America is largely unanimous in its support of the Israeli policy on the occupation and the settlements, it is better to avoid the topic. To strengthen solidarity between Catholics and Jews, a meeting took place in New York on January 19, 2004, that brought into conversation eight cardinals from various continents and key leaders of the international Jewish community. The participants thought that the meeting was a great success. The Middle East conflict was not mentioned.

On December 8, 2003, the leaders of the Canadian churches published a letter in which they condemned the recent manifestations of anti-Semitism in Canada and expressed their solidarity with the Jewish people on theological grounds.[42] They again express their sorrow over the hostility to Jews mediated in the past by Christian teaching, and remind Christians of the indebtedness of the Church to the tradition of Israel. "We declare our unqualified gratitude for the gifts of the Jewish people to world civilization in general and Canadian society in particular," the letter stated. The church leaders omit any reference to the Middle East conflict. Does solidarity with the Jewish people imply support for Israeli occupation of Palestine? Or may Christians express their objection to the occupation and the settlements, even if ardent defenders of these policies call them anti-Semitic?

The Intra-Jewish Debate

What is less known in North America is that there are Jewish groups and individual Jewish voices that offer strong support for the state of Israel but are critical of its policies towards the Palestinians. Rabbi Greenberg is one such voice. Many Jewish peace and justice groups in Israel and a few Jewish voices in North America advocate the withdrawal of Israel to the Green Line and reconciliation with the Palestinians, but their efforts are not reported in the mass media. Their books are brought out by small publishing companies that publish radical literature that is not reviewed in the major journals. An exception are two recent collections of essays and statements: *Wrestling with Zion: Progressive Jewish-American Responses to the Israeli-Palestinian Conflict*, edited by Tony Kushner and Alisa Slomon and published in 2003 by Grove Press, New York; and *Prophets Outcast: Dissenting Jewish Writings about Zionism and Israel*, edited by Adam Shatz and published in 2004 by Nation Books, New York.

It is my impression that in France, the inter-Jewish debate in regard to the Middle East conflict is carried out in the public media. Here are two examples. *Le Point* of October 3, 2003, featured a debate between two Jewish intellectuals, Rony Brauman and Alain Finkielkraut. The former claimed that one cannot criticize the state of Israel without being accused of anti-Semitism; the latter denounced the emergence of a new anti-Semitism disguised as a critique of the Jewish state.

The other example is the publication in 2003 of *La prison juive,* by the Jewish intellectual Jean Daniel, well-known editor of *Le Nouvel Observateur*, who lamented the worsening of the Israeli-Palestinian conflict, which is caused, he thinks, by the invocation of God's name. Jewish settlers believe that God gave them the land, and Palestinian suicide bombers trust that God will embrace them as holy martyrs. Faith in an Absolute, whether Jewish, Christian or Muslim, Daniel argues, is a spiritual prison. It makes believers unable to negotiate and arrive at a compromise, which is the only way to peace.

In Israel, the intra-Jewish debate over the occupation is very lively. The Internet provides web sites of a series of Jewish peace-and-justice organizations, some of which welcome Palestinian members. The North American press provides no information regarding these groups. Nor were they known by my Jewish friends, with whom I shared my discovery. These are the groups: Rabbis for Human Rights; *Oz VeShalom* (a peace-oriented Orthodox network); Israeli Committee Against House Demolitions; *Bat Shalom* (a women's movement for peace); Coalition of Women for a Just Peace; *Gush Shalom* (a grassroots movement founded by Uri Avnery), B'*Tselem* (Israeli Centre for Human Rights in the Occupied Territories); Israeli Council for Israeli-Palestinian Peace (ICIPP); Peace Now; Israel/Palestine Center for Research and Information, and Minerva Centre for Human Rights.

Allow me to cite the Principles of Faith spelled out by the Rabbis for Human Rights and their expression of loyalty to Israel's Declaration of Independence.

We, members of Israeli Rabbis For Human Rights, affirm [these principles] in our daily prayers and blessings:

God and Human Beings

God is sovereign over the universe. All humankind is created in God's image and is an active partner with God in perfecting the world (Shabbat 10a, 119b).

Abraham

When God chose our father Abraham, God promised, "All the families of the earth shall bless themselves by you" (Gen. 12:2) and that he would instruct his children and posterity "to keep the way of the Lord by doing what is just and right" (Gen. 18:19). As descendants of Abraham, we must fulfill his legacy of "compassion, generosity and sensitivity" (Yevamot 79b). In accordance with our Torah tradition, the world will declare in admiration, "what great nation has laws and rules as just as all this Teaching that I set before you this day?" (Deut. 4:8).

Torah

The essence of Torah, as summarized by Hillel: "What is hateful to you, do not do to others," reflects the historic experience and ethical consciousness of the Jewish people. Both this historic experience and ethical consciousness must sensitize us to defend the right of all who dwell among us. "When a stranger resides with you in your land, you shall not wrong him. The stranger who resides with you shall be to you as one of your citizens: you shall love him as yourself, for you were strangers in the land of Egypt: I am the Lord your God" (Lev. 19:33-34).

Kiddush HaShem

Exemplary conduct of Israel is a sanctification of God's name (Kiddush HaShem): shameful conduct is a defamation of God's name (Chilul HaShem).

Preserving Life

God's name is sanctified through the respect we show for the human worth and dignity of all God's creatures.

Sanctity of Human Life

Our Mishnah teaches: "Therefore was Adam created single, to teach you that the destruction of any person's life is tantamount to destroying a whole world and the preservation of a single life is tantamount to preserving a whole world" (Sanhedrin 4:5). And again in the words of Rabbi Akiva: "Beloved is Man who was created in (God's) image" (Pirkei Avot 3:18). In an ideal state, "We beat our swords into plowshares..." (Isaiah 2). With our concern for human dignity and the preservation of life, be they Jews or Arabs, we are deeply disturbed by and seek to remove excesses and abuses such as:

Expropriation of land.

Uprooting of trees.

Demolition of homes.

Torture through the use of "moderate physical or psychological pressure."

Coercion and torture to extract confession or to incriminate others.

Bullying and humiliating, which is demoralizing both to perpetrator and victim: and we wish to save our children from the temptation to these vices.

The exercise of double standards by, or the granting of relative immunity to those who wield political or military power and authority, in the pursuit of criminal proceedings in general, through delay, evasion, and protection.

Shooting to kill when life is not in immediate danger.

Collective punishment of "children for the sins of their parents" and "parents for the sins of their children."

Imprisonment without trial in administrative detention.

Removing the rights of residence through confiscation of identity cards.

Sale of weapons to aggressive regimes.

Undercover killings.

:::

As Rabbis of Human Rights in Israel, we are committed to the principles stated in Israel's Declaration of Independence "to foster the development of the country for the benefit of all the inhabitants, based on freedom, justice and peace as envisaged by the prophets of Israel: to ensure complete quality of social and political rights to all its inhabitants, irrespective of religion, race, and sex: to guarantee freedom of religion, conscience, language, education and culture; to guard the holy places of all religions: and to be faithful to the principles of the Charter of the UN."

We pray to bring nearer the day for the fulfillment of the prophecy: "The remnant of Israel will not act iniquitously, nor speak falsely; neither shall there by found in their mouths the tongue of deceit" (Zephaniah (3:13); "When nation will not lift up sword against nation, and no longer train for war" (Isaiah 2); "Who is mighty? One who transforms one's enemy into one's friend" (Avot D'Rabbi Natan 23).

When I discovered the websites of these organizations in November 2000, I was greatly impressed by the statements of their ethical principles, their analysis of the political situation in Israel, and their practical engagement in demonstrations against government policies and actions of solidarity with Palestinians. I downloaded a series of reports and statements from each of these organizations, 150 pages in all, to which I added an introduction of 20 pages and a conclusion of 15, in the hope of finding a publisher for the manuscript. I did not succeed. The manuscript was rejected by six publishers as being too controversial.

In the conclusion of my study I noted that while these groups were not in agreement on all political issues, they were all Zionists, they were patriots, they loved their country. Yet they held that their country, by occupying the land of another people, is betraying the Jewish ethical tradition that is to be an example to the nations. They argued that their commitment to social justice is not only for the sake of the unjustly treated Palestinians, but also and especially for the sake of the Jewish state that is in danger of losing its identity and moral legitimacy – and of entering a phase of violence that may become self-destructive. These groups sorrow over the violence committed on both sides. They record the acts of violence and the terror committed by the state of Israel in the occupied territories, and they do the same for the acts of violence and terror committed by Palestinians against citizens of Israel.

The statements made by these groups and their public gestures are hardly ever reported in the North American media. Gush Shalom, the organization directed by Uri Avneri, sends out e-mail messages on the activities of the Jewish peace and justice movements. In these messages, we hear of the repeated demonstration of Jewish Israelis protesting against the wall of separation that is presently being built.

Let me mention some of the North American Jewish centres committed to justice and peace that support the state of Israel, but are critical of its policies. These centres are in touch with the peace and justice groups in Israel.

The Shalom Center in Philadelphia, founded by Rabbi Arthur Waskow, brings Jewish tradition and spirituality to bear on issues of *tikkum olam* – pursuing peace, seeking justice, healing the earth and building community.[43] The Center works for peace between Israel and the Palestinian people. It provides a critical analysis of the political developments in Israel and reports the activities of the peace and justice groups in that country. The focus of the Center is spirituality. It tries to teach the Jewish community to integrate its concern for Israel into the life of faith and practice to which they are summoned by the Holy One of Israel.

In Vancouver a group of secular Jews publishes *Outlook*, a progressive Jewish review that supports the state of Israel but engages in an extended critique of its policies. In its editorials, *Outlook* opposes the occupation and the settlement. The review promotes a critical outlook on Canadian affairs and world politics from a democratic socialist perspective. It offers its pages to dissenting Jews in Israel and North America.

The Jewish Peace Fellowship takes a different approach, promoting a commitment to non-violence on theological grounds.[44] Like the other organizations mentioned above, the Jewish Peace Fellowship is in solidarity with the Jewish state but disagrees with its policies. The Fellowship is in touch with the Rabbis for Human Rights and other Jewish peace groups in Israel. A good introduction to the Jewish commitment to non-violence is the book *The Challenge of Shalom*, published by the Fellowship.[45]

Tikkun magazine, founded by Rabbi Michael Lerner, is a major publishing venture that brings together progressive political reflection and the Jewish spiritual tradition.[46] Because he wants to overcome the alienation of the Left from religious resources, Michael Lerner also invites Christian authors who acknowledge the link between faith and social justice to write articles for his magazine. To promote the spiritual commitment to peace, justice and respect for the environment, Rabbi Lerner has created Tikkun Communities in several regions of the United States, bringing together Jews who love justice and seek to relate their political perspective to the revealed sources of faith and practice.

The following text is an example of Rabbi Lerner's theology. In it he deals with the topic of atonement for the feast of Yom Kippur in 2000.

> *Tikkun* Magazine is urging Jews and Palestinians to atone for their actions in the past days. On the Jewish side, we are contacting rabbis and others and urging them to support silent vigils and fasting in protest of the excessive use of force by Israel. And we are asking them to include a special section of the Yizkor (memorial prayer for the dead) in memory of the Palestinians as well as Israelis who have lost their lives in the current flare up of violence in the struggle to end the occupation. And we are calling on Palestinians to take similar public actions of protest and atonement against those who are only responding with violence rather than seeking common ground. Yet we do not see these two as totally morally equivalent – the reality remains that the Palestinians have no army and are occupied by one of the most powerful military forces in the world.[47]

Michael Lerner's 2003 book, *Healing Israel/Palestine*,[48] offers a presentation of the Middle East conflict through the eyes of Jews and the eyes of Palestinians. Lerner records with sympathy the Jewish drama of a persecuted people seeking refuge in new land without sufficient respect for the local population, and the Palestinian story of a colonized people seeking to protect its cultural identity against Westernization without sufficient generosity towards the arriving refugees. The author wants to overcome the tendency on both sides to demonize the opponent, remain ignorant of the other's true history, and refuse to recognize the moderate voices in the other camp. The author is fully aware that in the present political climate, many Jews will be shocked by his critical analysis of Israeli policies, and many Palestinians will feel that he does not have sufficient sympathy for their struggle. The purpose of his book is to bring the moderates of the two sides into dialogue and invite the wider community, including Christians, to join this conversation.

Can there be respectful conversation on a topic that stirs up the emotions? A few months ago, a noisy conflict between Jewish and Palestinian students at Montreal's Concordia University erupted into violence. In response to the violent incident, a small group of Jewish and Arab students created an association of Moderates, people from different sides who are committed to justice and human rights and who wish to engage in civilized conversation about their political aims.[49] One concern of the Moderates is to prevent the Middle East conflict from disturbing the peace between people of Jewish, Muslim or Arab origin living in Canada. To foster the spirit of moderation, the Moderates have organized lectures and panel discussions at Concordia University, including interreligious conversation among Jews, Christians and Muslims.

Pope John Paul II highlighted the importance of respect and dialogue in the pursuit of peace:

> We commit ourselves to educating people to mutual respect and esteem, in order to help bring about a peaceful and fraternal coexistence between people of different ethnic groups, cultures and religions.

> We commit ourselves to fostering the culture of dialogue, so that there will be an increase of understanding and mutual

trust between individuals and among peoples, for these are the premise of authentic peace.

We commit ourselves to frank and patient dialogue, refusing to consider our differences as an insurmountable barrier, but recognizing instead that to encounter the diversity of others can become an opportunity for greater reciprocal understanding.[50]

However difficult it may be, interreligious dialogue, including Jewish-Christian dialogue, must go on.

5

Jewish and Christian Reflections on Divine Providence

After the horrors of World War II, many religious thinkers, Jewish and Christian, could no longer accept the traditional teaching on divine providence. They were unable to think of God as the ruler of the world who directed the course of history with loving care for his children. Theologians of my generation remember Adolf Hitler praising "the providence of the Almighty" that led him to become the chancellor of Germany. Is everything that happens in history a disposition of God's providence? Are all historical events providential?

Traditional theology saw the violence and oppression inflicted upon people as part of God's design as punishment for their sins, as pedagogy for their spiritual benefit, or as preparation for an extraordinary gift to be granted in the future. Official Catholic teaching insisted that God does not will evil directly, but only 'permits' it to happen as part of divine providence leading humanity towards its supernatural destiny.[51]

Jewish Theological Reflections

After the Holocaust, some Jewish rabbis were still willing to accept the traditional understanding of divine providence. A number of Orthodox rabbis held that God had permitted the mass murder of the chosen people as punishment for their growing indifference to the divine Law.[52] A liberal rabbi, Ignaz Maybaum,[53] tried to argue that the Shoah had been permitted by God in view of the positive developments after the war: the creation of the state of Israel, the freeing of the East European Slavic countries from century-old German domination, and the purging of the Western world from its fascist trends.

Yet the great majority of Jewish religious thinkers vehemently rejected these theories as caricatures of the Eternal One. They thought it more honourable, after the Shoah, to lose faith in the Lord of history. An atheism of protest was advocated by the American religious philosopher Richard Rubenstein,[54] who continued nonetheless to practise the Jewish religion. Why? Because the discourse and the rituals of Judaism sustained and revitalized Jewish identity. Some of Rubenstein's later writings suggest that an immanent divinity may in fact be at work in the process of humanization taking place in the human family.

An impressive reply to Rubenstein was offered by the Jewish philosopher Emil Fackenheim, who distinguished between two kinds of divine presence: the "liberating presence" revealed at the Exodus, and the "commanding presence" revealed at Mount Sinai where God handed down the Torah.[55] At Auschwitz, Fackenheim argued, God was present – not as liberating voice, but as 'commanding voice,' revealing to the surviving Jewish people a new law, holding primacy over all others, demanding of this wounded people a total commitment to its survival. While the idea of God's commanding voice speaking out of situations of massive historical evil appealed to Jewish and Christian theologians, hardly any

Jewish thinker endorsed Fackenheim's theory that the commanding voice at Auschwitz created a new law in addition to Torah.

Is it possible to question God's goodness? An accepted discourse in the Jewish tradition allows one to challenge God because of the suffering inflicted upon the innocent and accuse God of being unjust, neglectful and indifferent. In the Bible we read that Job was angry with God and indicted God of inflicting pain on the innocent; yet we also read that despite the misery sent to him, Job renewed his confidence in his Creator (Job 13:15). Still, humbly accepting one's own suffering is quite different from humbly accepting the suffering of others.

Elie Wiesel, the contemporary Jewish poet, has introduced his readers to the Jewish religious discourse that holds God responsible for the suffering of the innocent. In his famous play, *The Trial of God*,[56] situated in seventeenth-century Russia in the village of Schamgorod, a group of Jews who have gathered in the tavern, most of them victims of repeated pogroms, decide to put God on trial. The guests are to be the jury; the innkeeper volunteers to be the accuser; yet nobody wants to become God's defender. While the people feel sorry for their God because he has no friends, they are unwilling to defend him because in their hearts they think him guilty. Eventually a clever man walks in who is willing to become God's advocate, yet he cannot prevent the final verdict that finds God guilty.

Words of accusation and doubts about God's innocence are part of a religious discourse that help believers to keep their faith in times of persecution and the infliction of pain. There is no equivalent for this language of faith in the Christian tradition. Yet Christians have been impressed by Rabbi Irving Greenberg's statement that the Holocaust has brought an end to "untroubled theism."[57] Because faith in God generates love and compassion, believers extend their solidarity to the innocent victims and wonder how

God can choose to hide the divine face. The more strongly one believes that God is love, I wish to add, the more strongly one's faith is troubled and shaken in the presence of groundless misery. Christians lack religious sensibility if their faith in a loving God remains unchallenged as they watch on television people's suffering unto death – from hunger, violence and disease – in the vast populations of Africa and Asia. Christians may well acknowledge with Greenberg that faith in a merciful God includes an intermittent dynamic of doubt.

Is it possible to question God's power? The Jewish philosopher Hans Jonas has argued that God was unable to intervene at Auschwitz.[58] Why? Because in the creation of non-divine beings God freely ceased to be all-in-all, abandoned his omnipotence and, in a sense, relinquished his own divinity. God now suffers from his creation. God took the risk of creation without knowing the outcome. This God remains close to humans, cares for them, suffers with them and in this sense evolves in his divinity; yet he is not a king ruling history from above, capable of miraculous interventions to rescue his creatures from suffering. Despite his deep sorrow, God lacked the power to prevent the Holocaust.

The idea of God's freely chosen self-emptying in the act of creation, Jonas reminds his readers, is not wholly new in the Jewish tradition. Jewish mystics in the Kabbala spoke of God's self-withdrawal (*zimzum*) in creation, through which he exposed himself to an unknown fate. God willed to be a suffering God. Yet does this divine *kenosis* leave room for God's power revealed in the Exodus and at Mount Sinai? Hans Jonas is not clear on this point. One has the impression that Jonas's idea of God's self-chosen impotence voids the messianic promises recorded in Scripture.

Christian Theological Reflections

Among Christian authors we find similar anguished reflections. Some raise questions regarding God's goodness, while others challenge the idea of divine omnipotence.

Challenging God's Goodness

Two recent Christian authors believe that the Bible obliges us to say that God is the author of good and evil. Because they think that the biblical evidence for this case is overwhelming, the authors are critical of the theological mainstream and official Catholic teaching, which put the blame for historical evil purely and simply on the shoulders of human beings. This teaching, they argue, goes against the biblical proclamation of God's omnipotence and God's lordship over all of human history. God, they hold, is the creator of light as well as darkness. Catholic teaching, one remembers, has repudiated the idea that God is the author of evil. God does not cause evil, God simply 'permits' it to happen. Yet since, in Catholic teaching, evil is looked upon as devoid of substance, an absence of integrity, a metaphysical defect, divine 'permission' does not appear to imply divine authorship.

Who are the bold Christian authors for whom God is the author of good and evil? Walter Gross, an exegete, and Karl-Josef Kuschel, a theologian, published a major study in which they argue against the dominant theological trend that blames humans for all moral evil in history.[59] The book also opposes the contemporary trend, inspired especially by Jürgen Moltmann's work, to depict God as powerless and suffering. As the title for their book, the two authors chose a provocative passage from the book of Isaiah (45:7) *Ich schaffe Finsternis und Unheil* (I create darkness and woe), suggesting the divine authorship of evil. (I shall refer to this work as the book on God and darkness.)

The exegetical part of the book on God and darkness examines three passages: i) Isaiah 6:1-11, where God declares that he wants to harden the hearts of the people; ii) Isaiah 45:7, where God declares himself as the creator of evil; and iii) Psalm 88, the moving lament of an innocent person entrapped in a pit and tormented by pain, almost as if in a death camp, who holds God responsible for his suffering. What the exegetical section does not confront are the terrible passages in connection with the Exodus and the Conquest of the Promised Land, where God is presented as the divine warrior inflicting an escalating series of plagues upon the Egyptians, culminating in the death of the first-born sons (Exodus 12:29-30), drowning the Egyptian soldiers in the Red Sea, and creating terror among the nations, the inhabitants of Philistia, Edom, Moab and Canaan (Exodus 15:13-18). The LORD commands Israel not to make treaties with the inhabitants of the land and promises to help Israel to destroy all of them (Deuteronomy 7:1-24). The LORD is to be at war with Amalek in every generation (Exodus 17:14-16) and the Israelites are ordered to blot out the very memory of Amalek under heaven (Deuteronomy 25:17-19).

How are we to read these and other passages where God demands the death of entire peoples and punishes the Israelites who show them mercy? Already in the third century Origen argued that biblical passages that ascribe to God qualities at odds with the divine nature may not be taken literally, but must be interpreted in allegorical fashion.[60] He proposed that the water that drowned the Egyptians in the Red Sea symbolizes the grace God pours over his children in baptism to extinguish their aggressive propensities. Traditional exegesis has, for the most part, offered a non-literal interpretation of these violent texts. According to Martin Buber, these passages demand that Jews choose between God and the Bible: believers do not accept stories that are at odds with God's mercy and goodness.[61] I conclude that using biblical passages to prove that God is the author of historical evil is not a persuasive argument.

The theological part of the book, written by Kuschel, examines the traditional Christian teaching through St. Augustine, St. Thomas and the Church's official position rejecting the idea that God is the author of moral evil. Human suffering is only 'permitted' by God as punishment, as pedagogy, or as an antecedent of an unmerited gift. Calvin was more willing than his theological predecessors to ascribe to God authorship of human woe. Kuschel then presents an analysis of contemporary theologians who present God as unable to rescue people from their misery and instead as suffering with them and in them. Kuschel regards this trend as unacceptable, at odds with the biblical witness to God's action in human history. Even if incomprehensible to us, Kuschel argues, evil deeds making the innocent suffer are part of divine providence. We must overcome a naive understanding of God's goodness because God is sovereign and bears ultimate responsibility for the entire cosmos. Christians must put their trust in God's providence, which directs the entire course of human history. Christians must stand against evil and wrestle to overcome it, but they must also acknowledge that God, the totally Other, the Incomprehensible One, the creator and lord of the universe, transcends the distinction between good and evil.

Neither the biblical arguments for God as the author of good and evil nor the theological reflections elevating God beyond the categories of good and evil seem to me persuasive.

Challenging God's Omnipotence

Since the Holocaust, new thinking about God's relation to human history has emerged. We have mentioned Jewish religious thinkers who have questioned God's power. Several Christian theologians also concluded, quite independently from one another, that it is necessary to rethink what is meant by God's omnipotence. They argue that God is paradoxically both powerful and weak, that God enters in solidarity with those who suffer, and that God's gracious presence is the source of salvation and rescue. Divine providence reveals itself in the redemptive moments of human history.

Paul Tillich

An example of this development is found in the evolution of Paul Tillich's theology of divine providence from Volume I (1951) to Volume III (1963) of his *Systematic Theology*. In Volume I, Tillich adopts the traditional position that God directs the course of human history.[62] He defines divine providence as God's "directing creativity" as distinguished from God's "originating" and "sustaining" creativity. God directs every creature to its fulfillment, not by miraculous interventions but by releasing the creativity of human actors and their institutions. "God's directive creativity always creates through the freedom of man and the spontaneous and structural wholeness of all creatures."[63] Faith in divine providence provides an escape from the idea of blind fate and meaninglessness of life. Christians believe in loving protection and personal guidance. "*Special providence* gives the individual the certainty that under any circumstances, under any set of conditions, the divine 'factor' is active and that therefore the road to his ultimate fulfillment is open."[64]

There is also a *historical providence*, Tillich argues, since God is an actor in human history. "The experience of the great empires with their fateful power," he writes, "does not shake Jewish and Christian confidence in God's historical providence. The empires are stages in the world historical process, whose fulfillment is the Reign of God through Israel and the Christ"[65] – a fulfillment, he adds, that lies beyond human history. Tillich also offers a metaphysical argument for God's overall providence. "The certainty of God's directing creativity is based on the certainty of God as the ground of being and meaning."[66] Tillich admits that this trust in divine providence is often trust 'in spite of' the evidence of the senses. Still, the passages cited from Volume I of his *Systematic Theology* suggest that Tillich defended God's lordship over human history, even if the divine goodness often remains hidden.

I read quite differently Tillich's theology of divine providence in Volume III of his *Systematic Theology*.[67] Here he argues that only a theology that takes account of the Holocaust and other great historical horrors has the right to speak of divine providence.[68] In this context Tillich is more conscious of the sinfulness of the human situation. He introduces the idea of *kairos*: the special moment or hour of God's choosing that mediates a redemptive breakthrough in destructive historical circumstances. Tillich first speaks of *kairos* in a secular context, referring to the special constellation of historical factors when a revolution towards greater justice becomes a realistic historical project. In a theological context, *kairos* stands for the breakthrough of God's grace creating the new within the sinful, oppressive and destructive context of the present. "Something happened to some people through the power of God's kingdom as it became manifest in history, and history has been changed ever since."[69] The great *kairos* is the death and resurrection of Jesus Christ; in dependence on this redemptive Event, many other *kairoi* continue to occur in the history of humans and their communities.

In the light of this theology, divine providence refers to the saving acts of God. Not all events that occur in history are providential, but only God's redemptive actions creatively rescuing people from the power of evil. "Historical providence includes all [these] and is creative through [them] toward the new, both in history and above history," Tillich says.[70] Thus the horrors of the 20th century are not part of divine providence. They belong to the story of human sin. Yet the people who suffered in these dreadful events were not deserted by God: God remained with them as the power sustaining their faith that they continue to be in God's hands and their hope that their humanity will be fulfilled beyond present suffering.

If I understand these pages of Volume III correctly, Tillich here presents historical providence as the saving acts of God that at certain moments overcome historical evil. In an early book on socialism, Tillich had introduced the concept of 'expectancy,'[71] a faith-based attitude towards the future, without which no social movement can gather strength and eventually transform society.

Personal providence, according to Tillich, is God's presence in human life, especially in moments of greatest need, opening the door to spiritual growth, to what he calls the New Being, in this world or the next. According to a theme pursued by Tillich in several of his writings, it is in the eye of the storm, in the centre of human lostness, in the most crucifying circumstances, that God manifests God's transforming power, opening the door to the unexpected. For Tillich, we recall, God is not a divine super-person ruling the world from above, but the very ground of being sustaining and graciously rescuing humans on their way to fulfillment. While God's omnipotence remains hidden in the course of human history, except for certain salvific moments, God's omnipotence in people's personal lives is revealed in his ever-present care, sustaining them in a trust that will not be disappointed – a share in Christ's resurrection.

Eugen Drewermann

The horrible crimes committed during World War II opened Eugen Drewermann's eyes to the terrible cruelty operative in the evolution of life, where the strong conquer the weak and where all kill to eat and survive.[72] The biblical story of God as creator and lord of the universe has become unacceptable to Drewermann.[73] He believes instead that the God of whom the wisdom traditions in Old and New Testament speak and to whom religious people all over the

world address their prayers is an immanent divine power that rescues humans from their fears and their destructive behaviour and
empowers them to create a culture of love, justice and peace.[74] But
this God, Drewermann insists, may not be thought of as creator
of the evolving universe nor as lord of human history. This God,
therefore, bears no responsibility for Auschwitz.

Using the Kantian distinction between pure and practical reason,
Drewermann argues that the knowledge of the cosmos and human
history belongs to science (pure reason), while the knowledge of
a divine presence operative in the pacification of humanity belongs to wisdom (practical reason). This wisdom deals with the
practice of the good life and has nothing to say in the field where
science alone is competent. It is therefore an error to speak of
God as providentially involved in the shaping of human history.
Here Drewermann disagrees with the Bible and argues against the
Church. Yet since he acknowledges that the God encountered in
prayer rescues people from their destructive drives and transforms
their hearts, Drewermann seems to imply, in spite of himself, that
God acts graciously in the history of the human family. A generous
reading of this original thinker, softening his anti-metaphysical
bias and anti-ecclesiastical rhetoric, locates his thought within the
spectrum of traditional Christian theology.

Jürgen Moltmann

A suffering God has had a special appeal for Christian theologians.
As self-emptying or *kenosis* has been predicated of the Son of
God who divested himself of his divine prerogatives and became
obedient even unto the cross (cf. Philippians 2:8), so can *kenosis*
be predicated of God the Father, who in the act of creation has
freely bracketed the infinite divine totality. Divine *kenosis* makes
room for finite beings. In his important and influential theological
work, the Protestant theologian Jürgen Moltmann explored the
theme of divine *kenosis* in the light of Christian faith.[75] His ideas

have obtained a wide hearing in the Christian Church. He has argued that the traditional metaphysical idea of God – perfect, immutable and invulnerable – contradicts the scriptural witness to a God passionately involved in the lives of God's creatures and biased in favour of the poor and oppressed. Through the freely chosen divine *kenosis* in creating the world, God opened a space for the non-divine, restricted divine omnipotence and shouldered the terrible risk of human history. God here chose not to be omnipotent. When Jesus suffered and died on the cross, God suffered with him and in him: the Father grieved over the loss of his Son. On the cross, God has revealed both God's voluntary impotence and God's suffering solidarity with all human victims of injustice. God did not remain at a safe distance from Auschwitz, Moltmann argued, but was present there suffering with the inmates.

Despite his stereotyping of traditional metaphysics and his sometimes excessive rhetoric, Moltmann's original theology remains wholly within classical credal Christianity. He is aware of the Church's condemnation in 447 of Patripassionism, the idea that the crucifixion also causes God the Father to suffer.[76] A close reading of his work reveals that Moltmann distinguishes between suffering *ex carentia,* produced by the disruption of integrity, and suffering *ex abundantia,* produced by loving identification with those who are broken. According to Moltmann, God's suffers only *ex abundantia*, out of his infinite compassion, without any loss of divine integrity.[77] Yet that God is compassionate is traditional teaching. Moreover, a reading of his work reveals that for Moltmann – unlike Hans Jonas – the divine *kenosis* is a temporary disposition to be displaced at the eschaton by the glorious manifestation of God's omnipotence raising from the dead the victims of history and bringing about the final judgment.[78]

Moltmann's theology of God's suffering with and in human beings has been widely accepted among Protestant and Catholic theologians. Examples of the latter are Maurice Zundel,[79] Walter Kaspar[80] and Ottmar Fuchs.[81]

What is the meaning of divine providence if God has chosen to relinquish God's sovereign power? Moltmann has very little to say on this topic. He hints that God's liberating power manifests itself in history at special moments when the historical conditions are such that people suffering from injustice, empowered by the Spirit, are able to transform their society.[82] In my reading, this recalls Paul Tillich's idea that God's providence reveals itself in redemptive *kairoi*, the breakthroughs of grace in contexts created by sin.

Douglas Hall

In *God and Human Suffering*, the Protestant theologian Douglas Hall shows sympathy for Moltmann's theological approach.[83] Hall worries that a certain Christian imagination of God's omnipotence is based on the problematic human notion of conquest. He argues persuasively that conquest, the victory of some humans over other humans, has been the cause of evil and violence that has made human history into a slaughterhouse and that, for this reason, conquest should never be attributed to God. God's power is non-coercive and non-violent. God acts in history by touching people's hearts. For Douglas Hall, "providence is grace."[84] This recalls the curious fact that in the English language, calling an event 'providential' always means that it has been beneficial, at least in the long run.

My Own Reflections

When, in the late 1960s, I wrestled with the question of God's relation to humanity, I was greatly influenced by Catholic theologians, especially Maurice Blondel and Karl Rahner, for whom God was graciously immanent in human life and history. I recognized in this theology an affinity with Paul Tillich's idea of "God beyond

God." In my book *Man Becoming* (1970)[85] – the title reveals that I was as yet untouched by the feminist critique – I presented my own theological approach based on the idea of God's transcendent immanence in human history. God was not a divine person situated above history, ruling the world from his heavenly throne; rather, God was a mysterious personal power graciously present to humans and operative in their self-constitution as persons and as communities.

This approach allowed me to formulate a theology of divine providence that one could repeat without turning one's back on Auschwitz. Evil is purely and simply against the divine will. "God is light and in him is no darkness at all" (1 John 1:5). Theologians who regard God as the supreme being governing the world from above are obliged to say, however much they emphasize God's love and mercy, that evil is part of the divine plan of salvation. They must admit with a heavy heart that even Auschwitz has a place in God's providence. I prefer to argue that there is a radical opposition between God and evil. God does not permit evil; God stands against evil, condemns it and transcends it. God is constantly at work among humans, summoning them and strengthening them to discern evil; wrestle against it; be converted away from it; cooperate with others to overcome it; and if need be, sacrifice their life as a witness in opposition to it. Revealed in Christ's resurrection is that the transcendent divine mystery operative in the history of human self-making creates life out of death.

Since God is love, I felt it was necessary to rethink the traditional teaching on divine punishment. Theologians used to distinguish between God's 'antecedent will,' which intends universal salvation, and God's 'consequent will,' which is consequent upon human sin and which decrees plagues and punishments for sinful humanity. I prefer to think that God does not punish![86] As sin disrupts human integrity and creates chaos in human relations, sin devastates human well-being on the personal and social level and thus generates its own punishment. God's mercy, which in Scripture is also called God's justice, graciously offers to interrupt the connecting link between sin and its punishment, and to rescue sinners from the self-destructive consequences of their own deeds. Hell is the result of humans' self-exclusion.

Today, over thirty years later, I continue to hold that there is no shadow or darkness in God. In the words of Edward Schillebeeckx, God's presence is always healing and rescuing.[87] Where, then, does evil come from? We painfully discover evil as a dimension of our historical existence. According to the Christian tradition, the origin of evil is due to the sin of humans and the fall of angels. While St. Thomas recognized God as the *causa prima* of the universe, he designated humankind as the *causa prima* of evil.[88] The idea introduced into Christian theology by Jürgen Moltmann that in the act of creation God contracted God's own power and thus risked the emergence of counter-divine forces is very persuasive. We recognize that sin and evil are among us, and yet profess that God is good and in no way responsible for it.

While I have sympathy for the idea of divine *kenosis*, I hesitate to follow Moltmann's theology of God's powerlessness and his often unqualified reference to God's suffering.[89] Christians living in situations of historical terror – according to the witnesses living in Latin America – are consoled by the thought of God's omnipotence that will create justice at the end. They may hold that God is compassionate and grieves with them, but they cling to their faith that God is invulnerable, transcendent and out of reach of their oppressors. Adolfo Pérez Esquivel, who was imprisoned and tortured in Argentina and later, in 1980, received the Nobel Peace Prize, told the story of a religious experience that had sustained him in prison. As he was taken back to his cell after a session of torture, he glimpsed an empty cell with a blood-stained wall opposite the door, on which a prisoner had written with his finger the words *Dios no mata* – God does not kill.[90]

I prefer to continue to speak of God's omnipotence. Divine omnipotence here means that in whatever imposed or self-inflicted prison human beings find themselves, God's saving power accompanies them, enabling them to avoid a collapse into bitterness and despair, and bring to realization their human destiny in this life or the next.[91] Divine providence here means the acts of salvation in human history, culminating in the death and resurrection of Jesus Christ and present in the manifestations of divine grace rescuing people and their communities from evil. What God's omnipotence means to believers living in the midst of terror is that God sees their plight, God judges evil, God cannot be conquered, and God saves them in this life or in God's coming reign.

An Alternative Idea of Divine Providence

I conclude from the preceding discussion that many Christian theologians, reflecting on the Holocaust and other historical horrors, have arrived independently from one another at a new interpretation of divine providence. In one way or another, they agree with Tillich's idea of *kairos*. Not all historical occurrences are part of God's providence, but only the breakthroughs of divine grace.

While the whole of Christian theology recognizes God's incomprehensibility, the decision around where precisely we put the question marks has pastoral consequences. If we put the question mark behind God's goodness and think of God as in some way responsible for evil, we move in one spiritual direction; if we put the question mark behind God's power and recognize the divine *kenosis*, we opt for a different spirituality.

In my opinion, putting the question mark behind God's goodness creates spiritual problems for men and women afflicted by illness or other painful or debilitating hardships. How can we surrender ourselves to God in prayer when we have doubts about the divine goodness and think of God as in some way the author of our suffering? Opting for God's goodness without flaw or darkness creates a different spiritual situation. Many years ago, when I was sick over a period of several months, I found it impossible to surrender myself to God's will until it became clear to me that God was not the author of my illness; God was, rather, the gracious power that promised healing or a new spiritual life in a situation of physical handicap. I derived consolation from the Thomistic concept of God as *actus purus*, which implies that God, fully active, with all divine potentialities actualized, is creatively present in every passage from potentiality to act, including people's entry into their full humanity.[92] Here God is seen more as a verb than as a noun.

The tragedies in people's lives are not planned by God. They are not part of divine providence. What is providential is that people in these situations are accompanied by God's care and God's strength to manage their lives, act creatively and walk the way of healing, or trust in the newness after death. Was the death of Jesus on the cross in accordance with the divine will? God's will, I prefer to argue, was that Jesus become a prophet denouncing the alienating practices of the religious and political authorities, even if this meant endangering his life and suffering excommunication and crucifixion. At the end Jesus could have sought a hiding place, yet he surrendered himself to the divine will in remaining faithful to his prophetic mission even unto martyrdom. In raising his Son from among the dead, God rehabilitated all the victims of human history.

Putting the question mark behind God's goodness also has, I believe, problematic political consequences. For if in the face of massive injustices we invoke the providence of a God who is the author of good and evil, we may fail to be outraged by the misery inflicted upon others. Pope Pius X still believed that the division of society into rich and poor was part of divine providence. But if we hold that God is good and loving without qualification, then we recognize that social injustice is opposed to God's will and not part of divine providence. God is present to these tragic events as the divine summons empowering people to resist injustice and act collectively to reconstruct the social order. God's providence manifests itself in people's social passion that transforms them into critics and activists creating social movements in support of love, justice and peace.[93]

Opting for a God of love who bears no responsibility for evil and yet saves us from evil leaves an unanswered problem. What remains without adequate explanation is the presence of anti-divine forces in creation. What Christians believe is that God's providence overcomes these evil forces in part and that God's reign will triumph over them at the end of history.

My reading of the Our Father encourages me to sustain the theological option for God's unqualified goodness and God's radical opposition to evil. God the Father is 'in heaven' in the sense that God is beyond attack and cannot be harmed by the lords and masters of this world. We praise the name of God who is so different from us. Since it is by no means certain that God's will shall be done on earth, we pray that "[God's] will be done on earth as it is in heaven." We know what the divine will is: it is the coming of God's reign, the victory of love, justice and peace in a world wounded by sin. Thus we pray, "Thy kingdom come." Thinking of the starvation of peoples in famines, which for the most part have been produced by decisions made by the powerful, we pray that God may give humans their daily bread. Yet even though the masters of the world cause so much suffering and provoke our resistance, we do not want to hate them: we want to learn to forgive them as we ask God's forgiveness for our own sins. We pray that we may not be led into temptation: the temptation of despair over the dominion held by the unjust structures and powers that cause human misery – despair making us feel that there is nothing we can do to change the evil situation, despair that there is no alternative. The Our Father encourages me to think of divine providence as

God's acts of salvation, the *kairoi*, empowering people to see the truth, recognize evil, stand against it, be consoled, assume social responsibility, act in common, and enter upon God's life.

6

The Post-Secular Society:
A Proposal of Jürgen Habermas

On October 12, 2001, Jürgen Habermas, the famous German social philosopher, gave a public lecture in which he changed his mind about the role of religion in public life and advocated what he called 'the post-secular society.' The occasion of the lecture was the reception of the Peace Award, given to him by the German Book Trade. The text was published in the *Frankfurter Rundschau* of October 16, 2001. On a visit to Germany two weeks later, everyone I met in the theological milieu to which I belong was discussing Habermas's new proposal.

New Reflection on Secularization

Habermas's entry point into the topic was the heated debate on genetic engineering in Germany that is pitting two major voices against one another: the organized scientific community and the representatives of the Christian churches. The scientists demand freedom for research and new experiments and look upon the Church as obscurantist, opposing scientific progress in the name of irrational sentiments derived from a previous age. The churches in turn accuse the scientists of having a naive faith in progress and advocating a crude naturalism that undermines the ethical foundation of society. A third voice, Habermas notes, less prominent than the first two, represents what he calls "enlightened common sense," a form of intelligence that is willing to be taught by the sciences, yet opposes the orientation of science towards the instrumentalization of the world. As we shall see, this is where the German philosopher locates his own theoretical approach.

The present debate over genetic manipulation and the cloning of human beings, Habermas argues, calls for new reflection on the secularization of society. The modern state guarantees religious liberty and yet excludes religion as a public actor. At present, only secular voices receive a hearing. Should this change? Should the state listen to the voice of religion on public issues? Habermas calls for new reflection on this topic.

He reminds his audience that at the beginning, 'secularization' referred to the confiscation of ecclesiastical property by the secular authorities. Later, the term designated the gradual replacement of religious ideas, ways and customs by secular equivalents that were regarded as superior. The churches, on the other hand, interpreted this process as the alienation of illegally acquired property and eventually as the loss of their religious way of life. The 'replacement argument' offered by secular thinkers gave rise to historical optimism and trust in progress, while the 'alienation argument' put forward by the religious thinkers generated theories of cultural decline. According to Habermas, both of these positions reveal the same mistake: they presuppose that the tension between modernity and religion constitutes a zero-sum game, an all-or-nothing conflict where the victory of one side implies the defeat of the other.

This mistaken perception, Habermas continues, holds sway in secular society. The only religion acceptable in the modern state has been one that acknowledges the authority of the sciences and refuses to offer public resistance to what is regarded as scientific progress. If the churches want to be heard, they have to translate their religious convictions into secular discourse. They recognize that the modern state is partial and takes sides with the sciences against religion. Guaranteeing religious liberty, the secular state assures the freedom of individuals and their communities to practise their faith. Yet the state looks upon religious convictions as purely subjective, based on visions and values inherited from an earlier age, with no objective content that would deserve a hearing. Religious people who want to join the public debate are obliged to express their ideas in the one discourse recognized by secular society.

Is this the correct understanding of contemporary pluralism? In reliance on "enlightened common sense," Habermas proposes the thesis that the exclusion of religion from public life is undemocratic and ultimately harmful to society. The time has come to move beyond the secular society.

Communicative Rationality

What is this enlightened common sense? It is another way of naming the communicative rationality that Habermas has explored in his social philosophy of knowledge. Enlightened common sense is the hermeneutic intelligence that allows us to interpret other people's communications and arrive at an understanding of who we are ourselves. This intelligence is operative in the experience of daily living, 'the life world,' where we presuppose that we are interdependent subjects, acting freely with intention and holding ourselves and others responsible for the choices made. No scientific theory of behaviour, Habermas argues, has persuaded people to live their life differently. The experience of daily living with its manifold expectations, actions and reactions is immune to any determinist theory of human behaviour. Scientists who embrace a deterministic theory in their research continue to act in their own circle on the basis of common sense, recognizing the freedom and responsibility of their spouse, their children, their friends and their colleagues. People experience themselves as ethical beings: they hold moral values, have expectations regarding what they and others should do, regret their own faults and blame others for their moral failures. This realm of knowledge, Habermas argues, resists the impact of the sciences.

Enlightened common sense, Habermas continues, is critical of the (in principle) unlimited effort of the sciences to turn the whole of nature, including human beings, into objects – objects to be understood in terms of the laws operating within them and ma-nipulated in expectation of greater utility. That the sciences are ethically blind and advance the reification of the world is a criti-cism widely held in German philosophy: not only in the Frankfurt School, Habermas's own background, but also among philosophers associated with phenomenology. Habermas's contrast between science and common sense even recalls the distinction made by Kant between pure and practical reason. Habermas laments that today, brain research aims at objectifying human consciousness itself, an effort that seeks to depersonalize and dehistoricize human existence. The intentionality and normativity of human action are here being explained in neuro-biological terms. It may well hap-pen, Habermas suggests, that a person responsible for his or her actions will soon no longer be a scientifically acceptable concept. Because it fails to recognize it own limits, science here becomes 'bad philosophy.'

Enlightened common sense is open in two directions. It is will-ing to be taught by the sciences, yet refuses to regard them as the only source of knowledge. Common sense is keenly aware that the sciences are unable to account for human autonomy. They cannot grasp the drama of human existence. Enlightened common sense has a relationship to the religious traditions that is somewhat similar. With its emphasis on human freedom and responsibility, common sense resists the religious teaching that human beings are dependent on God and incapacitated without divine assistance. Still, common sense as hermeneutic rationality is able to understand the human meaning of many religious teachings. People without faith are quite capable of listening to and interpreting what religious communities are saying in the discourse proper to their tradition. Enlightened common sense, Habermas concludes, searches for truth and error in the realm of the sciences and in the discourse of the religions.

The Post-secular Society

In the name of this communicative rationality, Habermas demands that the democratic state remain neutral in regard to philosophy; refuse to identify itself with either side of the debate between the scientific establishment and the Christian churches; and yet be willing to listen to the voices of all parties, including that of religion. In Germany, the democratic process must pay attention to the voice of the Christian churches. Modern society, Habermas argues, must become a 'post-secular' democracy.

The famous German philosopher, who is now in his 70s, had in the past argued that the sacred has been transformed by communicative rationality into secular, authoritative discourse. The life-sustaining symbols and values of the Western religious traditions have been received and translated by the Enlightenment and are being handed on creatively by the historical project of modernity. The symbols and institutions that embody *liberté, égalité et fraternité* now provide people with ethical meaning and nourish their emancipatory aspirations. The religious traditions, Habermas then argued, have exhausted their creativity and social relevance, they have nothing pertinent to say to people wrestling with contemporary issues, and they will thus gradually drop out of the picture altogether.[94] His speech of October 12, 2001, showed that he had changed his mind.

The Canadian reader of Habermas's speech may wonder whether his description of the German state as ideologically secular and unwilling to listen to the churches is historically correct. To an outside observer the two churches, Protestant and Catholic, seem to be fully integrated into German society: they are publicly recognized social agents; they operate major social institutions such as social work agencies, health-care establishments and health insurance corporations; and they are among the most important employers in the country. Because their social function is indispensable, the government pays for religious education in the schools, finances theological studies at the universities, and collects the church tax that church members have to pay. (When Christians – the great majority in Germany – fill out their yearly tax declaration, they are legally bound to pay a specified amount in support of their church.) It seems to me that the secularization of German society has proceeded much more slowly than in other Western societies. Only in the eastern part of Germany, the former German Democratic Republic, has the dominant culture become fully secular. An outside observer finds it hard to believe that in a society where the churches are honoured public institutions and receive substantial support from public funds, the government refuses in principle to listen to their voice.

It is my impression that Habermas, deeply troubled by the current support for genetic engineering, including research on human cloning, is greatly afraid that the relatively small humanist camp to which he belongs will not be able to offer effective resistance. In our time, he argues, when science whittles away at the ethical foundation of society and the logic of the market invades ever-wider sectors of human interrelations, enlightened common sense welcomes the wisdom mediated by religion. Since he welcomes the voice of the churches, he finds himself obliged to rethink his theory of modernity. He calls upon Western countries to become post-secular societies where, following the democratic principle, all voices are being heard, including those of religious communities. The Enlightenment project of universal emancipation, he now argues, needs the critical co-operation of the world religions.

After September 11

The *Frankfurter Rundschau* reports that Habermas began to write his speech prior to September 11, and that he was subsequently obliged to relate his topic to the terrorist attacks on the World Trade Center and the Pentagon. By a curious coincidence, at the very moment when the celebrated philosopher wants to persuade the secular German public that religion is a source of wisdom, religion reveals its potential for rage, revenge and violence. Habermas recognizes that the terrorist attack on the symbols of American power was inspired by an extreme expression of religious faith, and that President Bush's rhetoric justifying the war against terrorism reveals his thinking to be guided by an apocalyptic religious imagination. Is this the right moment to defend the wisdom of religion before a secular audience?

After September 11, graffiti appeared on the wall of the Presbyterian College flanking McGill University, announcing in red letters that RELIGION KILLS. Many people have become afraid of religion. Even believers are disturbed by the ease with which religious faith explodes into violence. It deserves to be noted that the major churches in the US made public statements refusing to confirm the rhetoric of President Bush and instead counselling attentive reflection: they warned of revenge; agreed that the guilty parties be caught, tried and punished; yet demanded that no harm be done to the innocent. The churches defended Islam as a religion of peace. They also insisted that we owe it to the victims to investigate the reasons for terrorist violence and recognize that conditions of poverty and exclusion are breeding grounds for irrational rage.

How does Habermas relate the events of September 11 to his proposal of the post-secular society? He argues that these events confirm his idea that new reflection on the secularization of society has become imperative. What is the source of religious fanaticism? In part, at least, it is the enraged response to the systematic denial to grant religion a public voice. The refusal of Western governments to listen to the claims made by religious voices appears to representatives of non-Western societies as an ideologically motivated deafness that wants to exclude them from the global conversation. A principled secularism makes Western societies attribute universal validity to their own cultural evolution and prevents them from making an effort to understand non-Western cultures whose identity includes religious attitudes and symbols. The unwillingness to honour the public expression of religious meaning in other civilizations, linked to material conditions of exploitation, humiliation and exclusion, is capable of enkindling extremism among believers and stirring up fanaticism. Today the spread of secular modernity driven by neo-liberal globalization and a US-based culture of consumerism and entertainment represents a threat to religiously based civilizations. The war against terrorism, inspired by President Bush's sectarian Christian vision, is based on a total misunderstanding of the historical situation. Bombs on Afghanistan are as mute as terror attacks on New York and Washington; what is needed is communication.

Habermas argues that we must rethink the meaning of secularization in order to avoid 'the clash of civilizations' – Samuel Huntington's controversial argument that the world religions are at odds with each other and the great civilizations, generated and sustained by these religions, are thus bound to clash and turn into enemies of one another.[95] Habermas's reply to Huntington is a call for the 'dialogue of civilizations.' The hermeneutic intelligence with which humans are gifted enables them to listen to one another, enter into the perspective of 'the other' and try to understand what the unfamiliar discourse means to 'the other.' Thanks to this hermeneutic rationality, secular people are able to grasp the human wisdom expressed in religious language. Habermas does not want to impose his own secular values upon the world; all he demands – in the service of emancipation – is conversation, mutual understanding, and support for justice and peace. He transmutes the universal mission of Western Enlightenment into a worldwide promotion of dialogue.

Habermas Listens to the Churches

In his speech of October 12, Habermas wants to show what listening to the churches can mean to people without faith. He is impressed by the courage and inventiveness of the churches in Germany that put up with the dissonance of religious pluralism, the monopoly of truth claimed by the sciences and a state constitution based on secular presuppositions. As Christians have learned to listen to secular discourse, Habermas continues, secular citizens should make an effort to grasp the human meaning of religious discourse and inquire whether it provides wisdom for today's society. He himself offers two examples.

First, the religious discourse about sin, evil and forgiveness deserves sympathetic attention. Secular language, Habermas argues, does not permit us to distinguish between what is wrong and what is evil. Nor is the notion of sin fully equivalent with the juridical language of culpability. Even people who do not believe in God or the devil can recognize in this religious discourse something they need for a better understanding of their history. What Habermas has in mind is the continuing wrestling of the Germans with their recent past, especially the Holocaust. Even if sin and atonement are not part of the semantic universe of people who don't believe in God, they recognize that these symbols have a social meaning and a historical impact that render a service to German society. Secular people are able to recognize in the religious demand for forgiveness the non-sentimental wish to see undone the damage inflicted upon others. Of course, this damage cannot be undone. The slain remain slain. The only restitution that can be offered is solidarity with the victims by keeping their memory alive. While this is necessary, it is not sufficient. Secular people, Habermas argues, acknowledge that the religious discourse about these matters contains something of importance for society, even if it cannot be fully translated into secular language.

Second is the religious idea that humans have been created in the image of God. When the churches join the public debate about the treatment of the fertilized egg cell outside the womb, they speak of the human embryo as the bearer of fundamental human rights. This is their attempt to translate into secular language the idea of the *imago Dei*. But even people who don't believe in God realize that something is lost in this translation. For if we are told that God creates out of love, then we learn that humans created in the divine image have the freedom to love others and that mutual respect and solidarity belong to their very nature. Even secular people recognize that the religious discourse of divine creation differs in meaning from the emergence of humans in the evolutionary process. There is something in the story of creation, Habermas argues, that should be heard by society.

God as creator and redeemer, Habermas continues, does not operate like a technician according to the laws of nature nor as a communication expert according to the rules of a code. God operates in an ethically tuned universe: God determines human beings as free and responsible subjects. One does not have to be a believer to understand that it would be unacceptable if God were replaced by a human operator who interfered in the accidental combination of the parental chromosomes to produce a child according to the preference of others. Such an interference is unable to communicate freedom and love. Even atheists must object when humans want to play God. Genetic manipulation is the exercise of life-determining power of some human beings over others that undermines the equality of persons as free agents. The in principle unlimited thrust of the sciences to objectify the world leads here to the objectification of human life itself, and welcomes a controlling power that permits the self-instrumentalization of humanity. On this issue of genetic manipulation Habermas passionately takes sides with one party in the public debate in Germany.

Because of the increasing domination of instrumental reason and the omnipresence of the market discourse, society needs to listen to counter-voices that transcend utilitarianism, including, Habermas argues, the voice of religion. While he formerly believed that religion no longer had a pertinent message for modern society, he now insists that the semantic potential of religion is not exhausted. Leaving the secular ideology behind, society must become post-secular.

What Habermas does not tell us in his speech is how society decides what religious messages serve the well-being of society, and which religious messages have a harmful effect. I suppose that Habermas would argue that the religious voices be allowed to be part of the public debate, that the secular participants make a special effort to understand the religious discourse, and that in this debate the most intelligible and most life-supporting argument carry the day. Since the Catholic Church opposes divorce, birth control, abortion and homosexual love, the German audience of Habermas's lecture must have wondered how he would respond to these proscriptions. This is how I imagine he would formulate his answer. He would first set forth that the dominant individualism and utilitarianism, promoted by the free market system and an exclusively instrumental rationality, tend to undermine all bonds of solidarity and transform love, happiness and sexuality into commodities. Then he would argue that the Church's strict moral code deserves sympathetic attention since it reminds religious and secular people of the seriousness of the marriage bond, its stabilizing impact on society and its symbolic value of freely chosen, abiding solidarity. The Church's strict sexual teaching deserves attention – even though Catholics no longer interpret it in a literal sense – because it reminds people that sexuality is not a commodity, that it must not create a master-servant relationship, and that it calls for mutuality, tenderness and care. The Church's conservative voice is helpful, not indeed as dictating norms to be established by law, but as cultural opposition to the dominant cultural trend.

The Call for a New Pluralism

I wish to relate Habermas's proposal for a transition to a post-secular society to the conclusions of a recent dialogue on economic development, organized by the International Development Research Centre (IDRC) in Ottawa.[96] Here researchers from the South called for the recognition of a new pluralism.[97] They argued that the major development projects sponsored by donors in the North tend to end in failure largely because they have been planned in the North and hence take no account of the religious culture proper to the local community. The Western understanding of pluralism respects people's freedom to worship in accordance with their choice. Yet a more careful analysis reveals that Western pluralism assumes that the secular stance is the scientifically established, objective truth and that religions are purely subjective expressions of people's dreams and aspirations. Here the secular interpretation of the cosmos is affirmed as the universal truth, the exclusive key for understanding the world in which we live, invalidating all other perceptions of the universe. The participants from the South regarded this secular faith as an ideology of conquest intent on undermining and delegitimating the religious cultures of the non-Western world.

The researchers from the South argued that economic development must take the local religious culture seriously and invent innovative economic practices that assure a significant degree of cultural continuity. What is necessary, they argued, is that persons from the local community participate in the planning of development from the very beginning. Their presence will see to it that the project will not be wedded to Western secularism but honour an alternative vision based on the local religious inheritance.

The religiously oriented men and women at the dialogue had great respect for secular people who regard their own perception of the world as one perspective among others. Yet, all too often, people who don't believe in an invisible order slip – without noticing it – into an ideological secularism that sees itself as the only truth and claims universal validity. Such persons may regard themselves as open to pluralism because they respect their friends with religious convictions, yet they are simply open to tolerance since for them religious insights have no access to objective reality.

The dialogue at the IDRC supported the demand for a new religious pluralism that would honour the secular outlook as well as the religious perceptions of the world. The participants saw no conflict between science and religion. While science and religion look at the universe from different perspectives, they both aspire to modesty, they both recognize their limitations, they are both able to support development in the South so that people can live in conditions appropriate to their human dignity. Religion is able to nourish hope, generosity, solidarity, discipline and self-limitation, attitudes without which economic development is unable to sustain community life.

The events of September 11 remind us that it may be too early to endorse Habermas's proposal to invite the religions to join the public debate on the well-being of society and introduce the new pluralism advocated by many representatives of non-Western religious cultures. As a theologian identified with Roman Catholicism, I wish to argue that what is still necessary, prior to an entry into the new pluralism, is the systematic exploration, undertaken by believers, of the destructive potential of their religious tradition. The world religions will have to confront the elements of their tradition that divide humanity into masters and servants, princes and subjects, friends and enemies, the chosen and the non-chosen, and provide a credible rereading of their tradition that unveils it as a service to the pacification and emancipation of humankind. Only then will religious faith generate holy energy in the service of society. To achieve this goal, interreligious dialogue is a helpful practice, and critical engagement with the humanistic dimension of the Enlightenment is indispensable. The historical record shows that the emancipatory potential of religions has flowered only after an encounter of the Enlightenment. Since the Enlightenment itself is an ambiguous cultural movement promoting both human liberation and rationalistic domination, the engagement of religious faith with the Enlightenment must be critical. But this encounter is indispensable.

7

John Paul II and Benedict XVI: Contrasting Interpretations of Religious Pluralism and Modernity

In the early summer of 2005, a few months after Cardinal Joseph Ratzinger's elevation to the papacy as Benedict XVI, I read a book on truth and tolerance that he had published in Germany in 2002.[98] The volume, written in the author's magnificent German prose, is a collection of learned articles that analyze the unique place of Christianity in the history of the world religions and the threat to Christianity posed by the contemporary historical situation. Since I was well acquainted with the teachings of John Paul II, I was struck by the difference between the theology of these two ecclesiastical personalities, a difference that I thought was worth exploring. It occurred to me then that the difference between them was largely due to the fact that the Cardinal wrote as a theologian, while the Pope offered his teaching as universal pastor. I wondered at the time whether Benedict XVI, now shouldering papal responsibility, would continue to pursue his own theology or follow John Paul II's prophetic understanding of the Church. In his first homily of April 24, 2005, the new Pope said: "My programme of governance is not … to pursue my own ideas, but to listen, together with the whole Church, to the word and the will of the Lord, to be guided by Him, so that He himself will lead the Church at this hour of our history."

It seemed nonetheless appropriate to study Joseph Ratzinger's book published in 2002 and compare its theology with the pastoral teaching of John Paul II. In particular, I wanted to compare their different approaches to religious pluralism and to modern society. Several speeches given by the new Pope in the months after his consecration persuaded me that he had indeed changed his mind and now followed the teaching of his predecessor. Yet this was a hasty judgment on my part. Subsequent pronouncements of Benedict XVI reveal that he has remained faithful to his own theology.

Interpreting Religious Pluralism
Cardinal Ratzinger's Theology

In his book on Christian truth and the world religions, Ratzinger does not deal with the question that has preoccupied theologians over the centuries: namely, whether salvation is available in the world religions. With great confidence, the Cardinal simply refers to God's gracious presence in the whole of human history. Nor does he touch upon the urgent pastoral issue of how the Church should react to the new religious pluralism in European and American cities and what policy the Church should adopt in a world that is increasingly divided along religious lines. What interests the author instead is the place of Christianity in the history of the world religions. Here he offers an original interpretation, based on research he had done while still a professor at the university.

There were three ways, the Cardinal argues, in which people in antiquity escaped the arbitrary rule of the gods and the fear and superstition inspired by polytheistic religion. First was the mystical way present in the Hindu tradition. Here the spiritual guides came to believe that hidden in the many religious symbols was a single divinity, an incomprehensible divine presence, a gracious God to be encountered in faith: first as a 'thou' to be worshipped and finally as the true Self in which the human 'I' would disappear altogether. In this tradition the many gods are not discarded: instead, they are interpreted as symbols of different aspects of the one incomprehensible divinity. According to this mystical approach, all religions are in some way true; all mediate access to the one God, even if they formulate their faith in divergent ways. Seen from this perspective, the 'I-thou' relationship to God in the monotheistic religions appears as an arrested stage, destined to be transcended by the experience of the identity of 'I' and 'thou.'

We shall see later that Ratzinger regards this mystical approach as a dangerous challenge to contemporary Christianity.

Second was the classical Enlightenment represented by philosophers such as Socrates, Plato and Aristotle. Here, trust in the metaphysical competence of human reason led to the recognition of a single divine origin of all beings. The Greek authors reluctantly acknowledged the gods to whom the people prayed because these gods protected the values of society and thus fulfilled an important function, even though they had no being.

The third way to overcome polytheism was the monotheism of Abraham and his offspring: they recognized a single divinity, dethroned the pagan gods, and denounced as sinful all forms of idolatry. In this context, Ratzinger makes an interesting point: he argues that the early Christians, opposed to the polytheism of ancient Rome, regarded the classical Enlightenment as an intellectual ally. While theologians have often regretted the early Church's reliance on Hellenistic categories, Ratzinger recalls the liberating power of the Church's dialogue with the classical philosophers. Yet he also reminds the reader that, in modern times, reason has been reduced to scientific rationality and hence no longer discloses the meaning of human existence. Against this modern trend, Catholicism has defended metaphysical reason as an ally of biblical faith.

In today's world, Ratzinger regards the mystical way, first followed in the Hindu tradition, as a serious threat to the Christian Church. Monotheism presupposes a clear distinction between the Creator and the creation, between God and the human person. Even in the mystical tradition of Christianity, the 'I' of the believer is never fully dissolved in the divine 'thou,' ever retaining its personal identity for the age to come. Ratzinger fears that Christians in Asia are being tempted by the Hindu tradition and that even Christians in the West, urged by the idea of tolerance, come to believe that all religions are equally true, that all of them offer access to the divine mystery, and that debates about true or false have no place in the sphere of religion.

The Cardinal complains that there are even Catholic theologians who adopt a relativistic approach to religious pluralism and are unwilling to defend the absolute truth of the Christian faith. These theologians argue that more important than defending the truth is solidarity with humanity: they therefore search for a Christian discourse that serves reconciliation in a deeply divided world. They focus on 'orthopraxis' rather than orthodox belief.

To affirm the truth against this dangerous trend, Ratzinger's book tells us, the Roman Congregation of the Doctrine of Faith – which the Cardinal chaired – produced the document *Dominus Iesus*[99] and investigated the writings of the Belgian theologian Jacques Dupuis SJ, who had spent his academic life in India and wrote about the Asian religions with great sympathy.[100] *Dominus Iesus* reaffirmed the doctrine that the Catholic Church is the one true Church, and it referred to the other Christian churches and the beliefs of the world religions in terms that recognized their errors. Vatican Council II, as is well remembered, had emphasized the truths and values that the Catholic Church held in common with the other churches and shared to some extent even with the world religions. While the Council had urged Catholics to dialogue with other Christians and the followers of the world religions, *Dominus Iesus* warned Catholics of "the ideology of dialogue." Ecumenical and interreligious dialogue, it said, is not without danger, because dialogue with partners on an equal footing appears to imply the relativism of truth. Religious pluralism, it continues, exists only "in fact," not "in principle," since there is only one true religion. According to *Dominus Iesus*, Catholics must look upon ecumenical and interreligious dialogue as part of the Church's mission to proclaim the truth and invite outsiders to become Catholics. When, in response to this document, Protestants and Jews expressed their shock, they were told that *Dominus Iesus* was intended as a message to Asian Catholics not to water down the truth of Christianity.

For Ratzinger, the truth question is the central issue. Since two monotheistic religions, Christianity and Islam, lay claim to a truth that excludes the other, are we not inevitably heading for a major conflict? In his book, Ratzinger mentions this problem in a short paragraph, but does not deal with it. We shall return to this topic further on.

What bothered the Cardinal in his book was the possible misunderstanding of the assemblies at Assisi in 1986 and 2002, at which John Paul II and the representatives of the world religions he had invited, prayed together for peace of the world. To avoid having these two events interpreted as signs of religious relativism, the Cardinal distinguished between 'multireligious' and 'interreligious' prayer.[101] In 'multireligious' prayer, the participants are not joined together in prayer: instead, each prays in accordance with his or her own tradition. In interreligious prayer, the participants are united in a common prayer addressed to the same divinity. Catholics, the Cardinal argued, are not permitted to engage in interreligious prayer, since such a practice implies that all religions have access to the true God and hence fosters the evil of relativism. What happened at Assisi, the Cardinal insisted, was multireligious prayer: despite the appearances, the Pope and the invited representatives did not really pray together. To prevent any misunderstanding in the future, the Cardinal urged that gatherings of this kind not be multiplied. We shall see further on that, as Benedict XVI, he revised his judgment on this issue.

How did John Paul II understand the interreligious prayer meeting at Assisi? In his address to the assembled religious representatives on October 27, 1986, the Pope explained that the invited guests had not come to seek religious reconciliation in a common truth nor to make concessions to religious relativism. Then he continued,

> The coming together of so many religious leaders to pray is in itself an invitation to the world to become aware that there exists another dimension of peace and another way of promoting it, which is not the result of negotiations, political compromises or economic bargaining. It is the result of prayer, which, in the diversity of religions, expresses a relationship with a supreme power that surpasses our human capacities.

The last sentence suggests that John Paul II regarded the gathering as an occasion of interreligious prayer and did not feel the need to make the distinction introduced by the Cardinal.

The Teaching of John Paul II

John Paul II approaches the topic of the Church's relationship to the world religions quite differently. Needless to say, he professes – with the Cardinal and the entire Church – God's unreserved and definitive self-donation in Jesus Christ as the merciful divine gesture that embraces the whole of humanity. But prior to articulating the Church's faith, the Pope examines the present historical situation. Following the method of John XXIII and the Vatican Council, he searches for 'the signs of the times': the significant historical events to which the proclamation of Christian truth must now address itself.

The Pope recognized the increasingly divided world, marked by political conflicts and outbursts of violence, the fault lines of which include divisions over religion. The Pope worried about the tensions produced by religious pluralism in the cities of Europe and, more importantly, he feared the growing rift between the Muslim world and the West. He expressed his disapproval of American foreign policy and opposed the first as well as the second American war in Iraq. In response to Samuel Huntington's thesis of 'the clash of civilizations,' welcomed by the Christian Right in the United States, the Pope promoted 'the dialogue of civilizations' supported by the United Nations. In this dangerous historical situation, the Church's commitment to the absolute truth of the Gospel demands that it foster justice and peace, emphasize what the religions share in common and encourage interreligious dialogue.

In his encyclical *Redemptoris missio* (1990), John Paul II presented the Church's mission as the mission to give witness to Jesus Christ and invite all men and women to put their faith in the Lord. At the same time, he demanded that the Church engage in open and trusting dialogue with members of the world religions. In this dialogue, he argued, Catholics are guided by the faith that God's grace is operative in all religious and sapiential traditions.

> Dialogue does not originate from tactical concerns or self-interest, but is an activity with its own guiding principles, requirements and dignity. It is demanded by deep respect for everything that has been brought about in human beings by the Spirit who blows where he wills. Through dialogue, the Church seeks to uncover the "seeds of the Word" or "a ray of that truth which enlightens all men" found in individuals and the religious traditions of mankind. Dialogue is based on hope and love, and will bear fruit in the Spirit. Other religions

constitute a positive challenge for the Church: they stimulate her both to discover and acknowledge the signs of Christ's presence and of the working of the Spirit, as well as to examine more deeply her own identity and to bear witness to the fullness of Revelation which she has received for the good of all. (*Redemptoris missio*, 56)

This teaching differs from the theology of Cardinal Ratzinger, who denounced the ideology of dialogue, warned against the temptation of relativism and suggested that the purpose of dialogue was the conversion of others to Christian truth. John Paul II does not deny the paradoxical character of the Church's mission, sent by the Spirit both to proclaim the name of Jesus and, in today's world of conflict and violence, to honour religious pluralism and promote mutual respect, reciprocal understanding, and co-operation in the service of justice and peace. That the commitment to absolute truth of God's self-revelation in Jesus Christ demands that the Church respect otherness is an insight that is new in Christian history, brought about by the response of faith to a world threatened by violence.

One of the boldest documents published by John Paul II is the "Ten Commandments of Peace," composed in 2002.[102] The fifth commandments reads:

We commit ourselves to frank and patient dialogue, refusing to consider our differences as an insurmountable barrier, but recognizing instead that to encounter the diversity of others can become an opportunity for greater reciprocal understanding.

What John Paul II does not tell us are the principles that allow the Church in a particular situation to decide whether to proclaim the name of Jesus or to engage in interreligious dialogue. John Paul II has not always been consistent. One sentence pronounced by him produced great indignation throughout India: "Just as in the first millennium the Cross was planted on the soil of Europe, and in the second on that of the Americas and Africa, we can pray that in the Third Christian Millennium a great harvest of faith will be reaped in this vast and vital continent."[103] The evangelization of Asia remains nonetheless an open question. The Catholic Church in Indonesia has fully accepted the Indonesian constitution that respects the five religions practised in the country – Islam, Hinduism, Buddhism, Protestantism and Catholicism – and strictly forbids any proselytizing activity. Moreover, the Christian churches in the cities of Western Europe and North America, the home of recent immigrants from all part of the world, have decided to respect the religion of the immigrants, defend their religion against popular prejudices and hostile attacks, and abstain from any effort to convert them to the Christian faith.

The paradoxical character of the Church's mission in today's world is well expressed in a recent statement by the bishops of Quebec.[104] They ask the faithful to avoid religious relativism (supposing that all religions are equally true) as well as religious absolutism (supposing that no truth can be found in other religions). Commitment to the one truth of the Gospel, the bishops argue, obliges Catholics to show respect for members of other religions and foster dialogue and co-operation with them in the service of the common good.

The Words of Pope Benedict XVI

After the election of Benedict XVI, I followed his public speeches with great attention. Would he offer his own theology focusing on the danger of dialogue? Or would he follow the lead of John Paul II and commit the Church to ecumenical and interreligious dialogue? I was greatly impressed by Benedict XVI's early speeches.

In his address to the delegates of the Christian churches and representatives of the world religions on April 25, 2005, he committed himself to the approach of John Paul II in supporting the ecumenical movement and promoting interreligious dialogue in the service of justice and peace.

In the footsteps of my Predecessors, especially Paul VI and John Paul II, I feel strongly the need to reassert the irreversible commitment taken by the Second Vatican Council and pursued in recent years, also thanks to the activity of the Pontifical Council for Promoting Christian Unity. The path to the full communion desired by Jesus for his disciples entails, with true docility to what the Spirit says to the churches, courage, gentleness, firmness and hope, in order to reach our goal.... How can we not recognize in a spirit of gratitude to God that our meeting also has the significance of a gift that has already been granted? In fact, Christ, the Prince of Peace, has acted in our midst: he has poured out friendship by the handful, he has mitigated points of disagreement, he has taught us to be more open to dialogue and in harmony with the commitments proper to those who bear his Name....

I turn now to you, dear friends from different religious traditions ... I offer warm and affectionate greetings to you and to all those who belong to the religions that you represent. I am particularly grateful for the presence in our midst of members of the Muslim community, and I express my appreciation for the growth of dialogue between Muslims and Christians, both at the local and international level. I assure you that the Church wants to continue building bridges of friendship with the followers of all religions, in order to seek the true good of every person and of society as a whole.

The world in which we live is often marked by conflicts, violence and war, but it earnestly longs for peace, peace which is above all a gift from God, peace for which we must pray without ceasing. Yet peace is also a duty to which all peoples must be committed, especially those who profess to belong to religious traditions. Our efforts to come together and foster dialogue are a valuable contribution to building peace on solid foundations. Pope John Paul II, my Venerable Predecessor, wrote at the start of the new millennium that "the name of the one God must become increasingly what it is: a name of peace and a summons to peace" (*Novo millennio ineunte*, n. 55). It is therefore imperative to engage in authentic and sincere dialogue, built on respect for the dignity of every human person, created, as we Christians firmly believe, in the image and likeness of God.

Several weeks later, on June 9, 2005, Benedict XVI addressed a delegation of the International Jewish Committee on Interreligious Consultation.

In the years following the Vatican Council, my predecessors Pope Paul VI and, in a particular way, Pope John Paul II, took significant steps towards improving relations with the Jewish people. It is my intention to continue on this path. The history of relations between our two communities has been complex and often painful, yet I am convinced that the "spiritual patrimony" treasured by Christians and Jews is itself the source of the wisdom and inspiration capable of guiding us toward "a future of hope" in accordance with the divine plan (cf. Jer 29:11). At the same time, remembrance of the past remains for both communities a moral imperative and a source of purification in our efforts to pray and work for reconciliation, justice, respect for human dignity and for that peace which is ultimately a gift from the Lord himself. Of its very nature this imperative must include a continued reflection on the profound historical, moral and theological questions presented by the experience of the Shoah.

It has been widely recognized that, in the year 2006, Benedict XVI's theology of religious pluralism became more ambiguous. On the positive side, the Pope changed his mind in regard to the interreligious assemblies at Assisi initiated by his predecessor. In a letter to Bishop Domenico Sorrentino of Assisi, written on September 2, 2006, Benedict praises John Paul's interreligious initiative as having made "an important impact on public opinion, as constituting a vibrant message furthering peace and as an event that left its mark on the history of our time." Recognizing with his predecessor the dangerously conflicted world situation, to which religion often lends unholy passion, Benedict now lauds interreligious dialogue and prayer meetings in the service of peace and mutual understanding, as long as they do not lead to syncretism or relativism. In his letter to the Bishop of Assisi, Benedict expresses his commitment to the declaration *Nostra aetate* of Vatican Council II and fosters what John Paul II had called "the spirit of Assisi."

At the same time, Benedict XVI put the brakes on interreligious dialogue when he removed Archbishop Michael Fitzgerald as president of the Pontifical Council of Interreligious Dialogue and assigned the interreligious activities to the Pontifical Council for Culture. Since Archbishop Fitzgerald is a well-known specialist on Islam and has connections with Muslim scholars all over the world, the Catholic press interpreted his removal as a signal that the Pope was not happy with the Church's close association with Islam, introduced by John Paul II with the assistance of Archbishop Fitzgerald. John Paul II had repeatedly declared that Christians and Muslims believe in the same God and that in future Christianity and Islam must become communities in respectful dialogue, never more communities in conflict.[105]

Yet Benedict XVI was not certain of this. In an academic lecture on the relation of faith and reason given at the University of Regensburg on September 12, 2006, the Pope suggested that Catholics and Muslims have different concepts of God. The Pontiff quotes a sentence addressed by the Christian Emperor Manuel II to a learned Muslim, a few years before the long siege of

Constantinople at the turn of the fifteenth century: "Show me, the Emperor said, just what Mohammed brought that was new, and there you will find only things evil and inhuman, such as his command to spread with the sword the faith he preached." Insensitive to present interreligious tensions, Benedict does not immediately clarify that this is not how the Catholic Church looks upon Islam today. This quotation without commentary produced an outrage among Muslims everywhere, in some parts even outbursts of irrational violence.

Of greater theological interest is how Benedict uses this quotation. He reports that the Emperor continues the argument, saying that spreading the faith through violence is something unreasonable and, in fact, that violence is incompatible with the nature of God. Relying on a contemporary scholar, Benedict says, "For the Emperor, as a Byzantine shaped by Greek philosophy, this statement is self-evident. But for Muslim teaching, God is absolutely transcendent. His will is not bound up with any of our categories, even that of rationality." But is this really Muslim teaching? Do Catholics and Muslims really have a different concept of God and thus a different practice of their faith?

Let us follow Benedict's reasoning. "Is the conviction that acting unreasonably contradicts God's nature merely a Greek idea, or is it always and intrinsically true? I believe that here we can see the profound harmony between what is Greek in the best sense of the word and the biblical understanding of faith in God." This belief is held by the great theologians of Antiquity and the Middle Ages, including St. Augustine and St. Thomas. Yet Benedict admits that the mediaeval thinker Duns Scotus introduced a voluntarism into Catholic theology that eventually produced the idea of God's total freedom, not limited by reason – the idea, in other words, that God could have done the very opposite of what God actually did.

What Benedict did not know is that the same ambiguity, the same debate about the relation of reason and revelation, exists in the Muslim tradition. Early Muslim thinkers read the works of Greek philosophy in translation and produced the Mutazilah school of thought, which recognized a harmony between reason and revelation. While some of these thinkers became rationalists and were rejected by the mainstream, Mutazilite influence never disappeared. The reform movement in Islam, beginning with al-Afghani (d. 1897), acknowledged human intelligence as a divine gift and honoured the rationality implicit in divine revelation [106]

Benedict XVI did not realize that Muslims and Christians are heirs of the same internal debate about faith and reason and the influence of Greek thought, nor did he acknowledge that in significant moments of their history, not only Muslims but also Christians have instrumentalized their faith to legitimate violent aggression.

The outrage produced by his lecture on September 12, 2006, persuaded Pope Benedict to give a speech on September 25 addressed to the ambassadors of countries with a Muslim majority and the representatives of the Muslim communities of Italy. In this speech he did not return to the topic raised in his learned lecture: he simply reaffirmed the Catholic Church's respect for Islam, using the beautiful words drawn from Vatican Council II and the speeches of Pope John Paul II. He recognized the crucial importance of interreligious dialogue and co-operation in the present historical situation. He even added a sentence that could be read as an affirmation that Christians and Muslims worship the same God: "Christians and Muslims (must) manifest their obedience to the Creator who wishes all people to live in the dignity that he has bestowed upon them."[107]

Interpreting Modernity

We now turn to a different issue: the contrast between Cardinal Ratzinger's and John Paul II's evaluation of modernity.

The Cardinal's Evaluation of Modernity

In his book *Truth and Tolerance,* the Cardinal looks upon the modern age largely in terms of its scientific and technical achievements. The newness of modernity is the scientific world view and the technological control of the conditions of life. This technical culture, at first confined to Europe and North America, is now spreading to all parts of the globe. The dark side of this development is that reason has been reduced to scientific rationality and that empirically verifiable knowledge has become the only valid approach to truth. In modernity, reason has lost its metaphysical and ethical competence. Reason no longer opens people's minds to divine transcendence, nor does it provide ethical guidance. In this situation, people's values are chosen arbitrarily, following their taste or their self-interest. As a result, modern society is dominated by ethical relativism, and as the technical culture spreads across the world, destabilizing traditional wisdom and values, ethical relativism is becoming the universal condition.

In this condition, the Cardinal argues, people feel free to please themselves. Selfishness, greed, conquest, unjust practices, lying propaganda, cheating in business – all these have become acceptable because ethical norms have lost their authority and belief in God has been abandoned. Relativism or the absence of binding moral principles is the cultural source of the violent conflicts, terrorist acts, wars and genocides that define the present age.

We noted above that the Cardinal's principal worry regarding interreligious dialogue and co-operation was the spread of religious relativism. Now, in responding to contemporary culture, the

Cardinal sees the greatest danger in the spread of ethical relativism and indifference to truth.

The North American reader is puzzled by this analysis because the threat to world peace seems to come from powers that profess absolute truth. The religious discourse of radical Muslims blesses the jihad against the infidel West, and the discourse of the White House, the Christian Coalition and wide sectors of conservative American Protestantism legitimates present American foreign policy and its wars in religious terms. What frightens thoughtful people in North America more than compromise and relativism is the stubborn claim to absolute truth. They recognize that funda-mentalism in religion and other spheres has become a dangerous cultural phenomenon.

In *Truth and Tolerance,* the Cardinal offers no analysis of religious absolutism. He is not aware that many people in modern society are becoming increasingly afraid of religion. They fear that because religion claims to know the truth, it inspires contempt for heretics and infidels and produces a passion for truth that easily makes concessions to violence. That is why the statement of the Quebec bishops on religious pluralism, mentioned above,[108] warns against two attitudes towards religious difference: relativism as well as absolutism. No warning against the fundamentalist temptation is contained in *Truth and Tolerance.*

Did modernity, in addition to promoting relativism, also make a positive contribution to the human condition? To answer this ques-tion, the Cardinal offers his interpretation of the *Freiheitsgeschichte*: the history of human freedom, the struggle for emancipation culminating in modernity. He distinguishes between two different visions of human freedom. First, there is the freedom expressed in the democratic tradition of the Anglo-Saxon countries, includ-ing religious liberty and human rights, which – according to the Cardinal – has been derived from the Christian Gospel and is supported by the Catholic Church. What is new in modernity, he writes, is a more radical desire for freedom, the freedom to do as I please, to pursue my happiness and self-interest, to act in accordance with my own wishes, without responsibility for the people who surround me or the community to which I belong. This hidden longing produced by modernity is the wish to become independent and sovereign: to become like God, as was suggested by the serpent in Genesis 3:5.

Absent in the Cardinal's analysis of modern freedom is admiration for the men and women who wrestled against slavery, against tyranny, against colonial domination, against fascism, against apartheid, against communist dictatorship, against world hunger and against other forms of social evil. He praises the democratic freedoms, but does not acknowledge that the Catholic Church condemned them throughout the nineteenth and early 20th centuries, and that it was after a long struggle at Vatican Council II that the Church's official teaching accepted human rights and religious liberty.

Nor did the Cardinal acknowledge an affinity between the Gospel and the struggle for human emancipation. He has no sympathy for what the Latin American bishops have called "the preferential option for the poor," the Gospel imperative to look upon society from the perspective of its victims and offer public witness of solidarity with their struggle for greater justice.[109] In a few sentences, the Cardinal refers to politics as the sphere where there is no one truth, where decisions are made according to prudential judgments, and where Christian faith has no special competence. This view of the political order may be correct in some historical situations, yet there are also circumstances where Christian faith calls for political commitment. Following his Christian conscience, Joseph Ratzinger's own father repudiated the Nazi ideology spreading in his country. Yet the Cardinal criticized Latin American liberation theology because it "politicized" the Gospel and thus distorted its religious meaning. In his book, the Cardinal leaves no room for the Church's prophetic mission. As we shall see further on, John Paul II fully recognized the emancipatory dimension of the Christian Gospel.

What the Catholic faith offers us, according to the Cardinal, is to rejoice in God and the universe ordered by God. In his autobiographical reflections, Joseph Ratzinger recalls the profound religious experience he had as a boy in the liturgy of his village church, celebrating the ordered community in which God was graciously present. The vision of a society ordered by God, in which there is room for everyone, even if on different levels – imaged in the liturgy itself – has often been extolled in the Catholic literature of the past. Yet has this vision retained its attraction?

It is interesting to contrast the experience of the young Ratzinger in his village church with that of another young Bavarian German, Johann Baptist Metz, who later became a famous critical theologian. They were both boys during World War II. Metz remembers that in his village, the farmers went to Mass every morning before they bicycled to their fields where they did their daily work. Metz also remembers that thirty kilometres from his village was a concentration camp where the enemies of the Nazi regime were locked up and many of them killed. What deeply bothered Metz in subsequent years was that no one in his village and no priest at Mass ever referred to the camp. We never even prayed for the people who suffered there, he remembers. We did not know about the camp, and yet we all knew about it. The ambiguity of the ordered society celebrated in the liturgy has influenced Metz's critical theology.

John Paul II's Evaluation of Modernity

With the Cardinal, Pope John Paul II has lamented the cultural domination of scientific rationality produced by the spread of modernity, undermining people's trust in faith and in reason. The

Pope fully shared the Cardinal's worry about the spread of ethical relativism.

Pope John Paul's evaluation of modernity differed from the Cardinal's in two regards. First, as I mentioned above, the Pope recognized the positive dimension of modernity: the struggle for emancipation. Second, the Pope was keenly aware of the impact of institutions on human consciousness, and thus introduced the idea of 'social sin,' which is absent from the Cardinal's vocabulary in *Truth and Tolerance*.

Recognition of the Emancipatory Struggle

As a Pole, John Paul II was keenly aware that in the feudal-aristo-cratic order, his own nation had been colonized and divided up between empires, and that it was only the passage to modernity – the collapse of the monarchies – that allowed the reconstitution of the Polish nation. In his shrewd analysis of capitalism and communism, moreover, the Pope recognized the emancipatory starting point. The free market – freeing the market from the economic control of the Crown – opened the door to human economic creativity and produced great wealth. Yet when the free market was made into an ideology presenting it as the mechanism that would move history towards progress, it became an idol with harmful effects on the common good. Similarly, the nineteenth-century struggle of workers for conditions of justice was fully justified in ethical terms; yet when the struggle against the owners of the industries was made into an ideology presenting the class struggle as the mechanism that moved history towards the classless society, it became an idol with damaging effects on human well-being. In his criticism of these two modern ideologies, the Pope does not overlook the aspiration for freedom that gave birth to them.

In *Truth and Tolerance*, the Cardinal mentioned democracy and human rights only in passing, hinting that they were derived from the Gospel and supported by the Church. Yet the emergence of democracy and the recognition of human rights constituted a major breakthrough, a cultural revolution, which the Catholic Church opposed throughout the nineteenth and early 20th centuries and recognized only under John XXIII at the Vatican Council II. John Paul II agreed with the Cardinal that these modern values are ultimately rooted in the Christian heritage, yet the Pope recognized that implicit in them was a new understanding of the human person. He defined human beings as 'subjects,' historical agents responsible for themselves and the world to which they belong. For him, the human vocation includes a political dimension, the co-responsibility for society, a vocation enhanced by the preaching of the Gospel. Fidelity to Jesus Christ includes the commitment to justice and peace. Implicit in the Gospel is a social imperative. John Paul II is keenly aware of the Church's prophetic mission: her social teaching is part of the *kerygma*. "Teaching and spreading her social doctrine pertains to the Church's evangelizing mission and is an essential part of the Christian message, since this doctrine points out the direct consequences of that message in the life of society and situates daily work and struggles for justice in the context of bearing witness to Christ the Saviour" (*Centesimus annus*, 5).

Because he had suffered with other Poles under the totalitarian regime of his country, John Paul II became a passionate defender – in the name of Jesus Christ – of civil liberties and democratic freedoms. On his travels all over the world, he became a champion of human rights. Needless to day, the liberty he preached was not the freedom to do what one wishes (the freedom denounced by the Cardinal); it was rather the freedom to participate in the public debate and the decisions that affect the well-being of society. Believing that we are called by God to be free, to be "subjects," the Pope recognized the political dimension implicit in the Gospel.

While the Cardinal saw in modernity the spread of ethical relativism and the desire for the freedom to please oneself, the Pope also saw the positive dimension of modernity. Modernity is an ambiguous historical age that fosters relativism and individualism and, at the same time, contrary to these, human rights and responsible citizenship. In a sinful world, all historical ages are profoundly ambiguous. No reform movement nor any reconstruction of society, however dedicated in the service of justice, can ever escape the ambiguity that, according to Scripture, marks the human condition.

The Impact of Institutions on Human Life and Consciousness

Traditional Christian preaching analyzed people's virtues and vices and urged them, in the name of Jesus, to follow the path of virtue. Cardinal Ratzinger stands in this tradition. John Paul II, possibly due to his critical conversation with Marxism, realized that people's virtues and vices were related to the institutions in which they lived. Thus the Pope argued that the organization of labour in industry has an impact on the workers' consciousness. If they are treated as objects or instruments of production, they become frustrated and suffer damage in their humanity; yet if they are treated as subjects of production or responsible agents, they are able to enrich their humanity through their work. The Pope also analyzes the impact of the free market system on human consciousness: it fosters the spirit of competitiveness and self-promotion; it undermines concern for the common good; and it encourages people to look at all aspects of life, including love and loyalty, as commodities to be bought and sold. In the 1990s, John Paul became critical of the globalization of neo-liberalism, i.e. the extension of the free market to the entire globe, because it eliminates the traditional subsistence economies, undermines the inherited cultural and religious values, and widens the gap between the rich and the poor.

To render a theological account of the evil in the world, the Pope enlarged the idea of human sin and recognized, in line with critical theology, the reality of social or structural sin.[110] The awful things we humans do to one another are not simply the result of our malice; they are also the result of the institutions produced by us that have damaging effects on people's lives. For example, imperialism or colonialism that controls the destiny of other nations is a structural sin, as is organization of the national economy that allows massive unemployment. The ethical vocation of humans – and Christians in particular – is not only to grow in personal virtue but also to transform the sinful structures of society. Again, repeating the point made above, the Gospel message includes a political dimension. The deep yearning for justice and peace in the hearts of people, be they believers or not, is implicit participation in the prayer of Jesus that God's will be done on earth.

The Message of Pope Benedict XVI

Does Pope Benedict XVI follow the theology he offered as a Cardinal, or does he recognize the emancipatory dimension of the Gospel emphasized by John Paul II? Benedict's first encyclical, *Deus caritas est,* reveals that his theology has not changed. He presents the Church's mission as one of charity, of *diakonia*, of help extended to the poor and the needy, and makes it very clear that this does not include support for social justice and the defence of human rights.[111] He does not mention the preferential option for the poor. Political issues are important in themselves, he argues, but they are not the Church's concern. He writes, "Christian charitable activities must be independent of parties and ideologies. It is not a means of changing the world ideologically, and it is not a service of a worldly stratagem, but it is a way of making present here and now the love which humans always need" (31b). Following the Church's preconciliar theology, the encyclical makes a clear distinction between charity as a divine gift leading to salvation and justice as a natural virtue unrelated to salvation,[112] thus overlooking the Church's prophetic mission to denounce injustice and express solidarity with the victims of society.

Altogether remarkable and hard to explain is that Pope Benedict's message for the World Day of Peace on January 1, 2006, published a week after his first encyclical, offers a quite different theology of the Church's mission of charity. Here Benedict follows the pastoral theology of John Paul II. Benedict recognizes the mission of all Catholics and, in fact, of all humans to serve the reconciliation of the human family in peace, justice and truth. In a deeply divided world threatened by violent outbursts, the love of God revealed in Jesus Christ urges Catholics to become agents of peace, promoting a culture of dialogue, engaging in self-critical reflections, supporting international laws, opposing conditions of grave inequality and demanding the protection of human rights. Here Benedict XVI recognizes the political dimension of the Gospel. Yet since this message is so different from the encyclical, one wonder whether the Pope wrote it himself or allowed one of his collaborators to write it for him.

I am inclined to believe that Pope Benedict XVI does not fully appreciate the paradox of modernity: while keenly aware of modernity's dehumanizing dimension, fostering ethical relativism and the domination of instrumental reason, he fails to recognize its liberating dimension, generating the desire for emancipation and for democratic participation. Benedict XVI does not – at this time – share John Paul II's prophetic understanding of the Church's mission.

Part II

Economic Injustice

8

Social Injustice in Today's World

Does the present historical situation, so different from the recent past, demand that Christians rethink the meaning and practice of social solidarity? This is a question that many are asking in today's complex world. Let's look back at the initiatives of the past forty years and how these can shape or inspire efforts in the 21st century.

Vatican II and Social Democracy

At Vatican Council II (1962–1965), the Catholic Church, responding to lay movements all over the world, adopted a critical openness to modern society and encouraged all Catholics to engage themselves in the defence of human rights and the promotion of social justice. In the past, we used to make a neat distinction between the Church's supernatural mission, to offer people faith, hope and love, and the Church's temporal mission, to support peace and justice in society. In neo-scholasticism, charity was seen as a supernatural virtue, while justice was simply a natural virtue. At Vatican Council II, especially in *Gaudium et spes,* the Church recognized that faith, hope and love summon people to participate in society and involve themselves in cultural, social or political movements that promote freedom, justice and peace. The Council criticized the individualistic ethics contained in the manuals used in Catholic schools and seminaries (30). The famous first sentence of *Gaudium et spes* – "The joys and the hopes, the griefs and the anxieties of the men of this age, especially those who are poor or in any way afflicted, these are the joys and hopes, the griefs and anxieties of the followers of Christ" – was a declaration of solidarity addressed to the whole human family, beginning with the poor and the weak.

Gaudium et spes breathed a certain optimism. It repeatedly expresses the idea that, if people of goodwill act together, the economic order of the wealthy nations could be reformed, and with their help the poverty of the masses in less fortunate countries would be overcome. "For the first time in human history," we read, "all people are convinced that the benefits of culture ought to be and can be extended to everyone" (9). But are we certain that "all people" are convinced of this? The Council held that because God is graciously present to the sinful world, there is reason to hope that the liberal ideals of modern society – freedom, equality and fraternity – will come to be realized in all parts of the globe. The Council entertained a social democratic confidence that capitalism could be tamed and made to serve the common good of the global society.

A similar confidence pervaded the progressive social teaching of Pope John XXIII and his successors. They hoped that an interventionist government, a strong labour movement and an ethical culture of solidarity would be able to guide and restrain the free market system so that the wealth produced by industries would be distributed in accordance with the norms of justice. As late as 1987, Pope John Paul II, writing his encyclical *Sollicitudo rei socialis*, still believed that Western capitalism and Eastern European communism could be reformed: the former by strengthening the government's redistributive function, and the latter by granting more civic and economic freedoms.[113]

Medellín and the Option for the Poor

In 1968, three years after the end of the Council, the Latin American Bishops' Conference held its meeting at Medellín, Colombia. Looking at the expanding liberal world system from the margin, i.e. from the perspective of their impoverished continent, the Latin American bishops did not share the optimistic interpretation of the Council. With the emerging liberation theology, they feared that the spread of Western-style capitalism on their continent enriched a relatively small economic elite while pushing the majority of the population, the poor, into greater deprivation and dependency. The bishops, urged and supported by the base communities, declared themselves in solidarity with the poor and their struggle for greater justice.[114]

A principle emerged at Medellín that came to be called "the preferential option for the poor" by the next Latin American Bishops Conference at Puebla, Mexico, in 1979. This option involves a commitment with two dimensions: the hermeneutic dimension of reading society from the perspective of the poor, and the activist dimension of giving public witness of solidarity with their struggle for justice.[115]

Medellín pointed in a direction that was sustained and further explored by the base communities and, associated with them, by liberation theologians. Western-style economic development, they recognized, depended on capital from the wealthy centre, made use of sophisticated technology, created jobs only for the few, and produced goods, not to satisfy people's needs but for export to Western markets. The poor, and those in solidarity with them, demanded liberation from this system. They wanted an economic system that used local skills, employed a simple technology, involved everyone in production, and produced the goods and services needed by the people. These Christians applied a Marxist sociology of oppression without endorsing Marxist philosophical presuppositions. Their judgment upon the oppressive society and their hope for social transformation were drawn from Scripture, the Exodus event of liberation recorded in the Old Testament and the Resurrection of the humiliated Christ, in whom all the victims of society were rehabilitated. While the Latin American bishops and theologians were ill at ease with the liberal optimism of Vatican II, they were, in their own way, optimistic: they shared the expectation that was widespread on their continent that the 1970s were a *kairos,* a special historical moment, when a revolution for greater justice had become a historical possibility.

In the late '60s and the early '70s, liberation movements spread in Latin America and on other continents. People wanted a socialist economy: not the centralized economy of the communist countries, but a community-based economy adaptable to various forms of ownership. It was at this time that Pope Paul VI acknowledged that this sort of socialism was attractive to Catholics. While in the past socialism had been condemned by the Church, Paul VI now distinguished between different kinds of socialism, some based on principles at odds with Christian faith while others in conformity with Christian teaching.[116] Equally remarkable was the impact of Third World liberation theology on the 1971 World Synod of Bishops, which recognized that "a network of domination, oppression and abuses is being built up around the world which stifle freedom and which keep the greater part of humanity from sharing in the enjoyment of a more just world." The Synod also declared that the redemption Christ has brought includes "the liberation of people from every oppressive condition" and that "action on behalf of justice is a constitutive dimension of the Church's proclamation of the gospel."[117]

As a result of these developments, faith-and-justice Catholics in Canada and Quebec – and other developed countries – understood their social engagement in two different ways. One group, following a reformist vision, supported social democracy or democratic socialism; the other, following a radical perspective – this happened especially in Quebec – struggled with their secular comrades for a revolutionary transformation of society. The bold social teaching of the Canadian bishops, influenced by the Latin American Bishops and the World Synod of Bishops, can be read both in a reformist and a radical manner. Some Catholics supported the perfecting of social democracy in Canada while others struggled for the creation of an alternative society.

The Canadian bishops also proposed the idea (to which we shall return further on) that it may be more realistic to think of the struggle for greater justice in social rather then political terms.[118] They agreed with the social scientists of the period who argued that the preparations for the transformation of society were social movements: the old ones, such as the labour movement, and especially the new ones, such as the women's movement, the peace movement, the ecological movement, the co-operative movement and the movement against free trade.

Welfare Capitalism

The optimism of Vatican Council II was not unrelated to the achievement of the welfare capitalism that had reached a high point in the '60s. The industrialized countries were then enjoying economic growth, full employment and welfare for the needy. The successful middle-class societies of northwestern Europe – France, Germany, Belgium and Holland – were the home of most of the influential bishops and theologians of the Vatican Council. The present system, these men were inclined to believe, could be perfected and extended to the entire world.

What was the origin of the welfare state? We recall that unrestrained capitalism had revealed its failure in the Great Depression of the

1930s. Unemployment and poverty prevailed in the Western nations. It is no wonder that in those years many people turned to radical forms of socialism. In Canada, a new political party, the Co-operative Commonwealth Federation (CCF), was founded in 1933, the socialist policy of which was expressed in the Regina Manifesto. "No CCF government will rest," it said, "until it has eradicated capitalism." The '30s also saw the growth in Canada of the Communist Party, at odds with the CCF because of the latter's commitment to democracy. Canada's political future was uncertain.

It was only during World War II that countries such as Britain and Canada recovered from the economic slump and were able to solve their problem of unemployment. Because of the war, the government, now exercising greater power, was able to tell the national bank to assume the public debt and tell industry to produce the tools and goods the country needed to pursue the war effort. Government intervention here made the capitalist system operate more efficiently.

The economic elites also supported the interventionist policies of the government for other reasons. Since many of the soldiers who were risking their lives on the battlefield had been unemployed before the war, the governments of Britain and Canada now felt obliged to promise these men that they would find employment when they returned home. A certain national solidarity made the economic elites support this policy. The owning classes, moreover, were strongly opposed to socialism, whether democratic or revolutionary. They were therefore ready to enter into an unwritten social contract with the government that respected labour organizations and their right to collective bargaining, supported full employment and provided a safety net for people who, for one reason or another, were excluded from the market. The result was the birth of the welfare state.

In Canada, social democratic policies had been advocated in the 1930s by the CCF and the labour movement, but they were adopted only after the war by the Liberal Party thanks to the emergence of a new consensus. In Canada and western Europe, the welfare state eventually became part of the electoral platform of every political party. Their rhetoric was reassuring, yet the traditional parties were slow in implementing the reforms when they were in power.

The economic thinking behind this political development is attributed to the British economist and political thinker John Maynard Keynes. He was not the only one who had new ideas, but his approach garnered much attention. Roosevelt's New Deal, initiated in the '30s, was based on ideas that were to be fully developed by Lord Keynes. As a thinker, Keynes was greatly aware of the destructive forces in the world and hence regarded as absurd the idea of Adam Smith that the self-regulating market was steered by 'a hidden hand' to serve the well-being of society. In the '20s and '30s, Keynes observed these destructive forces operating in varying degrees in the Soviet dictatorship, belligerent Nazi Germany and the unrestrained drive for the maximization of profit that had produced the Great Depression. Keynes agreed with Marx that capitalism was an essentially unstable economic system oscillating between boom and bust. According to Keynes, the task of national governments was to protect their citizens from these destructive forces and create a region of security and social peace. He argued that to assure greater stability, governments should intervene in the economy, sustain the industries in periods of slackness (by grants, loans, tax breaks, etc.), and redistribute the wealth of society through a fair system of taxation. Keynes also wanted government to foster the loyalty of the labour force by putting in place a set of laws that protected the formation of labour unions and gave them the right to collective bargaining. In the long run, Keynes argued, these policies are economically advantageous. The rich shall not lose but win.

Keynesian capitalism was supported by a development in democratic theory. Political thinkers became convinced that equality or, more precisely, equal opportunity must be secured for all. To assure that people have the opportunity to develop their talents and, at the same time, become responsible and productive citizens, a democratic government should guarantee not only their civil rights but also their social rights, such as the right to work and to housing, health care and education. These services would strengthen democracy, the argument went, and would be also good for business. To foster production and commerce on any level, health and adequate training are of the essence. A political thinker associated with this interpretation of democracy was William Beveridge, the author of the Beveridge Report submitted to the British government in 1942. This Report provided the basis for the welfare legislation introduced by the Labour government after the war. These ideas were brought to Canada by the British political scientist Leonard Marsh, who wrote the Report on Social Security that oriented the social policies of the Canadian government.

Welfare capitalism was enormously successful. Some economists speak of the three 'glorious decades' (1950–1980) in which the Western nations produced great wealth and distributed more of this wealth to the labouring classes than ever before. At the same time, one must not idealize the welfare state: it also had its dark side. Society did not recognize that much of its wealth was produced by the production of arms. Militarism served the interests of the economic elites. Nor did society admit how much of its wealth was derived from natural resources bought at exploitative prices from the poorer continents. Nor did exploitation of labour disappear within Western society, despite its social democratic orientation. In Canada, the dependency on American capital steadily increased. The welfare state, moreover, became heavily bureaucratized so that it acquired oppressive features. Nor did society see that its phenomenal growth was a threat to the natural environment. While the movements challenging the racist and sexist character of society became very strong in the '60s, they were unable to liberate society from all forms of discrimination. The Native peoples remained excluded and forgotten. Still, the three decades of economic growth generated a cultural optimism that affected not only those who wanted to reform the existing society, but even the youth movement and other radicals who dreamed of replacing the realm of necessity by the realm of freedom.

The Unregulated Market

In the '80s it appeared that Keynesian capitalism no longer worked. Government investment in industry increased inflation and did not overcome unemployment. The public debt was beginning to rise. Economists are still arguing about exactly what happened. Was the crisis due to the sudden increase in the price of oil? Or was it the enormous expense of the arms race and the Vietnam War? Was it because wages were too high or social welfare demanded too much money? Did we live beyond our means? Was the growing unemployment the result of the new, electronic technology which succeeded in replacing more and more workers? Or was the crisis a propaganda victory engineered by the economic elites to increase their profit?

Whatever the complex causes, a new breed of economists, the so-called monetarists, now advocated a return to the laissez-faire capitalism of the last century.[119] The monetarists opposed government intervention in the economy; they criticized state policies that protected the national economy; they demanded the privatization of publicly owned institutions; they favoured the deregulation of services and industries that had been regulated for the good of society; they opposed labour unions as obstacles to the free labour market; they revived the nineteenth-century idea that unrestrained competition was the natural 'engine' that produced wealth, raised the standard of living and eventually improved the well-being of society as a whole. Ronald Reagan and Margaret Thatcher were the first political leaders who introduced the monetarist policies in their respective countries, the US and Britain. Canada's Brian Mulroney soon followed their lead.

The unwritten contract between capital and society made during and after World War II was unravelling. The corporations severed their loyalty to the society in which they were founded, whose working people had created their wealth and whose government had sustained them in times of slackness. As governments introduced legislation in support of free trade, many corporations became transnational: they expanded; moved to other countries; and produced their goods in parts of the world where labour was cheap, unions were weak or illegal, and environmental restrictions were minimal or non-existent. In this process, many transnational corporations became major powers. The national governments that had allowed them to grow were now beholden to them. Governments had to persuade major industries to remain in the country and woo others to come into the country, promising them favourable conditions such as building part of their installations, constructing new highways for transportation, and offering tax exemptions and other privileges. Thanks to their power, supported in each country by a strong business lobby (in Canada, the Business Council on National Issues), the government made laws that served the interests of the economic elites.

The monetarist policies first introduced by Reagan and Thatcher were called 'neo-conservative' because they first appeared in Conservative parties. Yet they were at odds with traditional political conservatism in Britain and Canada, which had defended community values and protectionist economic policies. John A. Macdonald, the Conservative premier of the newly founded Canadian state, set up the National Policy that introduced tariffs in support of the Canadian economy. Conservative politicians in Britain and Canada recognized that however important markets are, there are some concerns of society – education, culture, support for the poor and conservation of nature – that markets are unable to serve and that must be dealt with by government. In Canada, it is worth noting, it was the Liberal Party that, from the beginning, trusted the self-regulating power of the market and supported free trade with the US. Today, a reversal has set in: the Conservative Party advocates a return to the original laissez-faire liberalism of the nineteenth century. That is why in Quebec, in Latin America and on the European continent, the so-called neo-conservative policies are termed 'neo-liberal.' Neo-liberalism, as we shall see, is both an economic policy and a social project.

Since many people are confused by the terms 'neo-conservative' and 'neo-liberal,' allow me say a few more words about them. The word 'liberal,' we note, has been used in different ways. At the end of the eighteenth and in the nineteenth centuries, liberalism had two distinct meanings. 'Economic liberalism' opposed the control of the economy by the Crown and advocated the freedom of merchants to buy and to sell as they wished, thus fostering the growth of industrial capitalism. 'Political liberalism' also opposed the aristocratic order: it advocated popular sovereignty and democratic government; promoted liberty, equality and fraternity; and fostered the idea of responsible citizenship. While these two expressions of liberalism had a certain affinity – both of them struggled against the aristocratic order – tension exists between them. The reason for this is very simple. Economic liberalism stands for the unregulated market system and non-interference by government, while political liberalism expects government to promote the well-being of society and all its citizens. Thus monetarist policies are 'liberal' in the first sense, and Keynesian policies are 'liberal' in the second.

Thinkers called neo-conservative or 'neo-cons' are economic liberals who emphasize conservative social values such as law and order, women in their place, capital punishment and opposition to gun control.

The Globalization of the Neo-Liberal Economy

The globalization of the liberal economy is, as we have seen, a creation of governments and not, as its advocates claim, a spontaneous development. Governments created the global economy by making free trade agreements with other nations and by making laws that allowed corporations to escape their social responsibility. This fact is disguised by the neo-liberal rhetoric about 'getting the government off our backs.' Despite this insincere discourse, governments are expected to remain involved in the economy. To make the industries in the country more competitive – the new categorical imperative – government lowers their taxes, sustains them financially if necessary, weakens labour unions and puts the burden of the public debt on the weaker members of society.

One condition for the globalization of the economy I have not yet mentioned is the new electronic technology. Some writers attribute great power to the technology of production and communication. They claim that just as the steam engine and later forms of mechanical technology produced the industrial age and the nation-state, so will the new electronic technology produce a global economic system in which the nation-state will become weak and ineffectual. I fail to be convinced by such a deterministic theory, even though I recognize the powerful impact of the new technology on culture and society.

Worldwide communication has become almost instantaneous. This means, among other things, that the financial market has become truly global. Money crosses national borders without control and without being taxed. Speculation has become a universal phenomenon. The new technologies of communication, automation and transportation have allowed corporations to acquire a new flexibility, move from one continent to another and even decentralize the process of production, having certain parts produced in one country and other parts in another. Flexible capital and flexible industries call for a flexible work force. Hence the war against labour unions.

The new computer technology and various forms of automation derived from it allow corporations to reduce their staff considerably. It is convenient for neo-liberals to make the government's high public debt the primary worry in people's minds. Let me explain why this is so. The public debt is undoubtedly a problem. Yet there is little discussion of why the debt can become so large. Is it produced by high interest rates, by the arms race, by lowering the fiscal contribution of corporations, by incompetent management, or by financing social programs? The economists who assign primacy to public debt reduction usually assume, without proof, that the debt is due to the excessive costs of health care, education and public welfare. The Canadian federal and provincial governments have successfully persuaded the electorate that for the sake of rapidly paying the public debt, great sacrifices are required: reducing the health-care system, weakening educational institutions, eliminating support for cultural activities and pushing people on welfare into destitution. Governments also drastically downsize their own administrative offices. In the public rhetoric, downsizing was the theme song of the '90s. In this climate, corporations, banks and insurance companies also decided to downsize their staff. Even when their profits are very high, they may decide to automate their factories and offices and lay off large numbers of their employees. Millions of workers and employees have lost their jobs in the '90s. Some governments have the nerve to brag about how many jobs they have created, without mentioning the enormous numbers of jobs that have been lost. I fear that because of the new computer technology, we are not likely ever to see full employment again. Even if there should be an economic recovery, it promises to be jobless. We shall return to this topic further on.

What is taking place in Canada and other Western capitalist countries is the creation of a hierarchical three-sector-society. The first sector is made up of the economic and political elites and the professionals in their service. The second sector consists of people with secure employment: professionals and owners of small businesses who enjoy a reasonably good income. This sector, we note, includes unionized workers protected, for the time being, by a collective agreement. The growing third sector is made up of 'the excluded,' embracing the unemployed, the working poor (fully employed women and men whose low wages leave them in poverty), people precariously employed or in part-time jobs, and people too old or too weak to look after themselves. The sector of the excluded is not only growing in Canada and other industrial societies, it also promises to be a permanent feature of society. We note that the percentage of women and children in this sector is very high.

Karl Marx, we remember, expected that capitalist society would become divided into two antagonistic classes: the ruling class and the working class. He mentioned only in passing, and with a certain contempt, the few men at the bottom: the *Lumpen*, as he called them, the jobless vagrants. Marx did not anticipate the present situation, where the *Lumpen* constitute a growing sector of society.

What happens to a society with a permanent class of excluded men, women and children? John Maynard Keynes and many other social thinkers have argued that to do well and thrive, a society must avoid widening the gap between rich and poor and must do its utmost to allow all men – in his day, married women did not look for jobs – to participate in the production of wealth. Otherwise, society would become unstable and decline. Abandoned at this time is not only the Keynesian perspective but also the democratic theory of Beveridge and thinkers like him, who argued that a society that wants its members to be active and responsible citizens must support their health and their education. Betrayed at this time is also the Universal Declaration of Human Rights, promulgated in 1948 by the United Nations, which included among the human rights, the right to work and the right to social security (see Articles 22 and 23). What we are experiencing is a far-reaching decline of democracy. Many important decisions affecting society and its citizens are made today by transnational corporations and international financial institutions such as the World Bank and the International Monetary Fund. People who have not been elected shape the fate of our society, while the elected government claims to have no power to protect and promote the well-being of its citizens.

Political leaders in Canada and Quebec openly admit that in response to international market forces, they are obliged to introduce social adjustment policies: support free trade; offer natural resources and produce commodities for export; and, for the sake of enhancing the competitiveness of the industries, reduce their taxes, weaken the power of labour and cut social programs, health care and education. In 2001, Bill Phipps, then the Moderator of the United Church of Canada, launched a Consultation on Faith and the Economy because he believed that "the market was becoming God," ruling over us and entrapping us in a culture of consumerism.[120] Our political leaders claim that in introducing such policies, they bow to necessity, i.e. impersonal international market forces. In fact, behind these forces stand powerful actors and their institutions.

The structural adjustment policies, which our governments seem to introduce voluntarily, are imposed in much harsher ways upon the countries of the poorer continents by the policies of the World Bank and the International Monetary Fund. In addition, the governments of Canada and most other Western countries have reduced their support for Third World development and withdrawn part of the funding for non-governmental organizations that sponsor social and economic projects in these regions. Western society is deserting the poorer countries. The result is the widening of the gap between rich and poor countries and between the rich and the poor in every country. Many critical economists predict a bleak future for the world unless a radical change of orientation takes place.[121]

The neo-liberal world project is not imposed upon unwilling Western nations: their citizens readily vote for governments that promote the unregulated market system. People have been made to believe that we are forced by the public debt and global competition to pursue the present course. There is no choice, we are told. Alternatives do not exist. The neo-liberal world project is grounded in a social philosophy, an updated version of nineteenth-century Social Darwinism, and supported by a culture that legitimates public indifference to the common good. While it would be worthwhile to study this legitimating culture in detail, let me at least mention three contemporary cultural currents that undermine social solidarity. First, there is the self-serving individualism generated by universal competitiveness, which reduces all values to economic utility and makes people dream of enjoying more power and increasing their material gratifications. Second, there is the neo-conservative moralism, supported by many conservative Christians, which stresses private virtue yet fosters hard-hearted indifference to the social injustices that produce body and soul-destroying suffering among the many. Third, the ideas and the culture that define themselves as postmodern emphasize the particular and the different and consequently reject universal values, thus legitimating preoccupation with the small circle to which one belongs and effectively undermining universal social solidarity. Added to this is the fictional violence in films and on television that hardens our moral sensibilities and reinforces our indifference to the suffering of others. This solidarity-denying culture is communicated by the mass media, which are increasingly controlled by powerful capitalists and their corporations. The Canadian government has not resisted this trend. On the contrary, it reduces support to the Canadian Broadcasting Corporation (CBC) and assistance given to

Canadian publishers, cultural organizations and research institutes that promote an alternative vision of society.

Christian Responses to the New Situation

How should Christians respond to this new situation? They must not allow the present decline of cultural optimism to rob them of their hope in God's promises. Christians believe that because God is graciously active in human history and stirs people's hearts and minds, 'good things' continue to happen in the midst of social and cultural crises, even if they occur at first only among minorities. I have never forgotten a paragraph, written at the turn of the 20th century by the Catholic philosopher Maurice Blondel, which said that in every age, on account of God's redemptive immanence, humanity is in labour, giving birth to new ideas and practices. Blondel spoke of "the stirrings of parturition."[122] Christians, he wrote, must listen to these new developments, evaluate them in the light of the Gospel, and if they are compatible with it, learn from them and explore them further. Karl Polanyi, a secular political economist with sympathy for Christian social thought, has argued that whenever the well-being of society is being threatened by economic forces, social movements emerge among ordinary people that try to protect the community and its environment from disintegration.[123]

As Christians we believe that God is redemptively present in human history, a promise that is the foundation of our hope. In the darkness of today's world we must protect ourselves against depression and despair by spiritual practices, such as prayer, worship, meditation on the divine promises and participation in groups or networks of engaged Christians who, relying on God's solidarity with the poor, continue to believe that social transformation is possible. We will look for the good things that happen in society, test them in the light of the Gospel, recognize in them the divine initiative, and support them for the sake of greater justice. What we desire is that God's will be done on earth.

The practical questions that demand an answer are 'What are the good things happening in the Western world, especially in Canada and Quebec?' and 'How can Christians learn from them and offer them support?' I shall limit myself to four brief suggestions.

1) Christians join the effort to promote a critical culture,

2) they involve themselves in social movements,

3) they defend institutions that further the global common good, and

4) they support community development and the social economy.

1) The overwhelming power of the mass media helps to create a culture of conformity, persuading people that the present economic and political order is the only possible one and that expecting significant social transformation is unrealistic. To counter this complacency, a minority of thinkers tries to promote a critical culture that reveals the irrationalities of the present order and encourages thinking along alternative lines. The churches participate in this movement.

In 1996, the year dedicated by the United Nations to the elimination of poverty, the Catholic bishops of Canada, Britain and France published pastoral letters in which they lament the growing gap between the rich and the poor and denounce the neo-liberal policies adopted by their governments. The bishops want to make people aware of the lies and distortions mediated by the public discourse. It is wrong, they argue, to justify the neo-liberal policies, as this is done by governments and their apologists, by claiming that they are necessary in scientific terms, as if markets were natural forces, like forces in chemistry or biology that simply follow the laws of nature. We are free human beings, the bishops insist. Humans are the subjects of the economy: they are capable of making choices, they cannot hide behind necessity, they may not evade their moral responsibility.

This is not the place to list the many progressive pastoral statements made by Catholic bishops and the leaders of the Protestant churches in Europe and North America. The Catholic bishops of Quebec publish bold pastoral letters every year on Labour Day, which is celebrated in Quebec on the first of May. The pedagogical function of these publications is to promote a critical culture, making people question the existing order and fostering an alternative imagination. These documents confirm and support the manifold social justice engagements of Christians working in groups, centres, schools and associations to foster critical thinking in society: they do this through public acts of solidarity and through lectures, discussion and publications. This is where I locate my own theological work.

2) Important forces promoting the transformation of society are social movements organized by collectivities that experience injustice themselves or that recognize the damage done to society by the established order. The nineteenth century saw the creation of labour movements that exercised great political influence and the beginning of the women's movement struggling for emancipation. The second half of the 20th century saw the birth of new social movements, such as the peace movement, the women's movement, the ecological movement, the movement for gay emancipation and the movement against the use of torture. These movements promote a critical culture and sometimes succeed in producing significant changes in society. Christians test these movements in the light of their faith and, if they detect in them a spiritual affinity, they join them and lend them their energy.

In this connection, let me quote a remarkable sentence from John Paul II's encyclical *Laborem exercens* (1981).

> In order to achieve social justice in the various parts of the world ... there is a need for ever new *movements of solidarity of* the workers and *with* the workers. This solidarity must be present whenever it is called for by the social degrading of the subject of work, by exploitation of the workers, and by the growing areas of poverty and even hunger. The Church is firmly committed to this cause, for she considers it her mission, her service, a proof of her fidelity to Christ, so that she can truly be the "Church of the poor." And the "poor" appear under various forms; they appear in various places and at various times; in many cases they appear as a *result of the violation of the dignity of human work:* either because the opportunities for human work are limited as a result of the scourge of unemployment, or because a low value is put on work and the rights that flow from it, especially the right to a just wage and to the personal security of the worker and his or her family. (8, italicized in the original)

3) The taming of the transnational corporations and the international financial institutions cannot be achieved by national governments, yet they could be tamed by an international public authority such as the United Nations, equipped with the appropriate powers. Lawyers and political scientists are working out proposals to this effect that could become part of international law. As the United Nations has, in the past, composed human rights charters that have acquired the force of law, it could also create global charters that lay down conditions for transnational economic activities, aimed at protecting the public good. What has often been suggested is the creation of an effective Economic Security Council at the UN to which the World Bank and the International Monetary Fund must report, rather than, as is presently the case, to the G-8 nations. To contain short-term speculation from moving capital across national borders to the detriment of these countries, political scientists have proposed that these operations be taxed or that an international agency be set up with the power to monitor and control these operations. Reformist proposals of this kind are followed by church groups: in Canada, by the Taskforce of the churches on Corporate Responsibility.

In his encyclical *Pacem in terris*, John XXIII recognized that the growing economic and political interdependence of countries in the North and the South is creating conditions that demand reflection on the global common good. What is required is a rethinking of the international political order. The Pope thought that the United Nations offered a vision of a co-operative global society and fostered international agreements that favoured distributive justice and facilitated the peaceful resolution of conflicts. The Vatican has supported the United Nations with the appointment of a Permanent Observer. While the reform of the United Nations and the creation of international law regulating global economic operations lie in the future, an interest in these issues fosters a critical culture and provides a picture of the global future at odds with Western empire and American unilateralism. With the papacy, many Christians offer support for the United Nations and defend its social vision against the hostile propaganda spread by the political Right in the United States.

4) As we saw earlier, under the impact of neo-liberal policies, Western societies are becoming divided into three distinct sectors: the political and economic elites and the professionals allied to their cause; people with a comfortable income; and the unemployed, the working poor and those who are pushed to the margins because of their ethnic origin or culture. In most Western societies, the third sector is growing.

A new development in the third sector is the remarkable expansion of social and economic endeavours that have existed for a long time. Community development or the co-operative involvement of people to solve the social and economic problems created by their marginalization is becoming more intense and more widespread. The same is true of the social economy or the local democratically organized economic development that serves the community and allows its participants to escape from the poverty trap. Community development and the social economy reveal the creativity of men and women in the third sector who refuse to collapse into passivity or despair, who are willing to work together and use their intelligence to create institutions that provide them with the services from which society has deprived them. Because the people involved in these endeavours are critical of the political and economic institutions that have excluded them, their movement fosters a critical culture and generates a new political imagination.

Catholic social teaching has, as yet, not paid much attention to community development and the social economy. In chapter 11 I report the Canadian Catholic bishops' appreciation of this movement and argue in some detail why official Catholic social teaching should pay attention to this creative endeavour and encourage Catholic parishes and religious congregations to support community development and the social economy in their area. In Quebec, the support of these endeavours by several religious congregations of women is widely appreciated.

: : :

In the new situation created by globalization of the free market and the resulting unjust social conditions, people who love justice and respect nature are looking for new critical ideas and new forms of social engagement. Accompanying them are Christians called by the Gospel to stand for justice and serve the common good.

9

Resisting Empire

Since the end of the Cold War, a problematic political development has emerged. The one superpower has decided to become an empire exercising military, economic and cultural power over major sections of the globe. American military bases constitute a network of control across the continents; the globalization of the free market economy is promoted by the international financial institutions approved and supported by the United States; and the culture of consumerism and US-based entertainment spread by the mass media is undermining the cultural and religious traditions that have sustained the identity of peoples. We now live in an age of empire.

The emergence of empire has had an effect on the critical social sciences. New studies in various disciplines are focusing on the history of empires and the impact of colonialism on the colonized peoples and, more particularly, the impact of colonialism on the colonial powers themselves. This new interest has also affected biblical and theological studies.

The Imperial Domination of Israel[124]

Imperial domination plays an important role in the story of the people of Israel. First was the encounter with the Egyptian Empire. The rescue of the people of Israel from the oppressive conditions imposed by the Egyptian Empire, referred to as the Exodus, is the symbol of divine redemption in the Hebrew Scriptures. In the New Testament, Jesus adopts the Exodus as the symbol of his own redemptive mission. He is the new Moses; his Sermon on the Mount proclaims the new Law; and his bread from heaven is the new manna nourishing the people in the desert.

But Egypt was just the beginning. In its subsequent history, the people of Israel was colonized by several other empires: the Babylonian, the Median and the Persian. Yet the worst colonial oppression was imposed by the Macedonian army, led by Alexander the Great in 330 BCE. Biblical scholars agree that the vision of the four beasts recorded in the Book of Daniel refers to the successive empires, the worst of which was the Macedonian conquest.

> Daniel said, I have been seeing visions in the night. I saw that the four winds of heaven were stirring up the great sea; four great beasts emerged from the sea, each different from the other. The first was like a lion with eagle's wings and, as I looked, its wings were torn off.... And there before me was a second beast, like a bear, rearing up on one side, with three ribs in his mouth between its teeth. 'Up' came the command: 'Eat quantities of flesh.' ... And there before was another beast, like a leopard, with four bird's wings on its flanks, it had four heads and was granted authority. Next ... I saw another vision: there was before me a fourth beast, fearful, terrifying and very strong. It had great iron teeth, and it ate its victims, crushed them, and trampled their remains underfoot. It was different from the previous beasts and had ten horns. (Daniel 7:2-7)

Daniel predicts that the fourth beast, the Macedonian Empire, will oppress the faithful, try their faith and kill many of them. Yet in the end, the Empire will not last before God; it will be humiliated and God's people will be freed. In 175 BCE, the Macedonian Empire made an alliance with the Jewish priestly aristocracy, which was willing to promote the Hellenization of culture and the willing submission of the people to their colonizers. Fidelity to Torah and Temple led to the Maccabean Revolt in 168 BCE, recorded in the First Book of the Maccabees. Yet very soon the Maccabean or, as they were later called, the Hasmonean priests became the new aristocracy co-opted by the Empire. Then, in 63 BCE, the Romans conquered the entire area, privileged the Jewish aristocracy and created the Herodian client kings, who belonged to the Hasmonean dynasty. In 37 BCE, Emperor Augustus won the battle of Actium and imposed the strictest subjugation on the people of Israel. They were ruled by Jewish client kings, they had to pray tribute to the Emperor (non-payment was regarded as an act of rebellion and punished accordingly), and they saw their culture increasingly Hellenized by Jewish upper-class collaborators. This was the period of Jesus' public ministry. The Jewish Revolt (66–70) ended in the conquest and destruction of Jerusalem and the exile of the Jewish people from this area.

Jesus: Non-violent Radical

Jesus lived in a society marked by extreme violence. Thanks to *The Jewish Wars* by Flavius Josephus, we have a good idea of the conditions of repression and violent protest that prevailed in the Roman colony of Palestine. The imposed Hellenization of culture was resisted by various groups: 'the intellectuals,' who defended the faith tradition; the 'bandits,' who were dispossessed peasants roaming the region and robbing the rich; and the 'sicarii,' who kidnapped and murdered public personalities with their short daggers. Against these forms of resistance, the Empire inflicted new forms of repression. Since the Romans did not keep a large army in Palestine, they relied on the Jewish client kings to keep order; they also imposed terrible punishments on villages they suspected of harbouring the resistance. The Romans killed or enslaved the village inhabitants in the hope that this terror would frighten the people and make them subservient. Yet the large gathering of people at religious festivals continued to signal a time of unrest and danger. The high priests were nervous: they wanted these occasions to remain peaceful, to the satisfaction of the imperial government. They promoted a religion of temple worship, bracketing Israel's prophetic tradition.

The brutal colonization of peoples also affected the imperial society. Rome became increasingly a dictatorship, betraying the republican tradition and civic virtues it had admired in the past. While Rome let the colonized people keep their religion, the Emperor demanded that in addition to their gods, the people also worship him. The Empire's decision in 60 AD to introduce the imperial symbols in the temple of Jerusalem provoked the Jewish revolt, resulting in the destruction of the Temple and the exile of the Jewish people from the area.

How did Jesus react to the domination of Israel by the Empire, aided by the Jewish aristocracy? He announced the Gospel. In his Sermon on the Mount (Matthew 5), he presents himself as the new Moses, giving a new law as the foundation of a new and different society. Jesus is not a political leader; he is a prophet and more than a prophet who announces the new law of the Spirit, demanding the conversion of people to humility, love, justice and forgiveness, including the abolition of the *lex talionis*, society's right to retaliate. Jesus proposes an alternative to the Empire, a society that anticipates God's kingdom or God's non-violent reign making people brothers and sisters, living together in peace, willing to be selfless so that all will be well.

Jesus is opposed to violent action against Rome. At first he even avoids the kind of language that could lead to persecution and punishment. When his opponents tempt him by asking whether the people should pay tribute to Caesar, Jesus refuses to give a clear answer. Everyone knew that to resist the imperial tax was a crime equivalent to revolt and hence punishable by death. Yet Jesus' hour has not yet come. So he says, "Pay Caesar what belongs to Caesar – and God what belongs to God"(Matthew 22:21), words that have often been used to discourage Christians from speaking out against the government. Yet Jesus is a radical in the tradition of the Hebrew prophets. When his hour has come, he provokes the temple elite; he stands in judgment over the existing order; he speaks to Pilate as one who is not under his sway; and he prepares himself to suffer crucifixion, the capital punishment imposed by Rome upon rebels resisting the imperial power.

Social scientists distinguish between violent and non-violent radicals. During the '60s, Americans used to speak of 'power radicals' and 'flower radicals.' Power radicals hold that society has so many internal contradictions that it cannot be reformed; instead it will destroy itself. They are willing to commit acts of violence to symbolize society's ultimate collapse. Flower radicals also believe that society will destroy itself, yet they express this by challenging the authorities with symbols of non-violence. In the sixteenth century, the Anabaptists were radicals at odds with the churches and the Empire. A few of them committed violent acts, while the great majority practised non-violent resistance. When the police came to arrest them, they found the suspects sitting on the floor playing with toys like children. Using this terminology, one can say that Jesus was a flower radical: he responded to his powerful enemies by loving and forgiving them.

Why did this radical Jesus say to the people, "Repent, for the kingdom of heaven is close at hand" (Matthew 4:17)? Why did the poor, exploited and oppressed Jews have to repent? They were, after all, the victims, the sinned against, the objects of unjust and cruel colonial domination. This is a question that liberation theology has had to deal with. The sad truth is that exploitation and oppression have a soul-destroying impact upon the victims, making them liable to lose their innocence. Because of fear and frustration, the colonized often do mean and destructive things to one another. While they are the sinned against, they are nonetheless in need of repentance.

The Latin American theologian Ivone Gebara has created an original vocabulary to express this troubling reality. She distinguishes between 'transcendent' and 'immanent' evil.[125] Transcendent evil refers to the hurt and damage done by oppressive institutions that regulate people's lives in society, while immanent evil refers to the hurt and damage that the oppressed inflict on one another. As she lives among the poor in an urban neighbourhood in Brazil, she sees the destructive things that the poor do to themselves – the conflicts, the insults, the fights and the stealing – in addition to acts of generous assistance and spontaneous solidarity. These destructive reactions are provoked by despair over people's exclusion from the resources of life. Still, they rob people of their innocence. Hence the words of Jesus addressed to the victims of Empire: "Repent, for the kingdom of heaven is at hand." God is near; with God you will start a new way of life.

That oppression and persecution tempt victims to lose their innocence is an important ethical insight. The Afrikaner people conquered and humiliated by the British Empire in the Boer War were truly victims: they defended themselves and clung to their collective identity with all their might, producing an energy that would eventually be directed against the Black population. The Jews of Europe, persecuted, imprisoned and murdered by Nazi Germany, were truly victims: they courageously affirmed their collective identity with all their might, producing an energy that would eventually sustain the occupation of Palestine. Even victims struggling for liberation are called to engage in critical self-examination.

Christian Reactions to the Empire

The early Christians were in disagreement about the relationship between Gospel and Empire. One reason for this disagreement is that after the Resurrection, the followers of Jesus realized that what had taken place in him had a truly universal meaning: he was the new Moses who rescued the whole of humanity from enslavement to the powers of darkness. He was the promised Messiah whose death and resurrection rescued humanity from self-destruction and eternal loss. This theology allowed Christians to offer a purely spiritual interpretation of Christ's death on the cross: he died for our sins, took upon himself the punishment for our transgressions, rescued us from sin and saved us for eternal life. This interpretation bracketed the historical meaning of Christ's death and emptied the Gospel of its political message.

In the New Testament, there is disagreement regarding the attitude towards Rome. On the one hand, we have the Acts of the Apostles, written by Luke, in which Rome appears as the seat of justice. When Paul is accused of heresy in Jerusalem, he insists that he is a Roman citizen, he appeals to the Emperor, and he is subsequently sent to Rome to be tried by a secular court far removed from the Jewish elites who have accused him (Acts 22:25-29). The Acts of the Apostles seem to suggest that because the Roman Empire embraces the many nations, unites them through a common law and provides a system of communication among them, it opens the door for the Church to spread the Christian message throughout the world.

By contrast, the book of the Apocalypse offers the harshest condemnation of the Empire as Prostitute and Babylon the Great, the evil power that oppresses the nations and persecutes the saints.

One of the seven angels ... came to speak to me, and said, "Come here, and I will show you the punishment of the great prostitute ... with whom all the kings of the earth have prostituted themselves, and who had made all the population of the world drunk with the wine of her adultery." He took me in spirit to a desert, and there I saw a woman riding a scarlet beast which had seven heads and ten horns [*a reference to the seven hills of Rome and the ten vassal kings*]. The woman was dressed in purple and scarlet and glittered with gold, jewels and pearls, and she was holding a gold winecup filled with the disgusting filth of her prostitution; on her forehead was written a cryptic name: "Babylon the Great, the mother of all the prostitutes and all the filthy practices of the earth." I saw that she was drunk, drunk with the blood of the saints and the blood of the martyrs of Jesus. (Revelation 17:1-8)

In the history of the early Church, Christians continued to be at odds in their attitude towards the Roman Empire. As they suffered repression and persecution, many Christians regarded the Empire as an enemy and hostile power; well known among them was the apologist Tertullian (156–230). Yet other Christians looked upon the Empire as the work of God's providence, allowing the Church to preach the Gospel to the peoples around the Mediterranean. Christians who had suffered under persecution rejoiced when Constantine, after the battle at the Milvian Bridge in 312, recognized Christianity as the religion of the Empire. The political theologian Eusebius of Caesarea (263–339) went so far as to interpret this event as a consequence of Christ's victory on the cross and the fulfillment of the divine promises.

The young St. Augustine (354–430) showed a certain enthusiasm for the new Empire as the protector of the Christian order, but as he grew older he changed his mind.[126] The sack of Rome in 410 shocked the Roman world: it revealed the internal weakness of the Empire and raised the question of whether it would last much longer. The sack of Rome provoked Augustine to develop his critique of society in his book *The City of God*. He introduced the famous distinction between two cities created by two different kinds of love. On the one hand is 'the proud city,' 'the city of man,' produced by the love of self, expressed in the will to power and the desire for wealth; on the other is 'the humble city,' 'the city of God,' created by the love of God and neighbour, expressed in mutual assistance and works of justice. In some texts, Augustine identifies the City of God with the Church: these texts were used in the Middle Ages to claim the Church's superiority over the secular society. Yet other passages in *The City of God* offer a wider and more subtle meaning of the humble city, referring to any community in which people, in the name of God, love and serve one another and practise justice and peace. Augustine now looks upon the Roman Empire, the great society in which he lives, as the proud city marked by its origin, the practice of greed and domination. Yet he also recognizes that the existence of humble cities, small communities practising justice and love of neighbour, have a beneficial influence on the great society. He therefore sees the Empire as a *corpus mixtum*. It is a 'mixed body politic' because it is an unjust institution in which nonetheless many good things happen.

The Two Cities

I wish to use Augustine's theology of the two cities to interpret the reaction of Jesus to the colonial subjugation of his people. In his Sermon on the Mount, as I wrote above, Jesus announced that God would act through the poor and the humble to initiate an alternative society. The people whom Jesus calls blessed – the afflicted, the despised and the persecuted, all yearning for justice – were the oppressed population, the colonized Jews, subject to the culture of the colonizer, burdened by heavy taxes and betrayed by their religious leaders. Trusting in the divine promises, these men and women were to love one another, help one another, practise justice, forgive one another, abandon sentiments of hatred and revenge, and be ready to be persecuted. They were to create a new society, 'a humble city,' based on principles that were at odds with those of the established order, 'the proud city.' This alternative city, we note, was not to be a spiritual way for a few chosen souls. Jesus said to them, "You are the light of the world; you are the salt of the earth." What you do is significant for the entire social order: you constitute a social movement destined to reconstruct the dominant society.

We used to think that our political situation was quite different from the one in which Jesus lived. We did not live in a colony oppressed by foreign empire; we lived in a society that we honoured and wanted to improve. We were citizens of a democracy that allowed us to participate in the public debate and have a certain influence on the making of public policies. Christians committed to justice and peace supported reformist political parties that sought to serve the common good of society. At that time we did not recognize that the Sermon on the Mount was politically relevant: we interpreted Christ's urgent message in spiritual terms as a divine call to personal holiness. Many of us were also unhappy with St. Augustine's pessimism regarding the great society and his prediction that the Empire was about to collapse.

In the present phase of history, marked by the emergence of empire, Christians ask themselves whether our situation is like the situation in which Jesus lived and in which Augustine wrote *The City of God*. We have become deeply troubled by the oppressive features of contemporary society.[127] Reformist political parties no longer seem to be able to alter the direction of neo-liberal globalization, with its impact on the marginalization of people and its destructive consequences on the natural environment. Even social democratic governments seem to promote the neo-liberal agenda, foster deregulation and privatization, dismantle the welfare state, limit people's democratic freedoms, and refuse to intervene to protect the poor and excluded.

The only good news in the present situation is the ongoing creativity at the community level: a network of social movements guided by the vision of a more just and more caring society is promoting alternative practices that flout the logic of the dominant society. I am thinking here of the peace movement, the women's movement, the environmental movement, community development and the social economy, the anti-globalization movement, support groups for refugees and other marginalized people, and groups promoting an alternative lifestyle. Many Christians urged by their faith involve themselves in these movements.

These movements follow principles that are at odds with those operative in the greater society. They recognize the damage done by this society and the false values that drive it forward. Because they honour civil liberties, defend socio-economic human rights, promote the spirit of co-operation and self-restraint, and express humanity's yearning for greater justice, we may ask ourselves whether these movements are candidates for St. Augustine's 'humble city.' These movements are secular: they do not invoke the name of God, yet they are committed to justice and peace: they humanize the lives of the people involved in them; they offer help to millions of people in need; they do good things in an unjust society; and they invent models of social interaction that may one day generate a radically new society. Carried by a sense of hope, these movements believe that another world is possible.

The two cities are recognized in a recent book by Richard Falk,[128] a political scientist close to the United Nations, in which he offers an analysis of two disparate movements. The first movement promotes globalization from above – supported by transnational corporations, the international financial institutions and the governments of the United States and its allies – what I have called 'neo-liberal globalization.' The second movement promotes globalization from below. It brings together and organizes internationally a great variety of local critical social movements to offer a globalized opposition to the globalization from above and to find a common voice in the World Social Forums, the first one of which took place at Porto Alegre in 2001. According to Falk, the globalization-from-below movement is guided by an alternative imagination and sustained by ethical values and a proper spirituality. He studies the religious groups of various traditions that are involved in this movement and shows that even the secular people, the great majority, involved in this movement cultivate a spirituality. He describes in some detail their sense of transcendence, their commitment to solidarity, their option for non-violence, and their cultivation of friendship among the members, even when they are in disagreement.

In the past, Catholics were guided in their commitment to social justice by the Church's social teaching, in line with the Aristotelian-Thomistic tradition, aiming at the reform of their present society. Today, many of them are becoming increasingly Augustinian, distinguishing between the two cities and involving themselves in critical counter-movements.

10

The Priority of Labour over Capital: Pope John Paul II's Social Teaching

The needs of the poor must take priority over the desires of the rich, the rights of workers over the maximization of profits, the preservation of the environment over uncontrolled industrial expansion, and production to meet social needs over production for military purposes. (John Paul II, on his visit to Canada, 1984)[129]

Pope John Paul II's social teaching is theologically grounded. He developed his ideas in continuity with earlier papal teaching and in critical dialogue with secular thought, but the basis of his teaching is the Gospel. This differs from papal teachings in the past, which were based on natural law reasoning and bracketed reference to divine revelation. The popes did this in the hope of finding common ground with non-Christians. Pope John XXIII was the first pope to mention the Gospel in his social teaching. It was John Paul's II 'cosmic christology,' the idea that through Incarnation and Redemption Christ is related in some way to every human being, that accounts for the theological orientation of his social teaching. The Pope proposed this christology in his first encyclical,[130] expanding upon ideas set forth by Vatican Council II, and often referred to it on subsequent occasions. We have here the retrieval of a theological current of the ancient Christian authors, especially in the East, according to which the whole of humanity, or even the entire cosmos, has been elevated and assigned a supernatural destiny through Incarnation and Christ's death and resurrection. On the basis of this theology, the Pope speaks confidently of Christian principles, trusting that if they are expressed in simple language, people outside of the Church will understand them.

A practical consequence of this theological approach is that the commitment to social justice here receives a new location in the life of faith. When the Church's social teaching was based on natural law theory, social justice belonged to the order of the natural virtues and did not involve the order of faith, hope and love. At that time, spirituality and the intimate life of faith did not include commitment to justice and the transformation of society. The spiritual books then used in seminaries and religious communities testify to this: they did not trouble their readers with the problems of their society. With John Paul's social teaching, universal solidarity and commitment to social justice were lifted into the life of faith, hope and love and thus become a part of Catholic spirituality. There is a mystical dimension in the sorrow over the suffering of others and the public engagement to reconstruct the social order. The Pope's teaching, one might add, reflects the religious experience of vast numbers of Christians committed to social justice in various parts of the world.

The Purpose of This Essay

Since Pope John Paul II has produced an extensive literature developing his social teaching, a single essay cannot cover the full range of his thought, but will have to focus on a particular topic. I wish to concentrate on a theme in his teaching, often overlooked in North America, that made him a critic of Eastern communism and Western capitalism. During the Cold War, John Paul II adopted a position, rarely defended in North America, that called for the spiritual, moral and structural conversion of communism and capitalism. While he opposed the totalitarian regimes in the Soviet bloc countries, denounced their militant atheism and criticized the imperialist outreach of the Soviet Union, he did not envision the collapse of these systems, but advocated their reform. Nor did he think that the world was threatened by Soviet imperialism alone. In his first encyclical, *Redemptor hominis* (March 1979), he denounced the involvement of the two superpowers in Third World countries, accusing them of exploiting the local populations, fomenting conflicts between them, supplying them with weapons to wage war, and exercising neocolonialism of one kind or another. Then he added that this criticism is likely "to offer both 'sides' an occasion for mutual accusation, each overlooking its own faults" (16).

Since John Paul II's social teaching is so bold and so rarely heard, I will have to offer many quotations from his speeches and encyclicals; otherwise the reader might think that these radical ideas are drawn from other sources. First, I shall deal with the Pope's encyclical *Laborem exercens* (September 1981), in support of the Polish labour movement, *Solidarnosc*, which called for reforms in the existing communist and capitalist societies. Second, I will offer a brief account of Rome's relation to Latin American liberation theology. Third, I shall study the encyclical *Sollicitudo rei socialis* (December 1987), which offers a critical analysis of the two superpowers and, far from anticipating the collapse of communism, urges the reform of the two existing economic systems. Finally, I shall examine the Pope's teaching after the collapse of Eastern European communism in 1989, both in his encyclical *Centesimus annus* (May 1991) and in his speeches delivered in Poland and other countries formerly members of the Soviet bloc.

Laborem exercens

Let me begin with a brief account of the political philosophy of the Polish solidarity movement supported by both secular and Catholic workers. In her detailed study, *The Polish Solidarity Movement,* Arista Maria Cirtautas examines Solidarity's affirmation of social rights and its relation to capitalism.[131] She offers a careful analysis of the debate among workers and intellectuals over the basis for their opposition to Poland's communist government, and then shows that they eventually agreed on a value-rational position that she designates as "a fusion of communist and Catholic humanism."[132] She confirms this conclusion in her study of the writings of Adam Michnik, the influential secular socialist,[133] and of Jozef Tischner, the Catholic social thinker.[134] These intellectuals articulated humanistic positions that, though distinct, were close enough to lay the foundation for solidarity in a joint struggle for communist reform. In his encyclical, John Paul II, conscious of this secular-Catholic co-operation, expressed his thought in a Catholic discourse that addressed at the same time the secular workers. The Pope's message was fully heard as support for the joint struggle. Responding to the encyclical in the name of his colleagues, Michnik wrote that the Pope did not confront them with a choice between faith and atheism; instead, he proposed a set of common values with which they readily identified.

What was the aim of the Polish labour movement? It was certainly not to introduce Western-style capitalism into Poland. *Solidarnosc* fought for independent labour unions, a more participatory society with freedom of speech, a more open space for economic initiatives and the creation of free markets; at the same time, it supported a strong central government to regulate the economy and assume the redistribution of wealth. Thinking that communism was reformable, the movement struggled for a socialism with a human face.

In *Laborem exercens* John Paul II defines human beings as workers. "Work is one of the characteristics that distinguishes humans from the rest of creatures, whose activities for sustaining their lives cannot be called work. Only humans are capable of work, and only human work, and in doing so occupy their existence on earth" (Introduction). "Human life is built up every day from work, from work it derives its specific dignity, yet at the same time work contains the unceasing measure of human toil and suffering and also of the harm and injustice which penetrate deeply into social life within the individual nations and on the international level" (1). The Pope wrote his encyclical "to highlight – perhaps more than has been done before – that human work is a key, probably the essential key, to the entire social question" (3). This is in fact a new discourse in papal social teaching.

The encyclical introduces the important distinction between the *objective* and the *subjective* pole of labour. The objective pole refers to the product of work, which in one way or another transforms the earth, while the subjective dimension refers to the self-realization of the workers through their work. It is to the latter that the Pope attributes priority. "Human beings work as persons, performing various actions belonging to the work process. Independently of their objective content, these actions must all serve to realize the humanity of the workers, to fulfill the calling to be persons that is theirs by reason of their very humanity" (6). Humans are divinely destined to realize and constitute themselves through their work. What follows from this is that workers are *subjects,* not *objects,* of their work. "The sources of human dignity of work are to be sought primarily in the subjective dimension, not in the objective one" (6).

This understanding of human work respects what the Pope refers to as "the primacy of the spiritual." This primacy, we note, is not an otherworldly principle; it refers rather to the preeminence of the spiritual dimension in the constitution of human beings and their societies.

Continuing his argument, John Paul II writes, "At the beginning of the industrial age, work was understood and treated as a sort of 'merchandise' that the industrial worker sells to the employer, who is the possessor of the capital, i.e. of all the working tools and means that make production possible" (7). When workers are not respected as subjects, their work is deeply alienating, preventing them from fulfilling their human vocation. The encyclical argues that workers' movements and social reforms were able to transform the original situation at the beginning of the industrial age and produce various forms of capitalism and socialism. Still, "the danger of treating work as a special kind of 'merchandise' or as an impersonal 'work force' needed for production always exists, especially when the whole way of looking at the question of economics is marked by the premises of materialistic economism" (7).

Is the Pope here speaking of the communist East or the capitalist West? Here is what he says: "When the human is treated as an instrument of production ... whatever the program or name under which this occurs, should rightly be called 'capitalism'" (7). By implication, the Pope here accuses the existing communist society of being a form of state capitalism. "The error of early capitalism can be repeated wherever workers are treated on the same level as the whole complex of the material means of production" (7). John Paul II here formulates an ethical principle that is applicable to all industrial systems, namely "the priority of labour over capital" (12).

In several of his writings and speeches, the Pope tries to set the origin of capitalism and socialism into their historical context.[135] At the industrial revolution, "a break occurred" through which "labour was separated from capital and set in opposition to it, and capital was set in opposition to labour, as if they were two impersonal forces" (13). "Considering human labour solely according to its economic purpose, was a fundamental error that can be called ... economism" (13). "It was this practical error that struck a blow first and foremost against human labour, against the working man, and caused an ethically just social reaction" (13), "an impetuous emergence of a great burst of solidarity between workers, first and foremost industrial workers" (8). This outburst of solidarity, as we shall see further on, produced reform movements within capitalism and generated socialism in various forms, most of them affected by the same economistic error. This error is corrected by the application of "the priority of labour over capital."

Almost the entire social teaching of John Paul II in the period of the Cold War was formulated in such a manner that it offered a theologically grounded, ethical critique of the existing communist and existing capitalist societies. I have called this 'the double orientation' of his teaching. This does not mean, of course, that he put the two competing superpowers and their allies on the same level. The totalitarian regimes of the Soviet bloc countries and their militant atheism created oppressive conditions over against which the Western democracies appeared as realms of freedom, despite their own oppressive practices. Yet, as we shall see, the Pope did not overlook the imperialism exercised by the superpower of the West.

Space does not allow me to offer a detailed analysis of *Laborem exercens*. To illustrate the Pope's brilliant double-oriented economic and political ethics, I simply wish to give two examples: i) the ongoing need for a labour movement supported by all who love justice and ii) the conditional character of the ownership of the means of production.

First, since in all industrial societies the subjectivity of labour and the living conditions of workers continue to be threatened, labour movements, including the unionization of labour, are indispensable elements of society, gifted with a historical vocation.

> In order to achieve social justice in the various parts of the world … there is need for ever new movements of solidarity of the workers and with the workers. This solidarity must be present whenever it is called for by the social degrading of the subject of work, by exploitation of the workers and by growing areas of poverty and even hunger. The Church is firmly committed to this cause, for it considers it to be its mission, its service, a proof of its fidelity to Christ (8).

That this struggle differs from the Marxist idea of class war is clear: first, this social struggle does not aim at the conquest of the owning classes but at conditions of greater justice; and second, this struggle calls for the solidarity *of* workers and the solidarity *with* workers of all citizens who love justice and hence transcends its location in the working class.

The second example is the Pope's bold interpretation of ownership that radicalizes anything taught on the subject by previous popes. Applying the principle of 'the priority of labour,' the encyclical argues that unless the ownership of the means of production, whether it be personal or collective, intends to serve labour, or more widely the labouring society, the ownership loses its legitimate title. This is a subversive principle questioning both capitalist and communist societies. Here is the remarkable text.

> Isolating the means of production as a separate property in order to set it up in the form of 'capital' in opposition to 'labour' – and even to practice exploitation of labour – is contrary to the very nature of these means and their possession. They cannot be possessed against labour, they cannot even be possessed for possession's sake, because the only legitimate title to their possession – whether in the form of private ownership or in

the form of public or collective ownership – is that it should serve labour (14).

Implicit in this understanding of ownership is the realization of the ancient Christian teaching usually formulated quite abstractly as "the universal destination of goods and the right of common use of them" (14).

Laborem exercens had a strong influence on the social teaching of the Canadian bishops, especially on their *Ethical Reflections on the Economic Crisis* (1983).[136] When the Pope visited Canada in 1984, he supported the radical critique of the existing economic order by a number of strong statements, one of which was quoted at the very beginning of this article. Here is another strong statement on North-South relations made by the Pope on his Canadian journey.

> Poor people and poor nations – poor in different ways, not only lacking food, but also deprived of freedom and other human rights – will sit in judgment on those people who take these goods away from them, amassing to themselves the imperialistic monopoly of economic and political supremacy at the expense of others.[137]

The Pope here calls for the conversion of heart and mind of the powerful elites. His radical call for the reconstruction of the global society recognizes the primacy of the spiritual.

Liberation Theology

The evaluation of Latin American liberation theology by Pope John Paul and the Congregation for the Doctrine of Faith is a complex one, not free of contradictions, that has never been carefully studied and would deserve book-long exploration. On the one hand, Latin American liberation theology has been able to shift the focus of ecclesiastical teaching – at the Latin American Bishops' Conference at Medellín (1968), at the World Synod of Bishops (1971) and in

Paul VI's *Octogesima adveniens* (1971).[138] Pope John Paul II himself repeatedly endorsed 'the preferential option for the poor,'[139] a concept taken from Latin American liberation theology. Sometimes the Pope preferred to speak of 'the preferential love of the poor,' which is an option within the order of charity, demanding that in its pastoral and charitable service the Church assign priority to the poor. 'The preferential option for the poor' belongs to a different order. It is implies a double commitment: i) to read historical events and the texts associated with them from the perspective of the poor and ii) to give public witness to their struggle for greater justice. This is what the Pope did on many occasions. On his visits to Third World countries, he sided with the poor, the great majority, and told them that, in their name, he denounced the unjust structures that oppress them.

A famous example is his speech at Cuilapan, Mexico, in January of 1979, addressing several hundred thousand Native people from Oaxaca and Chiapas.[140] Here the Pope promised that he would be their voice, the voice of those who cannot speak or who are silenced, expressing their prolonged suffering and their disappointed hopes and accusing the men in power responsible for the oppressive conditions that cause hunger and misery among the poor and rob them of their dignity as God's children. The Pope here read Mexican society from the perspective of the poor and gave public support for their struggle for justice. Here he proclaimed the Christian Gospel as God's merciful act of love rescuing the people from the enemies of their lives.

An alternative emphasis is made by John Paul II in his opening statement at the Latin American Bishops' Conference at Puebla (1979).[141] Here he insisted that the starting point of Christian reflection must be the doctrines of the faith, and only the second step is the turn to the misery of the poor inflicted by unjust conditions. Here he criticized liberation theology and even a trend among the bishops to regard solidarity with the poor as the first step, taken in the name of Jesus, and then only to explore the meaning of Christian doctrine from the perspective of these oppressed people. After this criticism followed two declarations made by the Congregation for the Doctrine of the Faith (1984, 1986).[142] The first declaration was highly critical of liberation theology, suggesting that it made "an insufficiently critical use of Marxism," while the second adopted a more positive approach, even while warning against the adoption of Marxist principles. To what extent these critical observations apply to the different types of liberation theologies produced in Latin America deserves careful study. In a letter to the Brazilian bishops (March 13, 1986) who were puzzled by the Roman position, John Paul II seemed to clarify his own attitude: "The theology of liberation can and must exist … we must proceed with this reflection, update it and deepen it more and more."[143] Liberation theology is acceptable, he continued, as long as it respects the primacy of the spiritual, recognizes the struggle of the poor for social justice as grounded in Christian values, and remains faithful to the Church's social teaching. The Pope's concern here is the same as in *Laborem exercens*: the struggle against injustice and oppression must preserve the primacy of the spiritual and understand itself as an ethically grounded movement sustained by the Gospel, and not as the necessary product of the class conflict built into the material dynamics of history as Marxists have interpreted it.

The entire topic of Rome and liberation theology deserves major study that takes into account both the various ecclesiastical texts and the differences among liberation theologians. The topic is even more complicated because Rome also seemed to criticize the Latin American bishops for their sympathy with liberation theology, even if their own public statements were more moderate. The new bishops appointed by Rome were often conservative churchmen who did not share the spirit of Medellín and did not follow the option for the poor as expressed at Puebla. Students of this period of history, puzzled by this shift in Roman policy, have focused on the US government's opposition to liberation theology and episcopal teaching in Latin America and have raised the question whether Rome had consented to an agreement with President Reagan.[144]

Sollicitudo rei socialis

The encyclical *Sollicitudo rei socialis* was published in December 1987, commemorating Paul VI's *Populorum progressio,* written twenty years earlier. In 1987, it was already clear that a shift had taken place in the orientation of the Western economy. Under the impact of the policies adopted by Margaret Thatcher, prime minister of the United Kingdom, and Ronald Reagan, president of the United States, the national economies in the countries of the West had abandoned the Keynesian policies favouring regulated capitalism and the welfare state and instead introduced monetarist policies that called for the deregulation of capital, the privatization of public goods and the globalization of the free market. The encyclical concludes that since 1967, the conditions of the poor countries had deteriorated.

What is remarkable is that the encyclical in no way anticipates the collapse of Eastern European communism that would take place less than two years later, in 1989.[145] In 1987 John Paul II still believed, as he did in *Laborem exercens*, that the two opposing economic systems and their respective societies could be reformed, made more just and more human, and then live peacefully side by side. In 1987 the Pope was still preoccupied with the impact of the Cold War, especially on the countries of the Third World. "If their situation is examined in the light of the division of the world into ideological blocs … and in the light of the subsequent economic and political repercussions and dependencies, the danger is seen to be much greater" (10).

Space does not allow me to summarize John Paul II's bold and original social teaching in *Sollicitudo rei socialis*. Rather, I wish to demonstrate the double orientation of the encyclical: the formulation of a spiritual, ethical and structural critique of society that was relevant for the communist and capitalist world. Again, because the Pope's proposals are so daring, I will quote his very words.

Sollicitudo rei socialis begins with a survey of contemporary conditions, focusing especially on the Third World (11–19). Using several statistical criteria, such as the production and distribution of foodstuffs, hygiene, health, housing, availability of drinking water, working conditions (especially for women), life expectancy, indebtedness, and other social and economic indicators, the Pope concludes that the gap between rich and poor is increasing and that the majority of humanity is now worse off than in 1967, when Paul VI published *Populorum progressio*.

Among the oppressive features of contemporary society, John Paul II mentions the spread of unemployment in capitalist countries and the suppression of people's right to economic initiative in communist countries. In this context the Pope explored the concept of 'subjectivity,' already applied to workers in his *Laborem exercens*, by expanding it to all citizens and, more generally, to members of any organization. No institution has the right to suppress the spirit of initiative, reliance on personal creativity, and the sense of co-responsibility, for these belong to a person's 'subjectivity.' The immediate reference is here to the command economy in communist countries that stifles people's economic initiative and fails to recognize the indispensable role of markets. The Pope adds an interesting sentence on bureaucratic domination that has universal relevance. "In the place of creative initiative there appears passivity, dependence and submission to the bureaucratic apparatus which, as the only 'ordering' and 'decision-making' body – if not also the owner – of the entire totality of goods and the means of production, puts everyone in a position of almost absolute dependence, which is similar to the traditional dependence of the worker-proletarian in capitalism" (15).

According to the encyclical, the situation of Third World peoples is strongly affected by the tension between the two superpowers,

> [...]the existence of two opposing blocs, commonly known as the East and the West. The reason for this description is not purely political but is also, as the expression goes, geopolitical. Each of the two blocs tends to assimilate or gather around it other countries or groups of countries, to different degrees of adherence or participation. The opposition is first of all political, inasmuch as each bloc identifies itself with a system of organizing society and exercising power which presents itself as an alternative to the other. The political opposition, in turn, takes its origin from a deeper opposition which is ideological in nature. (20)

> In the West there exists a system which is historically inspired by the principles of liberal capitalism which developed with industrialization during the last century. In the East there exists a system inspired by Marxist collectivism which sprang from an interpretation of the condition of the proletarian classes made in the light of a particular reading of history. Each of the two ideologies, on the basis of two very different visions of man, and of his freedom and social role, has proposed and still promotes, on the economic level, antithetical forms of the organization of labour and of the structures of ownership, especially in regard to the so-called means of production. (20)

It was inevitable that by developing antagonistic systems and centers of power, each with its own form of propaganda and indoctrination, the ideological opposition should evolve into a growing military opposition and give rise to two blocs of armed forces, each suspicious and fearful of the other's domination. International relations, in turn, could not fail to feel the effects of this 'logic of blocs' and of the respective 'spheres of influence'.... Sometimes this tension has taken the form of 'cold war,' sometimes of 'wars by proxy', through the manipulation of local conflicts and sometimes it has kept people's minds in suspense and anguish by the threat of an open and total war. (20)

John Paul II further developed the analysis expressed in the above paragraphs at other occasions. He argues that because industrial capitalism produced both wealth and freedom for the middle classes, they were tempted to turn private property and the free market into a principle of universal validity, an ideology that accounted for the evolution of history and defined its orientation towards the future. Ideologies are deadly – the Pope refers to them sometimes as 'idols' – because they are taken as infallible guides for policies and actions without attention to their destructive empirical consequences. John Paul II is fully aware that thanks to the labour movement and reform-minded political parties, capitalism has assumed new forms, sometimes allowing workers substantial degrees of participation.

Conversely, the Pope argues that the ethically justified struggle of workers to achieve more just conditions and the respect of their rights has tempted Marxists to turn the working class struggle into a principle of universal validity, an ideology that accounts for the evolution of history and defines its orientation towards the future. Again, this ideology has become deadly because it guides policies and actions without attention to the devastation they produce. The struggle of workers for greater justice, the Pope holds, is an ethical undertaking, an outburst of solidarity, that deserves the support of all classes and the Church itself. In line with the Polish Solidarity movement, the Pope believes that an ethical, non-ideological form of socialism is a political possibility. The rigidity of communist governments has prevented this from happening.

The opposition between the two superpowers, John Paul II argues, has been transferred to the developing countries, creating hostilities between them and prompting them to arm themselves, prepare for war, and spend their limited resources on the expansion of their military. "This is one of the reasons why the Church's social doctrine adopts a critical attitude towards both liberal capitalism and Marxist collectivism" (21).

While the East-West tension seems to be declining, the Pope believes that a new development has begun to threaten the well-being of the developing countries: the global interdependence between rich and poor countries or the globalization of the free market system, unrestricted by any ethical principles. "The results are disastrous consequences for the weakest. Indeed, as a result of a sort of internal dynamic and under the impulse of mechanisms that can only be called perverse, this interdependence triggers negative effects even in the rich countries" (17). *Populorum progressio* already foresaw the possibility that under such a system the wealth of the rich would increase and the poverty of the poor would remain (16).

John Paul II, we note, was not opposed to the process of globalization brought about by the development of technology and universal exchange. On the contrary, he praised globalization as long as it is regulated by social justice, respect for the culture of others and a universal commitment to solidarity.

In the rich social teaching of *Sollicitudo rei socialis*, John Paul II touches upon many issues of great importance, such as the international debt, the arms trade, refugees, unemployment, the culture of consumerism, population policy, abortion, and threats to the natural environment. He is encouraged by some positive developments (26): i) the attention to human rights fostered by the United Nations and other international organizations; ii) the growing awareness of the limits of nature and the need for environmental protection; and iii) the growing realization that the entire globe is vulnerable to the same threats, that humanity shares a common destiny and that universal solidarity is indispensable.

John Paul II also offers a theologically grounded theory of human development that takes the economic dimension with utmost seriousness and at the same time emphasizes the primacy of the spiritual. The spread of global interdependence must be guided by the spirit of solidarity. There exist no solutions of the world's problems and no remedy for the human suffering caused by these problems, apart from a commitment to universal solidarity. What is required is a conversion of the heart and mind.

I wish to draw attention to the emphasis of *Sollicitudo rei socialis* on 'evil mechanisms' and 'structural sins' that create and perpetuate injustices and damage the lives of human beings. Thus we read in reference to the international debt that changes made in the international financial markets "have turned into counter-productive mechanisms" (19). "The mechanisms intended for the development of peoples has turned into a brake upon development instead, and in some cases has aggravated underdevelopment" (19). Or we read that "a world divided into blocs, sustained by rigid ideologies, in which instead of interdependence and solidarity different forms of imperialism hold sway, can only be a world subject to structures of sin" (36). What we must wrestle against demands therefore collective action and public engagement to reconstruct institutions that do grave harm to people. The primacy of the spiritual may not be interpreted as if the divine summons to social justice simply means that each person should become more holy in his or her private life. "All you need is love," a popular song says, but love is not enough. What is needed are social movements grounded in preferential solidarity with the victims and oriented towards the renewal of human society as a whole.

Centesimus annus

Centesimus annus (May 1991) is the first encyclical the Pope wrote after the "unexpected" collapse of Eastern European communism in 1989.[146] It is not surprising that the demise of the Soviet bloc gave him great joy. The totalitarian regimes with their official atheism had been overcome, and the doors had been opened for the public celebration of the Christian faith and new social and economic developments in the liberated countries. This encyclical has much to say that is important for the contemporary world. What I wish to focus on is the continuity of the Pope's social teaching. What interests me, therefore, is the continued relevance of *Laborem exercens* and *Sollicitudo rei socialis* after the collapse of the Soviet bloc.

We read in *Centesimus annus* that in the world of 1991, Pope John Paul II saw three distinct socio-political projects that people or their governments attempt to translate into reality (19). I wish to describe these projects, though not in the order in which they are discussed in the encyclical. One of these projects the Pope dismisses very quickly. There are governments, he writes, that oppose Marxism for ideological reasons and set up "systems of national security aimed at controlling the whole of society in a systematic way in order to make Marxist infiltration impossible" (19). These societies sin, the Pope argues, as did the Marxist system by robbing the citizens of their freedom.

A second societal project is "the affluent or consumer society that seeks to defeat Marxism on the level of pure materialism by showing how a free market society can achieve greater satisfaction of material human needs than communism, while equally excluding spiritual values" (19). While it is true that the existing socialist societies were economically inefficient, the ideological defence of capitalism "reduces man to the sphere of economics and the satisfaction of material needs" (19). It is based on an economistic misunderstanding of the human being. "There is a risk that a radical capitalist ideology could spread which refuses to consider that vast multitudes are still living … in great material and moral poverty, in an *a priori* belief that … blindly entrusts the solution of these problems to the free development of market forces" (42). Or again, "it is unacceptable to say that the defeat of 'real socialism' leaves capitalism as the only model of economic organization" (35). Why is this unacceptable? Because today "it is necessary to break down the barriers and monopolies which leave so many countries on the margins of development" (35).

Two issues related to this second societal project preoccupy the Pope: the market as possible 'idol' and the culture of consumerism.

While markets are necessary in a free and economically efficient society, markets have their limits. "There are collective and qualitative needs which cannot be satisfied by market mechanisms. There are important human needs that escape its logic. There are goods that by their very nature cannot and must not be bought and sold. Certainly the mechanisms of the market offer secure advantages … yet they carry the risk of 'idolatry' … ignoring the existence of goods … which cannot be mere commodities" (40).

The encyclical, we note, offers high praise for the free market. "On the level of individual nations and of international relations, the free market is the most efficient instrument for utilizing resources and effectively responding to needs" (34). This positive evaluation is immediately followed by a paragraph emphasizing the limits of the market. First, the free market is acceptable only for things that are by nature 'marketable,' and second, the free market is a useful instrument for the distribution of goods only among people who have money to pay the price. For the distribution of basic needs to the poor, one must find institutions other than markets. "It is a strict duty of justice and truth not to allow fundamental human needs to remain unsatisfied and to allow those burdened by such needs to perish" (34).

In what the Pope calls liberal, rigid or ideological capitalism, the logic of the market invades every sphere of human life and creates a culture where 'having' has priority over 'being.' "Consumerism occurs when people are ensnared in a web of false and superficial gratifications rather than being helped to experience their personhood in an authentic way" (42). The culture of consumerism is promoted with the help of mass media by industrial and commercial institutions intent upon extending the market and increasing their profit.

> Alienation is also found in work, when it is organized so as to ensure maximum returns and profits with no concern whether the worker, through their own labour, grows or diminishes as a person, either through increased sharing in a supportive community, or through increased isolation in a maze of relationships marked by destructive competitiveness, in which he is considered only a means and not an end. (42)

This second societal project described in the encyclical – which I shall call Model A – appears to refer to the neo-liberal globalization of the free market which, as I indicated above, was already being promoted in 1991. Model A is brought about by the deregulation of capital; the privatization of publicly own goods; the unlimited rights of private property; the unrestricted global mobility of capital and goods; and the reliance on market forces to regulate education, public health and cultural development and to solve the problems created by ecological damage, social inequality and the exclusion of the poor.

What does John Paul II call the third societal project that he discerned in the world of 1991? In one place he speaks of "democratic societies inspired by social justice" (19). Such societal projects, he wrote, try to preserve the free market mechanisms, the harmony of social relations, and the citizens' economic initiative to build a better future for themselves and their families. At the same time, these societal projects "avoid making the market mechanisms the only point of reference for social life; they also tend to subject these mechanisms to public control which upholds the principle of the common destination of material goods" (19). These societies recognize the role of labour unions, provide welfare for the needy and encourage political participation. In the special language of the Pope, these societies enhance 'the subjectivity' of its members. This third societal project, which I shall call Model B, is character- ized by what the Pope calls "a modern business economy" (32). Here freedom is exercised in the economic field as it is in other fields; at the same time, economic activity is only one sector in a great variety of human activities. The market is here surrounded by other social forces, and competition is restrained by a culture of co-operation and solidarity. Moreover, "it is the task of the state to provide for the defence and preservation such as the natural and human environment, which cannot be safeguarded simply by market forces" (34).

At one point in the encyclical John Paul II asks whether, after the failure of communism, capitalism is now the one victorious social system that should be the goal of countries that presently wish to rebuild their economy (42). His answer is very clear. If capitalism is understood as referring to the second social project described above – our Model A – with its rigid capitalist ideology, its unregulated free market system, and its economistic concept of the human being, then the answer is negative. But if capitalism is understood as referring to the third social project described above – our Model B – with its free market economy regulated by government and contained by labour organizations and a culture of solidarity, then the answer is positive.

Since Model A remains predominant or, in the Pope's words, "since marginalization and exploitation remain in the world, especially the Third World, and alienation continues to be real in the more advanced countries" (42), the struggle for greater justice must continue, "to which the Church lends her voice" (42). That is why the labour movement continues to play an essential role in society: it must wrestle against Model A capitalism. "It is right to speak of a struggle against an economic system, if the latter is understood as a method of upholding the absolute predominance of capital, the possession of the means of production and of the land, in contrast to the free and personal nature of work" (35). The Pope here refers to his *Laborem exercens*. To struggle against such a system, he writes, is not an attempt to reconstruct the old socialism, which in fact was state capitalism, but to create a society of free work, enterprise and participation. "Such a society [our Model B] is not directed against the market, but demands that the market be appropriately controlled by forces of society and by the state, so as to guarantee that the basic needs of the entire society are satisfied" (35).

According to John Paul II, the experience of the Polish labour movement offers an important lesson for contemporary social movements that struggle against the unjust structures of society (24). First, such movements must engage in their struggle with non-violent means; second, they must understand their struggle as not simply aimed at greater economic benefits, but also and above all as oriented towards a more dignified and responsible human existence; third, such movements must set a limit to their demands, allowing them to opt for negotiations at the right time.

With *Laborem exercens* and *Sollicitudo rei socialis*, *Centesimus annus* calls for a commitment to solidarity with the excluded and unjustly treated at home and abroad.

Speeches in Formerly Communist Countries

In the speeches of John Paul II given in countries formerly integrated into the Soviet bloc, we find repeated warnings – in line with his encyclicals – against Model A capitalism with its consumerist culture. This capitalism is promoted by forces in the West and has begun to appeal to great numbers in the East. Against this trend, the Pope calls for a political commitment to a socio-economic project in keeping with Model B. Here are some examples.

In a speech given in Poland on June 8, 1991, John Paul II cited with approval a paragraph written by an Italian political thinker, Rocco Buttiglione, whom he greatly esteemed. "The Polish people could either enter the [European] consumer society and occupy there the lowest place before this society closes its doors to new arrivals … or they could contribute to the discovery of the great, profound and authentic tradition of Europe by opting simultaneously for the free market and for solidarity."[147] Speaking to the bishops of Poland in 1991, the Pope said, "In the past, Poles found in the Church the defense of their human rights; now Poles find in the Church a defense against themselves, against a bad use of their freedom, against wasting a great historical moment."[148] In a sermon delivered in Poland in 1997, the Pope said, "Political leaders and men of the economy have the grave responsibility for a just distribution of the goods on the national and international level…. Solidarity must conquer the unbridled desire for profit and the application of the laws of the market that do not take people's human rights into account."[149]

Addressing an audience at the University of Riga, Latvia, in 1993, John Paul II made the following observations.

> While the Church has vigorously condemned 'socialism,' it has also, from Leo XIII's *Rerum novarum* (2) on, distanced itself again and again from the capitalist ideology, holding it

responsible for grave social injustices. In his *Quadragesimo anno* (109) Pius XI employed clear and strong language to denounce the international imperialism of money. This line of thinking has been confirmed by the most recent magisterium, and after the historical collapse of Marxism, I have not hesitated myself to raise serious doubts regarding the validity of capitalism, if one understands by this not the simple 'market economy', but a system where the freedom in the economic sphere is not circumscribed by a juridical framework capable of making the economy serve integral human freedom.[150]

In the same speech the Pope had this to say about Marxism.

The problems from which Marxism historically arose were very grave indeed. The exploitation which an inhuman capitalism had inflicted on the proletariat from the beginning of the industrial age represented a social evil that was openly condemned by the Church itself. This protest is the grain of truth in Marxism, thanks to which it could present itself as a solution attractive even in the countries of the West. But this solution proved a total failure.[151]

According to John Paul II, wrestling for justice in solidarity with the exploited and marginalized remains an abiding task.

In 1997, the Pope called upon the Polish people to examine their conscience. He warned them that "the decadent forms of the concept of the human person and of the values of human life have become more subtle and, for this reason, more dangerous. What is needed today is great vigilance."[152]

Despite the Pope's warnings, Poland and other countries formerly of the Soviet bloc have opened themselves to Western-style capitalism with the inevitable result of unemployment and a growing gap between rich and poor. In his book on John Paul II published in 1994, Alain Vircondelet wrote, "Seduced by the European economy, Poland no longer listens to warnings of the Pope against the capitalist system which is today the source of major evils in the world, the damage of which has affected Africa as well as America itself."[153]

The critique of Western capitalism in *Laborem exercens* and *Sollicitudo rei socialis* is taken up and extended by John Paul II in his encyclical *Centesimus annus*. What he recommended for today's world is above all a conversion of the heart, a commitment to social solidarity. What we are to struggle for, following his teaching, is a free market society in keeping with Model B, where the market forces are regulated by government, making them serve the common good, and where the logic of capital is contained by the labour movement and a culture of solidarity. There are only hints in these encyclicals recommending more involvement by citizens, the strengthening of civil society, the importance of solidarity movements at the base, and the promotion of community economic development – topics discussed in today's critical literature that have already received the attention of some bishops' conferences.[154] With the globalization of the free market system, the world has become a new and dangerous ball game, the consequences of which reach into every area of human life. The world is deeply troubled by many as yet unanswered questions. The brilliant social teaching of John Paul II will support social movements in various parts of the world, reaching out for the globalization of solidarity from below and aiming at the reconstruction of society in greater conformity with God's will.

11

Alternative Models of Economic Development

Catholic social teaching offers a progressive message. It recommends a market economy where markets are constrained to serve the common good by government regulations, publicly owned corporations, a strong labour movement, and a vital culture of cooperation that will not allow competition to become the dominant value. This proposal has a certain affinity with social democracy, even if the Catholic emphasis on the role of culture, including the place of religion within it, is original.

John Paul II's *Laborem exercens* (1981) contains certain radical positions that move far beyond social democracy. I am thinking especially of chapter 6, on the subjective meaning of work. Here the encyclical recognizes that work, the daily activity at which most people spend their best energies, has a profound impact on their self-understanding. The organization of labour in the factory will dispose workers to see themselves either as tools (or 'objects of production') or as responsible agents (or 'subjects of production'). This radical humanistic principle challenges the organization of work not only in the factory but in all offices, chanceries and administrations.

In this essay I wish to rely on this ethical principle of economic activity to make the proposal that Catholic social teaching offer support for 'the social economy,' the economic creativity of people at the community level.

Alternative Models of Economic Development

In their pastoral statements of the late 1970s and early '80s, the Canadian Conference of Catholic Bishops (CCCB) urged Catholic activists to imagine "alternative models of economic development." In these statements the bishops used Catholic social teaching to formulate a radical critique of the emerging neo-liberal capitalism and, at the same time, warn Catholics against an uncritical reliance on Marxism.[155] The cultural revolution of the French-speaking province of Quebec, beginning in 1960, gave rise to a strong social solidarity that expressed itself in a search for an appropriate form of socialism. In Quebec of the '70s, Marxist political organizations had a wide appeal. Quebec was probably the only North American society in which Marxism was taught in high schools. Catholic Marxists set up their own association, called *les politisés chrétiens*.[156]

In the pastoral letter of 1977, "A Society to be Transformed," the Catholic bishops repudiated neo-liberal capitalism and ideological Marxism, praising at the same time the political pluralism in the Catholic community. They wrote,

> Some people in your neighbourhood will choose to continue reforming our present capitalist system in the light of the Gospel, others will choose to participate in socialist movements, trying to reconcile them with the teaching of Jesus, while still others, rejecting these options, become involved in searching for some alternative socio-economic order based on Gospel principles.[157]

The bishops repeated their call for experiments in alternative forms of economic development on other occasions. In a pastoral statement made in 1983, they wrote, "The challenge before us is to search for alternative visions and models for future development of the socio-economic order." According to the bishops, "there are built-in problems in our culture that limit our capacities for social imagination: for instance, the restricted ideological choice between two systems, either capitalism or communism, tends to stifle social imagination."[158] New models of economic development deserve Catholic support:

Across this country, there are working and non-working people, men and women, in communities – small farmers, fisherpeople, factory workers, forestry workers, miners, native people, office workers, people on welfare, public services workers, small business people, and many others – who have a creative and dynamic contribution to make in shaping the social and economic future of this country. A clear social commitment is required to enable these people truly to become subjects of production and subjects of their own history.[159]

Community Development and the Social Economy

The paragraph cited above is undoubtedly a reference to social activities called in Quebec *le mouvement communautaire* and *l'économie sociale* and in the rest of North America 'community development' and 'community economic development.' The extended debate about the precise definition of these terms and their equivalence in French and English does not interest me at this point. Social scientists agree that these movements reveal the creativity of people belonging to 'the third sector' of contemporary society: that is to say, the growing sector of unemployed workers, part-time workers, occasional workers and underpaid workers – men and women pushed to the margin of society. Their multiple forms of self-organization are a protest against the existing economic order that has no place for them.

Community development (*le mouvement communautaire*) produces an ever-expanding network of self-help groups, co-operatives and non-profit organizations. Some of these groups have a political purpose: they are formed to exert pressure on city hall to protect a neighbourhood park or demand the repair of dilapidated streets, or to stage public protests against government policies harmful to the poor. Other groups have social purposes: responding to local needs, they set up daycare centres, shelters for abused women, educational courses for the unemployed, storefront offices counselling uninformed citizens regarding their rights, and centres helping newly arrived refugees in trouble with the immigration authorities. Still other groups have an economic purpose: responding to local needs they set up co-operatives, loan associations, jointly run stores, community kitchens, house repair teams, backyard gardening and other collective initiatives, some of them very large.

In many places, community economic development has become a significant network of enterprises that produce goods or offer services for society and, in addition, create paid employment. In Quebec, the provincial government has set up centres of economic initiative in neighbourhoods of high unemployment that try to bring people together, explore their as yet undiscovered potential, and support them in economic projects that serve the community and provide jobs.[160] Because Quebec's cultural tradition communicates a strong sense of social solidarity, the social economy has become a major social movement. A report written in 2001 registers as part of the social economy in Quebec 4,764 businesses (2,303 co-ops, 2,461 non-profit) with a total revenue of 4.2 billion Canadian dollars and providing 49,450 jobs.[161]

Community development and the social economy are managed according to principles at odds with the dominant capitalism:

decisions are made democratically, with each member having one vote; and production is not for profit, but is aimed at serving the community. Yet in a capitalist society the social economy remains fragile. Co-operative projects usually need a certain financial support, at least at the beginning, which is sought from government agencies, banks and corporations, and in Quebec from labour unions and religious communities. These enterprises also need, at least at the beginning, skilled facilitators who know how to generate a common spirit and organize the co-operative effort. The facilitators are often trained and paid by public or private organizations that support community development and favour the growth of the social economy. Most importantly, community development and social economy are dependent on the goodwill and co-operative spirit of its members.

Community development relies on volunteer labour. Unemployed men and women offer their time and energy to work together to help themselves, transcend their depression, find friends, discover meaning in their lives and express their vision of an alternative society. They are supported in their work by volunteers, people with a secure income and some free time, who want to express their solidarity with the marginalized. While at a certain point the social economy is able to provide paid employment for a good many individuals, it still offers people the opportunity to participate as volunteers.

In this context, volunteering takes on a new meaning. In the past, volunteer work was an expression of charity. In fact, volunteering used to be criticized by social democrats, who believed people should be paid for their work; by the labour movement, who feared that volunteering would replace paid employment; and by feminists, who observed that women were constantly asked to volunteer without ever being invited to participate in decision-making. In community development and the social economy, volunteering has a political meaning: it expresses an impatience with the present economic order and a desire for an alternative model of economic development. Here volunteering is a concrete symbol of justice, not charity.

Community economic development has attracted criticism and generated an interesting debate.[162] Because many people give themselves totally to this work, exhaust themselves and sometimes experience burnout, the social economy has been criticized as the self-exploitation of the poor. Because governments may offer financial support to the social economy with the intention of having the services it offers replace the more expensive publicly funded services, critics have argued that the social economy may further weaken the welfare state. Because the social economy honours dedication, selflessness and sacrifice, women have argued that it will foster an unhealthy self-understanding that women have been trying to overcome. These criticisms are useful warnings: they urge the participants in this movement to become more reflective and avoid the pitfalls that will cause harm.

Catholic Teaching

The social economy as an alternative model of economic development has not received much attention from Catholic social teaching. In addition to the short texts of the Canadian bishops, a relevant paragraph is found in the American bishops' pastoral letter "Economic Justice for All":

> Self-help efforts among the poor should be fostered by programs and policies in both the private and public sectors. We believe that an effective way to attack poverty is through programs that are small in scale, locally based, and oriented toward empowering the poor to become self-sufficient. Corporations, private organizations, and the public sector can provide seed money, training and technical assistance, and organizational support for self-help projects in a wide variety of areas such as

low-income housing, credit unions, worker co-operatives, legal assistance, and neighborhood and community organizations. Efforts that enable the poor to participate in the ownership and control of economic resources are especially important.[163]

Catholic social teaching has praised the co-operative movement. Well known is the strong support for co-operative enterprises in John XXIII's encyclical *Mater et magistra*.[164] The Quebec bishops have repeatedly supported the co-operative movement in their society.[165] Yet what is absent in these texts, and possibly even in the American text quoted above, is an interpretation of co-operatives as an alternative to capitalist and socialist economic development. In the ecclesiastical texts, co-operatives are appreciated as institutions that offer help to people in areas where the dominant economic system is ineffective. The texts do not clearly say that co-operatives allow workers to be the subjects of production and therefore differ from the capitalist and communist industries. Only more recent pastoral statements interpret co-operative ventures as alternative models of economic development challenging the existing order as well as socialist theory.[166]

Humans as Subjects

In this essay I wish to suggest that the social economy is an alternative model of economic development that deserves the support of Catholic social teaching. It is the only model that allows workers to be truly subjects of production, to assume collective responsibility for the organization of labour and for the kind of goods to be produced. John Paul II made the point that for most people work is the daily activity in which they invest their best energies and that, as a consequence, the work situation has a strong influence on people's self-understanding. In the social economy, people not only recognize themselves as subjects of production, they also become keenly aware of the deficiencies of the dominant economic system. The social economy makes the participants critical of their society and therefore has an important political meaning. It initiates people into an alternative model of economic development that may one day affect the self-organization of the major industries and produce a more just and more humane society.

The political meaning of the co-operative movement was promoted by two priests, Jimmy Tompkins and Moses Coady, the founders of the Antigonish Movement in Nova Scotia in the 1920s. They argued that co-operatives were at the same time schools of adult education. The planning and organization of the co-operative project introduced the members to new skills, made them literate, led them to reflect critically on the established order and persuaded them that they were responsible agents of their social existence. In a pamphlet entitled "Knowledge for the People," published in the 1920s, Jimmy Tompkins anticipated some of Paolo Freire's educational principles, and in *Masters of Their Own Destiny*,[167] published in the 1930s, Moses Coady offered a radical critique of capitalism and presented the co-operative movement as an alternative model of economic development. His dream for Canada was a national economy, one third of which was publicly owned, one third was co-operatively owned and managed, and one third was privately owned and operated for profit. Yet in the 1940s, the Antigonish Movement lost its critical political character and simply became a school training activists to set up co-operatives in their regions.

When I studied the Antigonish Movement in the 1970s, I was amazed by the title of Coady's book.[168] Where did he learn to think of people as masters of their own destiny? This did not sound Catholic to me. After all, this is a principle that challenges all hierarchical institutions, including the Catholic Church. Neither Coady nor Tompkins indicated the sources of their ideas. Coady assured his readers that his social perspective was in keeping with Leo XIII's *Rerum novarum*, yet he did not provide a single quotation to back up his argument.

That we are divinely intended to be masters of our destiny or, better, 'subjects' of our collective existence is an idea that entered official Catholic teaching only in the 1980s, in the encyclicals of John Paul II. Here the Pope recognized people's 'subjectivity'[169] – their vocation to assume co-responsibility for the institutions to which they belong. He also insisted that the governing authorities of these institutions must honour the subjectivity of their members. Even if an authoritative decision is made in the service of the common good, it is unethical if it has excluded participation or consultation of the people. John Paul II applied this radical democratic principle to the industries of the future, where workers would be entitled to share responsibility for the organization of labour and the choice of the goods to be produced – and eventually to become co-owners of the giant workbench at which they labour.

Since humans spend most of their best energies at the work they do, their work has a profound influence on their self-understanding. Where does this principle come from? It is not Marxist: Marxists believed that it is social class that determines the workers' consciousness. Neither is it social democratic: social democrats believe that rational persuasion is able to affect the workers' political convictions.

Proudhon and Karl Polanyi

That the work people do affects their consciousness was a principle dear to Pierre-Joseph Proudhon (1809–1865), the French social philosopher and activist whom historians refer to as an anarchist. Convinced that people's daily labour determines their self-understanding, this original French thinker called for a co-operative organization of labour that allowed workers to share in the decisions that affect their work. This practice, which he called "mutuality,"[170] would deliver people from their narrowly private concerns, reveal to them their co-responsibility for the common project, and persuade them that society itself must be based on mutuality, the co-operative organization of the people.

Proudhon mistrusted power exercised from above. He questioned the authority of the state and was suspicious of Marx's socialism organized as a political party eager to gain power. Proudhon did not even support the struggle for universal suffrage in France: since people's consciousness had not been prepared for this responsibility, he argued, they were as yet unable to guide the commonweal. The struggle for a just society, according to Proudhon, was in the first place a social movement, a movement affecting the organization of labour and generating a new social consciousness, before it could become a political movement to change the structure of society.[171] The struggle for justice must begin with the practice of mutuality at the place of work.

Proudhon's ideas were revived in an original way by the Vienna-born Hungarian Karl Polanyi (1886–1964), a social economist and historian, whose magnum opus *The Great Transformation* was written and published in the US in 1944.[172] According to Polanyi, the destabilizing effect of capitalist production was what he called "the disembedding" of labour from social relations. In the past, people's daily work, the activity demanding most of their energy, took place within their community, re-enforced the existing social bonds, and assured a respected place for individuals in the community. Labour in the new industries lifted the workers out of their villages, put them to work with people with whom they did not share their lives and made them give their best energies for a purpose that had nothing to do with their community. According to Polanyi, disembedding people's work from their social relations created isolation and alienation. Nationalizing the ownership of the industries was no solution at all: the communist experiment left workers frustrated and powerless.

Polanyi admired the effort of Richard Owen (d. 1892) to set up industries in which workers became members of a community and had access to cultural development. If England and, later, Europe had further explored Owen's experiments, Polanyi believed, the history of industrialization might not have been as dehumanizing as it turned out to be.

Polanyi agreed with Proudhon that the struggle for justice and equality had an important cultural and ethical dimension. This struggle would at first have to take the form of a social movement, a movement at the base of society, making people's daily labour produce social bonds and contribute to the well-being of the community. Re-embedding their daily work, Polanyi believed, would affect their consciousness, make them socially minded and concerned about the common good, and thus lay the foundation for a political movement to change the structure of society.

The principles of Proudhon and Polanyi have an affinity with Catholic social teaching, especially with the radical proposal of John Paul II that the structure of daily work as the place where people spend their best energies has an impact on their self-understanding. Catholic social teaching should offer support for the social economy since it is an effective school of adult education producing a critique of liberal and neo-liberal capitalism and an ethical sense of co-responsibility for the common good. The Antigonish Movement of the 1920s and 1930s recognized the critical political dimension of co-operatives. The founders of the movement, as mentioned above, saw co-operatives as alternative models of economic development, different from capitalist and socialist patterns.

It is worth mentioning that Muslim believers living in Western societies are also ill at ease with capitalism as an economic system disconnected from moral norms. They ask themselves what positive steps they can take to promote economic development in keeping with their faith. Tariq Ramadan, the important Western Muslim religious philosopher, makes the following proposal. The rejection of neo-liberal capitalism on religious grounds, he writes, makes it

> absolutely vital that Muslims study closely and deeply the dynamics of resistance that are already in process in the United States, [Canada] and Europe. Muslims are neither the first nor the only ones who reject the dominant economic system: many studies have been published, and development co-operatives, alternative banks, and ethical businesses and investment funds are functioning and putting forward 'something else.' Muslim citizens should take inspiration from these writings and experiences and get involved in multidimensional, complementary and long-term partnerships.[173]

The spread of unemployment in the heavily industrialized countries, in part caused by the industrialization of India and China, has produced anxiety among many observers in the West. Thoughtful people recognize the importance of developing an economy from the bottom up. In this situation, the Church's social teaching should urgently foster economic creativity at the community level: the democratic self-organization of people to produce the goods and services to fulfill their needs. It is not unrealistic to hope that this joint social and economic activity, supported by distinct ethical or religious traditions, will produce a critical social consciousness and thus lay the cultural foundation for a new political movement – a movement to replace the gravely inefficient neo-liberal system with an alternative model that respects the humanity of workers and redistributes wealth and power in society.

The Nobel Prize for Muhammad Yunus

In this essay I have dealt with community development and the social economy in the capitalist countries of the North. Yet sustained community self-help projects are of even greater importance in the countries of the South. In Canada, the Catholic Organization for Development and Peace supports community development and the social economy in these countries. In every country, proponents of this movement at the base of society rejoiced when the Nobel Peace Prize 2006 was awarded to Muhammad Yunus, an economist in Bangladesh, who founded the Grameen Bank, a rotating loan fund, that offered credit to people too poor to qualify for loans from traditional banks. By providing micro-credit, the Grameen Bank allowed thousands upon thousands of marginalized people to pursue small economic projects, discover their creativity, and escape the destitution in which they had lived. The World Council of Churches addressed a letter to Mr. Yunus that expressed admiration for his work and told him of its own ongoing support for the social economy. "The World Council of Churches, through its programme activities on economic justice, contributes to the enhancement of life by improving people's economic welfare, by broadening opportunities and solidarity linkages, and by the enrichment of life through the deepening of people's spirituality and the upholding of just and sustainable communities."

12

The Common Good in a Pluralistic Society

In this essay I wish to demonstrate the extraordinary evolution of the idea of the common good in Catholic social teaching and then make a few remarks showing its contemporary relevance. When I was a young student of theology in the 1950s, we were suspicious of the idea of the common good, since it was invoked by the Church's official teaching to repudiate the civil liberties of modern society, in particular the freedom of religion. The common good, according to ecclesiastical teaching at the time, included the common culture and the common religion of society, and governments were thus obliged to prohibit currents of thought at odds with this spiritual inheritance. At that time, the Church was not yet reconciled to a pluralistic society.

The Common Good as an Argument against Pluralism

The history of the Church's resistance to modernity is well known. Right after the French Revolution and the Declaration of the Rights of Man in 1889, Pope Pius VI (1775–1799) condemned the civil liberties in the breve *Quod aliquantum* of March 10, 1791. After the revolutionary unrest in 1830s, Gregory XVI (1831–1846) published the encyclical *Mirari vos* on August 15, 1832, defending the feudal-aristocratic order, ordering Catholics to obey their prince and repudiating, in the name of the common good, civil liberties, including religious freedom. In 1864, Pius IX (1846–1878) published the encyclical *Quanta cura*, accompanied by the famous Syllabus of Errors, vigorously reaffirming the condemnations of popular sovereignty, the separation of Church and State, democratic freedoms and religious pluralism. The biblical text repeated in the ecclesiastical documents was Romans 13:1-2: "Everyone is to obey the governing authorities, because there is no authority except from God and so whatever authorities exist have been appointed by God. So anyone who disobeys an authority is rebelling against God's ordinance."

With Leo XIII (1878–1903), the Church's political stance was beginning to change. On February 16, 1892, he addressed the encyclical *Au milieu des solitudes* to French Catholics deeply attached to the monarchy, asking them to acknowledge and respect the republican government. This request was called *le ralliement*. Leo XIII argued that the Church is able to live and flourish in any form of government as long as its freedom is respected. At the same time, when Leo XIII spelled out the Catholic idea of a just society, he opposed the separation of the Church and State, rejected popular sovereignty and repudiated civil rights and religious liberty. The Pope tolerated the approval of American Catholics for their secular government, but when he feared that this exception was being raised to a universal principle, he published the encyclical *Testem benevolentiae* of June 22, 1899, condemning as "Americanism" the preference for a secular government that respects religious pluralism. The subsequent popes, Pius X (1903–1914), Benedict XV (1914–1922) and Pius XI (1922–1939) continued to use the idea of the common good to resist human rights and democratic pluralism.

The Evolution of Jacques Maritain's Thought

It is interesting that when Jacques Maritain became a Catholic in 1906, he repudiated liberal modernity, human rights, pluralism and democracy, and joined the ultra-conservative movement l'Action française under the leadership of Charles Maurras. Maritain justified his rejection of modernity in the book *Antimoderne*, published in 1921. When Pius XI condemned l'Action française in 1926, Maritain was deeply shaken. A year later, in 1927, he published *Primauté du spirituel*,[174] in which he revealed his own personal anguish, analyzed the crisis in the French Church, defended the teaching authority of the Pope and pleaded with Catholics to accept the recent condemnation. He argued that l'Action française had been condemned not because of its courageous resistance to political liberalism, but because Charles Maurras, as a professed atheist, was not a suitable leader for a Catholic movement. Maritain tried to console his Catholic readers by invoking the abiding truth of the Syllabus of Errors and other papal documents condemning liberal errors: popular sovereignty, parliamentary democracy, the value-neutral state, and the superiority of personal freedom over truth and justice.[175] Still, in this little book Maritain also suggested that to overcome the errors of modernity, Catholics should return to the sources of their faith and move forward in a new and original way.

Maritain's next book, *Du régime temporel et de la liberté*,[176] published in 1933, offers two new ideas. First, drawing upon the Aristotelian-Thomistic tradition, Maritain presents philosophical reasons for human freedom and human self-responsibility. Gifted with intelligence, moral consciousness and free will, people are never simply subjects of a temporal regime; they always transcend the regime as responsible agents. Human freedom is the ability to discover an objective order and to do the good. Maritain here offers a metaphysical foundation of human rights, different from the utilitarian arguments proposed by classical liberal theory.

In the same book, Maritain also makes a distinction between two different historical contexts in which the Church exercises its pastoral ministry: the sacred order of medieval and baroque society, and the profane order of modern society marked by the pluralism of ideas and values. The Church's conservative social teaching was appropriate while the Church was located in the sacred order, yet as it is moving into the profane order of the present, this teaching must be rethought and reformulated.

On the basis of these two ideas, Maritain wrote his major study, *L'humanisme intégrale,* in 1936, which carried on an open dialogue with modernity. Recognizing the new context for Catholic social teaching and relying on his understanding of the human person, he offered Catholic arguments in support of political democracy and religious and ideological pluralism. At the same time, he continued to reject liberal capitalism and called upon social and political actors to keep the economy firmly within a moral framework. A visible symbol of Maritain's extraordinary evolution was his public support of the Republicans during the Spanish civil war against Franco's Nationalist forces. In 1943, during World War II, while a refugee in New York City, Maritain published *Christianisme et démocratie,*[177] in which he defended the liberal ideas of democratic pluralism and human rights as secularized values derived from the teaching of Jesus.

The evolution of Maritain's thought was to have a profound impact on the Church's official teaching.

John XXIII's New Definition of the Common Good

A breakthrough came with Pope John XXIII (1958–1963). This Pope had listened to the ideas of progressive Catholic thinkers such as Jacques Maritain: Pope John also had been deeply affected by the horrors committed during World War II and the subsequent Universal Declaration of Human Rights promulgated by the United Nations in 1948. In 1963, John XXIII published the encyclical *Pacem in terris*, which recognized the high dignity of every human being, affirmed civil rights and religious liberty, and offered a new interpretation of the common good.

Acknowledging the dignity of every person is not part of the Church's traditional position. Because of its egalitarian implications, ecclesiastical teaching had avoided it. Traditional society recognized the honour of its members. They were all to be honoured, even if in accordance with different levels of respect: first the princes, then the higher clergy, then the bourgeois, and finally craftsmen and peasants. We remember this honouring on different levels in our solemn Catholic liturgy, when the respect for the participants is expressed with different strokes of incense: three and two for the different degrees of clergy and one for the laity.

Pope John XXIII offered theological arguments in his defence of human dignity. This in itself was new. Until then, Catholic social teaching had been formulated in purely rational terms, avoiding any reference to divine revelation, because the popes wanted to address the whole of society, not just Catholics, and believed that the rational language based on Aristotelian-Thomistic concepts was universally understood. John XXIII broke with this tradition. He and the subsequent popes invoked the Scriptures in their social teaching.

In *Pacem in terris* John XXIII offers two biblical arguments for the high dignity of the human being. The first, drawn from the book of Genesis, claims that humans are created in God's image (5); the second, drawn from the Pauline letters, claims that in the death and resurrection of Jesus, all humans are called to become friends of God (10). The encyclical then turns to an argument based on reason:

> Any human society, if it is to be well-ordered and productive, must lay down as a foundation the principle that all human beings are persons, endowed by nature with intelligence and free will, and that, for this reason, they have rights and duties that flow directly from their nature. These rights are universal, inviolable and inalienable. (8)

We have travelled a long way. I shall show further on that this doctrinal evolution represents no concession to liberalism: the Catholic understanding of human rights differs substantially from classical liberal theory. But first, let us look at what *Pacem in terris* says about the common good. From the preceding remarks it is clear that the common good of society must include the promotion of human rights and protect cultural and religious pluralism. *Pacem in terris* develops the idea of the common good at great length and then offers a definition of it in a single sentence:

> The common good embraces the sum total of those conditions of social living whereby human beings are enabled to achieve their own integral perfection more fully and more easily. (58)

This brief statement needs explanation. The sum total of social conditions refers to the values, customs, laws and institutions that order human interaction in society. The sum total of these social conditions constitutes the common good if the values, customs, laws and institutions serve the well-being and the development of all members of society. A superficial reading of this text suggests that the reference to people's own integral perfection reveals an individualistic concept of the human being. Yet a careful reading reveals that the text presupposes the social nature of human beings and, in fact, their inescapable interdependence. According to this definition, any social exclusion of people from well-being and any form of discrimination harms not simply the disadvantaged groups, but also the common good of society.

According to this definition, unemployment is not only a threat to the personal well-being of the unemployed, it also damages the common good and disgraces society as a whole. The colonial treatment of the Native peoples by the Canadian government is here seen not simply as harm inflicted on them, but also as damage inflicted on the common good of society as a whole. Why? Because the conditions of social living prevent the Native peoples from developing their humanity. It follows that racism and discrimination of minorities offend the common good and shame the whole of society. The new definition of the common good protects cultural and religious pluralism in society. The political task of the citizens is to promote values, customs, laws and institutions that facilitate and foster the human development of all members of society.

In *Pacem in terris,* John XXIII makes a remark that deserves special attention. He argues that because of the new means of communication and transportation and the ever-increasing interdependence of the various parts of the world, it has become necessary to think of the universal common good: the common good of the entire human family (140–141). Catholic social teaching had recognized the tradition of international law, going back to Francisco di Vitoria and Francisco Suarez, but the popes had never repudiated the colonial conquests of the Christian Empires. Emmanuel Kant is often cited as the first philosopher who imaged a peaceful world ordered in accordance with ethical principles. John XXIII's call for the promotion of the universal common good challenged the wealthy nations of the world. This challenge was repeated by Pope John Paul II on his visit to Canada when he said, "Poor people and poor nations ... will sit in judgment on those people who take the goods away from them, amassing to themselves the imperialistic monopoly of economic and political supremacy at the expense of others." [178]

John Paul II Deepens the Idea of the Common Good

Pope John Paul II added his own thoughts to the new understanding of the common good. In *The Acting Person*,[179] written prior to his elevation to the papacy, he demonstrated that dissent in society can be a service to the common good. Living in communist Poland, where conformity was imposed and the government tolerated no public criticism, Karol Wojtyla recognized that the authorities, any authorities, are in need of being challenged: public dissent obliges them to take a critical look at themselves and, if need be, change their policies. Of course, dissenting voices may also be destructive. According to him, dissenting opinions deserve attention when they are based on solidarity with the society. That dissent may actually serve the common good is an idea that Wojtyla applied only to secular society; he did not introduce this idea in the Church when he became Pope. Still, in the evolution of Catholic social teaching that I have just outlined, the dissension of Catholic authors has played a significant part.

Living in communist Poland also persuaded John Paul II that the traditional teaching on the organic nature of society was not universally useful. Critical thinkers have always recognized that looking upon society as a body has problematic political implications. Bodies have many members, each with its different function: the head, the hands, the feet and so forth. Here the feet cannot say to the eyes, I want to see. If society is seen as a body, its members have clearly defined tasks to perform. Those exercising lower functions, such as workers and farmers, may not say to the ruling classes that they want to be co-responsible for public policies. John Paul II knew that it would be a mistake to look upon Poland as an organic society, for then the working people had no right to challenge the public authorities and protest against their oppressive measures. Polish society was conflictive, not organic. The Pope supported the independent labour union *Solidarnosc* in its struggle for greater justice and the recognition of human rights. In his encyclical *Laborem exercens* of 1981, he recognized that the Polish struggle revealed a universal principle applicable to all societies: the disadvantaged must stand together and struggle for greater justice.

> In order to achieve social justice in the various parts of the world, in the various countries and in the relationships between them, there is a need for ever new movements of solidarity *of* the workers and *with* the workers. This solidarity must be present wherever it is called for by the social degrading of the subject of work, by exploitation of the workers, and by the growing area of poverty and even hunger. The Church is firmly committed to this cause, for it considers it to be its mission, its service, a proof of its fidelity to Jesus Christ. (8)

These carefully phrased sentences make it clear that this position is not identical with what Marxists have called the class struggle. The principal appeal of the encyclical is not to the self-interest of the exploited class. Instead, it offers an ethical argument calling for a twofold solidarity: the solidarity of workers and the disadvantaged among themselves, supported by the solidarity extended to workers and the disadvantaged by all citizens who love justice, including the Church. Operative in history is the ethical call to justice, which is ultimately an echo of God's voice.

John Paul II's social teaching comes close to what in secular language is called social democracy. He makes this clear in his encyclical *Centesimus annus,* published after the collapse of the Soviet Union, where he argues that in the market society of the future, the markets must be constrained and guided by public law, a strong labour movement and a culture of co-operation preventing competition from becoming the dominant value. John Paul

II repudiated neo-liberal capitalism, i.e. the unregulated market system, because surrendering the economy to market forces alone endangered the common good of society.

Comparing the New Catholic Social Teaching with Classical Liberal Theory

The new Catholic teaching on human rights, the common good and democratic pluralism is an original development of the Catholic tradition and differs radically from classical liberal theory. We owe a great deal to John Locke (1632–1704), the British philosopher and activist who opposed the authoritarianism of the Stewart monarchy and laid a theoretical foundation for democracy, pluralism and human rights. What seems problematic to us is that he defends this foundation with utilitarian arguments. He recognizes that people have a natural right to defend their life and their property with their sword and, at the same time, that owners of property in the growing cities live in constant fear, seeing that their life and their goods are increasingly threatened by the criminal elements in society. To sleep peacefully at night and know that their property was protected, these people should enter upon a contract, found a society, choose a government, define its constitution, and then concede to this government their own right to defend their life and property. For the sake of self-protection, the citizens should hand their sword over to the government, invest it with the power of these swords, and demand that it police the city and protect their life and property. Now they can sleep well at night. They do not have to love their neighbours, they may even have little in common with them, but they are no longer afraid of them.

For John Locke, society was created by a contract made by free men because it served their material interests. The citizens are the source of political sovereignty: they choose the government and its rules, and they demand that government protect their rights and their property. They do not see the government as the promoter of the common good! In fact, there is no common good in classical liberal theory, for each person has his or her own idea about what is good. The government is here not entitled to define the good for society. In this social vision, people are good citizens because it suits their purpose, not because they are in solidarity with their neighbours.

At first, only property owners were part of the social contract: they alone had the right to vote. But the desire to participate in political decision-making made non-property owners – employees, workers and women – struggle to be included in the social contract and acquire the right to vote.

Then the question arose whether classical liberal theory can justify government involvement in issues of social justice. Is such intervention possible on utilitarian grounds? In the second part of the nineteenth century, liberal thinkers in England argued that the widening gap between rich and poor creates dissatisfaction and social unrest, which has a bad effect on business. Business profits from social stability. There are thus utilitarian reasons for advocating a more just distribution of wealth. The liberal thinkers also argued that labourers should be paid higher wages so that they are able to become customers and contribute to the profit of the owning classes. After World War II, liberal thinkers in England favoured social welfare legislation for utilitarian reasons. They argued that industrial development depended on educated and healthy workers and, similarly, that democratic government depended on educated and healthy citizens. There are thus good utilitarian reasons for the government to finance public education on various levels and introduce public health programs. These were the arguments of the Beveridge Report published in England in 1942, recommending the welfare state that was subsequently introduced by the Labour government after the war. In 1943, Leonard Marsh, a student of Beveridge, produced the Report on Social Security for Canada that was used by the Liberal Party to introduce the welfare state in this country.

We are grateful to classical liberal theory when it is used to promote greater justice. Yet the utilitarian basis makes this theory problematic. What happens if there are no utilitarian arguments to promote justice? It was not inconsistent with liberal theory that the American Revolution did not extend the dignity of citizenship to people with black skin. There were then no utilitarian arguments for the emancipation of slaves. It was not inconsistent with liberal theory that the great democracies of Britain and France exercised anti-democratic domination over their overseas colonies. There were then no utilitarian arguments for an alternative policy. We are grateful to liberal theory because it introduced democracy in Western societies, but we admit its vulnerability. In changed historical circumstances, political liberalism may well turn to policies at odds with human welfare and social justice.

The important difference between classical liberalism and Catholic social theory is that the latter is grounded not in utilitarianism, but in metaphysics. We saw that Catholic social theory recognizes the dignity of human beings and their human rights on religious and rational grounds. Some conservative voices in the Catholic Church have accused recent Catholic social theory of having succumbed to liberal influence because it bases its idea of society on individuals and their rights and thus fosters an individualistic culture. This accusation deserves a careful reply. It is quite true that the new Catholic social theory pays primary attention to individual persons, yet it defines persons not as free-standing, unencumbered individuals, but as historical agents responsible for their social world. Persons are here regarded as social beings. They are members of various communities and institutions that contribute to their historical existence and for which they bear a certain responsibility. This is far away from individualism.

To make this point very clearly, John Paul II introduced a new vocabulary in Catholic social teaching. He called human beings "subjects" – that is to say, historical agents co-responsible for their world – and he called the co-responsibility for the world their "subjectivity."[180] This was a new usage of this term, derived from Hegel. In traditional Catholic discourse we distinguished objectivity and subjectivity, where the latter referred to inner states of mind. We were asked not to rely on subjectivity, but to pay primary attention to the objective reality. John Paul II uses the word "subjectivity" quite differently, referring to people's co-responsibility for the institutions to which they belong. Thinking of his experience in communist Poland, the Pope demanded that all governing authorities respect the "subjectivity" of their people. People have the right to be consulted and participate in the decisions that affect the well-being of their communities and the great society to which they belong. We have here a theological anthropology that calls for the practice of democracy.

We notice again the extraordinary evolution of Catholic social theory. In the past, papal teaching, in conformity with traditional practice, distinguished between the authorities and the people: the authorities were responsible for justice, law and order in society, and the people served the common good by their obedience to the authorities. John Paul II's definition of subjectivity was a radical innovation. Some may question why John Paul II did not introduce respect for the subjectivity of the faithful within the Catholic Church, his own organization. His theological anthropology would seem to have demanded this. Yet this is a question for which I have no answer.

In Praise of Catholic Social Theory

Still, I am very proud of the evolution of Catholic social teaching. The Catholic Church changed its position on Jews, Muslims and followers of other religions when it recognized that its relations to them were issues of social justice and hence could not be defined in purely religious terms. I regret that the Church's official teaching has not yet admitted the equality of men and women as an issue of social justice. Despite this lacuna, I am grateful for the evolution of Catholic social theory because it is faithful to a great ethical tradition, listens to the Gospel of Jesus, and records the insights of socially engaged Christians. It allows me to become a critical citizen based on my Catholic faith; it teaches me that the damage inflicted upon minorities wounds the common good of society as a whole; it helps me to defend ethical values and practices at odds with the culture of capitalism; it summons me to deflate my personal problems and be troubled by the suffering of others.

The Need to Defend Democracy

Catholic social theory promotes the global common good and supports democracy, pluralism and human rights in the present situation, where anti-democratic ideas and practices are again defended in the public debate. I am not merely thinking of the return of torture and other violations of human rights in countries with a democratic tradition; what I have in mind are anti-democratic theories produced by scholars that influence political thinking. We tend to assume that democratic values are well protected in Western societies, yet a closer look at the political science literature reveals that many of the values we take for granted are presently being challenged.

Let me begin with the thought of Leo Strauss (1899–1973), a Jewish classical scholar, an American citizen born in Germany. Strauss studied the thought of the ancient Greek philosophers and compared it with modern ideas. He was greatly impressed by Plato's philosophy and, in particular, his contempt for Athenian democracy. This contempt was due, in part, to the corruption that had affected the Athenian government; yet it was also produced by the elitist philosophy of antiquity, according to which the majority of people were blind and ignorant, and only a minority of wise men were able to know the truth. Most people, according to Plato, lived in a dark cave, separated from reality, and seeing only a vague reflection of it through a small opening. Truth is discovered by an elite that stands apart from the crowd and strives after wisdom. This elite, Plato believed, should be the rulers of society. What society needed for its own good was a philosopher king or at least an oligarchy of enlightened men.

Leo Strauss, for many years a professor at the University of Chicago, believed that Plato was right: truth is available only to a minority of dedicated thinkers. Plato recognized that government by an elite is difficult, because to assure social peace in society the people have to be in agreement with the government. Without consent there is no social stability. To create this consent, at least according to Strauss' interpretation, Plato recommended that the ruling elite lie to the people – tell them stories that flatter them and disguise the government's true intentions. Plato called these stories "noble lies": they were noble because they protected the common good of society.

Several followers of Leo Strauss holding influential positions in the US defend the rule of a clear-sighted elite, look upon democratic participation as a social handicap, and justify the noble lie as an efficient method to create consent. The extensive public debate on the thought and the influence of Leo Strauss deserves attention.[181] It is of particular interest for Catholics because Strauss denounces liberalism and relativism, holding that reason has access to truth – positions defended by Catholic thinkers – while he arrives at a political philosophy at odds with contemporary Catholic social theory.

A more vehement repudiation of parliamentary democracy was offered by another German thinker, this time a Catholic scholar named Carl Schmitt. In the 1920s, Schmitt was a conservative legal thinker who praised the Church as an institution, but rejected the Catholic natural law tradition. After Hitler came to power in 1933, Schmitt became a member of the Nazi Party. Why should one show any interest in an author whose life and thought have been discredited? The reason is that certain aspects of Schmitt's anti-democratic political philosophy have been taken up by contemporary political thinkers on the right and on the left.

In the 1920s, Carl Schmitt repudiated the parliamentary democracy of the German Weimar Republic and the Geneva-based League of Nations because they were both based on the optimistic idea, which he called "liberal," that people are guided by reason and goodwill, and that therefore conflicts in society can be resolved by negotiation and compromise. But people, he argued, are not reasonable; they are selfish, greedy and will do anything to promote their own interests. Plato thought ordinary people were ignorant; Schmitt, invoking the doctrine of original sin, argued that people were evil. The majority must therefore be prevented from exerting political influence.

Parliamentary democracy, Schmitt went on, involves endless talk, reports written by committees and counter-reports written by subcommittees, resulting in the inability to arrive at clear decisions at the moment when historical conditions demand them. In the past, we had kings capable of making rapid decisions; now, Schmitt argues, we must find other sovereign leaders. A new kind of dictatorship is required.

Who, according to Schmitt, is a sovereign leader? In parliamentary democracies, political leaders must respect the constitution and follow the law. Only at exceptional circumstances of great danger, for instance during a military conflict, can a democratic government break the law to protect its country and its people, promising at the same time to return to the rule of law as soon as normal times permit it. Democratic governments, Schmitt argues, act with sovereignty only in "exceptional circumstances," a few moments of their history. Yet, he continues, there are no "normal times"; the threat to society's well-being is constant; nation stands against nation, each seeking to increase its power. True government must be sovereign all the time, capable of making decisions beyond constituted law; it must exercise dictatorship.

Schmitt objected to the Catholic natural law tradition because it locked political decision-making into a set of fixed moral norms. Instead, he introduced a clear separation between ethics and politics: ethics having to do with the distinction between good and evil, and politics with the distinction between friends and enemies. Here Schmitt rejected again the optimistic or "liberal" opinion that negotiations with neighbouring states and discussions with internal dissidents will eventually arrive at a compromise and a peaceful resolution of conflicts. To be realistic, Schmitt argued, government must recognize that society is constantly threatened by external and internal enemies, make a clear distinction between allies and opponents, attract the support of friends and engage with them in a struggle against enemies. In fact, he continued, society needs enemies for its own well-being: fighting enemies fosters internal unity, strengthens society's self-affirmation and increases people's willingness to make personal sacrifices for what the government defines as the common good. In this struggle, internal enemies must be silenced, imprisoned or even eliminated, and external enemies must be threatened with war or other forms of military aggression. Because of the radical distinction between ethics and politics, Schmitt sees no contradiction between the cultivation of piety and personal virtue and the total disregard of ethics in the field of politics.

Critical political scientists in the US believe that the anti-democratic political theories of Leo Strauss and Carl Schmitt help them to interpret American politics, its unilateralism, its suspicion of the United Nations, its ample use of the noble lie, its clear definition of the enemies, its effort to control public opinion and thwart the career of dissenting intellectuals and the combination of evangelical piety and family values with indifference to ethical values in international relations determined according to changing definitions of friends and enemies.[182]

In today's political context, contemporary Catholic social theory, with its understanding of the common good, deserves to be heard in the political debate regarding national and international affairs.

13

Critical Theology in Canada

In the 1960s, following the decolonization movements in Asia and Africa, liberation movements multiplied in Latin America. These movements, which protested the growing poverty and misery of the masses, wanted to delink the economy from capitalism, with its centre in the US, and build a new economy along socialist lines, in accordance with the natural resources of the regions and the needs and talents of the local population. Christians who participated in this movement produced theological reflections on their social engagement, which they called liberation theology. Vast numbers of Latin Americans believed that a special historical moment, a *kairos*, had arrived, making a radical transformation of their societies a realistic possibility. The engaged Christians were able to influence their churches. In 1966, the Church and Society Conference[183] held in Geneva persuaded the World Council of Churches to develop its theological theory and practice along liberationist lines. In 1968, the Latin American Catholic Bishops' Conference at Medellín[184] adopted several principles derived from liberation theology. The Latin American theological movement created by Catholic and Protestant thinkers[185] had a substantial impact on Christians in

North America, including Canada and Quebec. Since many of the faith-and-justice Christians wanted to respect the Latin American context of liberation theology, they preferred to speak of political theology, an expression used at that time by German theologians of the left.[186]

Critical Theology in the 1970s

If liberation meant anything in English-speaking Canada in the early '70s, it was the struggle of a ginger group in the NDP, called "the Waffle," which advocated a consistent democratic socialism, economic independence from American capital and the replacement of the American-owned industries by publicly owned corporations. Nationalist aspirations were heightened by Kari Levitt's 1970 book, *Silent Surrender*,[187] which documented the absence of resistance to the American takeover of Canadian industries. Even though the Ontario New Democratic Party (NDP) expelled the Waffle in 1972, the ideas proposed by that group influenced many Christians who read the Gospel as a divine summons to social and economic justice. Their commitment was in keeping with the thrust of liberation theology and political theology.[188] In the mid-'70s, the faith-and-justice movement touched the Canadian churches themselves, producing great vitality in all the churches. This is a story that has not yet been told. Thanks to the ecumenical stance adopted by Vatican Council II (1962–1965), the Canadian churches – Catholic, Anglican and Protestant – were now able to assume joint responsibility for ministry in the service of social justice. They published a number of joint statements addressed to the government[189] and created a series of interchurch coalitions that dealt with justice issues in Canada. Their remarkable work is recorded in the book *Coalitions for Justice*, edited by Christopher Lind and Joe Mihevc.[190]

Since I am not a historian and since I have not kept a diary, I am writing about the birth of critical theology in Canada from memory.

My report is undoubtedly incomplete.[191] I will not have space to mention many friends who made contributions to critical theology, nor report on some major faith-and-justice events in the United Church and other Protestant churches. In 1971 I had just returned to Toronto from the New School of Social Research in New York City, where I studied sociology and witnessed radical Christian opposition to the war in Vietnam. I had an intense friendship with Rosemary Ruether at that time. When I was invited to join the editorial board of the international Catholic review *Concilium*, I had the chance to meet Johann-Baptist Metz and Jürgen Moltmann from Germany, and Leonardo Boff and Gustavo Gutierrez from Latin America.

In the early '70s, I had the impression that the faith-and-justice movement was a vital force in the Canadian churches. In 1967 the Catholic bishops had founded Development and Peace, an organization designed to support development projects in Third World countries and educate Canadian Catholics regarding the origin and extent of Third World poverty. The Jesuits founded their Social Faith and Justice Centre in Toronto, and other Catholic religious orders, male and female, created committees to promote social justice. A similar vitality occurred on the Protestant side. A group of Reformed Christians founded Citizens for Public Justice, an organization that sought to link faith in Jesus Christ to social responsibility. Groups and networks in the Protestant churches, especially the United Church, promoted the cause of economic justice in the name of faith; they analyzed the oppressive features of the dominant system and fostered the spread of a Christian Left in Canada. I have good memories of Catholic and Protestant friends, men and women with whom I had the pleasure to plot and plan.

In the mid-'70s, Roger Hutchinson and I were greatly impressed by the critical papers produced by church groups in the various regions of Canada. We hoped to persuade one of the Christian colleges at the University of Toronto to set up an institute that would collect these reports, folders and pamphlets – the kind of literature not kept in libraries. Roger Hutchinson succeeded in setting up at Emmanuel College the Centre for the Study of Religion in Canada (later renamed the Centre for Research in Religion), which focused mainly on United Church documents.

In the early '70s, *The Ecumenist*, a theological review promoting Christian unity I had started in 1962, gradually turned to critical theology. It published articles on liberationist themes by Rosemary Ruether and Rudolf Siebert. I still remember the Karl Barth Colloquium held at Victoria College in 1972, where Markus Barth gave a lecture on the socialist interpretation of Karl Barth's theology, offered in Wilhelm Marquardt's *Theologie und Sozialismus* (1972). While Markus Barth was critical of certain aspects of Marquardt's work, he approved of the socialist interpretation of his father's theology. The explosive lecture was made available in the proceedings of the colloquium,[192] edited and introduced by Martin Rumscheidt, through whose subsequent writings the critical perspective of Barth and, more especially, Helmut Gollwitzer obtained a hearing in Canada.

Because of the growing Christian concern for social justice, Ben Smillie, a well-known prairie radical in the United Church and professor at St. Andrew's College, organized the Saskatoon Conference on Political Theology in March 1977. The conference brought together many Christians from English-speaking Canada and Quebec.[193] It was a stimulating event, even if it had its limitations. Several invited speakers were secular scholars with little knowledge of the Christian movement. The most exciting theologian present was Dorothee Soelle from Germany. The dominant themes of the conference were the defence of Canadian sovereignty and identity, the critique of the existing capitalism, and support for a socialist society. The spirit of the Waffle was alive and well at Saskatoon! While most participants at the conference supported socialism, they were not in agreement on the correct political theory. Some, including Ben Smillie, supported the original CCF socialism defined by the Regina Manifesto, while others preferred a Marxist discourse. CCF socialism differed from Marxism inasmuch as it was deeply attached to parliamentary democracy and freedom of speech and offered ethical arguments in defence of its radical political policies. The moral character of CCF socialism allowed Ben Smillie to appeal to the Scriptures and offer interpretations of biblical stories that condemned the unjust structures of society and promised God's blessing on the effort of reconstruction. At the same time, Smillie lamented that the New Democratic Party had abandoned the platform of the CCF, out of which it had evolved in 1961.

The Marxist voices at Saskatoon were not united. Yves Vaillancourt from Montreal, a founder of the socialist group Politisés chrétiens,[194] advocated an Althusserian Marxism – Marxism simply as science – while Dorothee Soelle, at that time an active member of Christians for Socialism in Europe, denounced Althusserian Marxism for betraying the humanistic current in Marx's thought. Kai Nielson, a secular philosopher invited to give a paper, revealed himself as a Fabian socialist: he thought it was possible to prove, following a utilitarian logic, that a socialist organization of the economy was more rational than the capitalist one.

I had the opportunity at the Saskatoon Conference to present a theme I have repeated and documented many times: the shift to the left of Catholic social teaching, beginning at the Medellín Latin American Bishops' Conference (1968) and the World Synod of Bishops held in Rome (1971).[195] In the early '70s, Pope Paul VI had replaced the taboo on socialism by a teaching that socialism existed in many forms, some of which are in keeping with Catholic social teaching. The Church's official teaching now recognized the class-divided character of capitalist society and supported the struggle for greater justice exercised by the disadvantaged classes, seconded by people of all classes who love justice. Patrick Kerans, the author of *Sinful Social Structures* (1974),[196] who was present at Saskatoon, supported my interpretation, while Yves Vaillancourt felt that these ecclesiastical documents were not trustworthy since they were contradicted by the Church's practice. Still, in subsequent years, the Canadian Catholic bishops produced a number of radical pastoral statements that seemed to recommend a Christian socialism.

There was great confidence in socialism of one kind or another at the Saskatoon Conference. Yet a few non-socialist voices were also heard. Remarks made by the Protestant pastor Vernon Wishart from Edmonton reflected Max Weber's social theory, according to which the alienation experienced by people in modern society is largely the result of their imprisonment in 'the iron cage,' the tight envelope produced by technology and bureaucracy. Wishart's critical intervention may even be interpreted as an echo of the Frankfurt School, according to which the domination of instrumental reason in ever-increasing facets of daily life is becoming the real threat to freedom and self-determination. May not socialism turn out to make things worse? When the revolution comes, Weber said in the early 1900s, it will set up the dictatorship not of the proletariat, but of the bureaucrat. That Marxist sociology did not provide a critique of bureaucratic administration turned out to be a tragedy in the Soviet bloc countries. 'The iron cage' was a threat to both capitalist and socialist industrial societies.

In general, the human damage done by non-economic factors received little attention at the Saskatoon Conference: neither the subjugation of women, nor the oppression of the Native peoples, nor the devastation of the environment. Nor did the speakers explore the problematic nature of Canada's relationship to the Third World. These topics came to be developed in the 1980s.

What Is Critical Theology?

In my book *Religion and Alienation,* I define critical theology as theological reflection on the emancipatory meaning of the Christian Gospel.[197] I prefer to allow liberation theology to stand for the new Latin American theological movement and political theology for the German theology developed by Metz, Moltmann and Soelle. Critical theology is, of course, intimately related to both these theological movements. Like them, critical theology is grounded in an emancipatory commitment embracing in solidarity the victims of society.

That thinking influences action is generally admitted, but that action has an impact on thinking is not usually recognized by philosophers. This impact was first noticed by sociological thinkers. Some of them, influenced by Marx among others, argued that unless an intellectual investigation is guided by a commitment to human liberation, it will offer support for the ideology that legitimates the structured injustices of the existing order. Intelligence alone is not enough. Only engaged thinking can be of service to humanity.

The starting point of critical theology is solidarity with the victims of society. It begins with an act of love and thus returns to the perspective of St. Augustine, who was suspicious of reason unless it was based on *agape*, the love of God and neighbour. Love is the guide of the intellectual life. Since critical theology uncovers society's structured injustices and explores God's summons to compassion and solidarity, it offers not abstract theory but theoretical understanding that sustains emancipatory action. If the word 'praxis' is used to indicate the interaction between practice and theory in the service of human liberation, then critical theology belongs to 'praxis' as its cognitive dimension.

Needless to say, emancipatory reason is not a monopoly of academics. Since critical theology is an exercise of intelligence based on faith, hope and love, it is being practised by Christians without theological training who wrestle for greater justice in reliance on the Gospel. Christian faith-and-justice groups, of which there are many all over Canada, reflecting on how to act in their local situation are in fact practising critical theology. Yet in this essay my main preoccupation is with critical theology produced by professional theologians.

It is important to stress that critical theology is not a theory or a system of thought; it is rather a method of doing theology, including a variety of procedures. It includes a) listening to the voices of the oppressed and marginalized, b) dialogue with social and political scientists, and c) attention to biblical scholars and church historians. Some authors have presented critical theology as an entry into a hermeneutical circle made up of several steps.[198] Such a circle might include i) listening to the cries of the poor or, more precisely, listening to the people at the bottom and at the margins of society who demand freedom and justice; ii) analyzing the social structures that produce these injustices; iii) analyzing the secular ideologies that legitimate these structures; iv) analyzing the religious ideologies that lock people into submission and social passivity; and v) rereading Scripture and tradition to formulate Christian teaching so as to bring out the emancipatory meaning of divine revelation.

These steps can be modified and expanded, but they always constitute a circle, since changes in society or a new listening to the excluded may demand a new inquiry into the structures of injustice. The steps of this circle indicate that critical theology is not the work of a single discipline; it is constituted, rather, by studies in different disciplines. Contributions to critical theology are therefore made by theologians and social thinkers belonging to a variety of fields.

The Saskatoon Conference engaged in critical theology in the Canadian context. I wish to mention some of the specifically theological points made on that occasion. That mainstream theology and popular piety have curtailed the social meaning of the Gospel is a point strongly made in the writings of J.-B. Metz.[199] The emphasis on personal salvation, he argued, reinforced modern individualism, and the emphasis on eternal life persuaded Christians that the divine promises had no impact on finite history. To correct this one-sidedness and find the proper balance, Metz developed his political theology. At the Saskatoon Conference, Dorothee Soelle articulated her own critique of mainstream theology and popular piety inasmuch as they offer cultural protection of the status quo, despite its injustices. She made four proposals.

There is, first, the widely held distinction between the vertical and horizontal dimension of Christian life, assigning priority to the relationship to God and a subordinate role to human action in society. By contrast, critical theology must emphasize the presence of God in history and the unity of the love of God and neighbour. There is, second, the commonly held theology of divine providence that tends to reconcile Christians with whatever happens in history. By contrast, critical theology must understand divine providence as God's redemptive will for the whole of humanity, manifesting itself in moments of personal and social rescue from the powers of destruction. There is, third, a certain theology of original sin that stresses the inevitability of human defection and thus anticipates the failure of all movements of social change. By contrast, critical theology must interpret original sin as the distortion of human consciousness through the structured injustices of the society into which humans are born. There is, fourth, the proclamation of Christ as the Lord of history that may encourage people to look for lordly or authoritarian forms of government. By contrast, critical theology must proclaim Christ as Liberator, setting people free to assume responsibility for their own society.

Critical theologians insist that the emancipatory commitment, the starting point of their theological project, is an act of obedience to the Gospel. In May 1984, Harold Wells and I offered a joint presentation at the meeting of the Canadian Theological Society at the University of Guelph, in which we defended this faith-based nature of the primary commitment – Wells from a Protestant perspective and I from a Roman Catholic one.[200] Wells wanted to remain faithful to the *sola scriptura* principle of the Reformation. He recognized that the Bible can be read in various ways, that its message depends on what passages are taken as central and what presuppositions are being brought to the text. He acknowledged that biblical passages can be used to legitimate injustice. It all depends on the hermeneutical key employed in reading the Bible. The correct hermeneutical key, Wells argued, is "God's option for the poor" – God's merciful intervention to save Israel from Pharaonic oppression; God's solidarity with the poor and weak revealed in the prophetic books; and, finally, God's condescension in Jesus Christ, who embraced the unlettered people of the land and provoked the wrath of the established classes. Since the very key for reading the Scriptures is revealed, the *sola scriptura* principle remains intact. We are to read the Bible in solidarity with the poor and oppressed.

Since Catholics base their Christian faith on Scripture and tradition, I argued, they are able to give theological weight to people's religious experiences, past and present. Latin American Christians experienced the power of Jesus Christ in their struggle against the forces of oppression. This spiritual experience sustained the poor in their struggle and summoned the non-poor to join them in this effort. Since religious experiences are uncertain guides, they must be tested by Scripture, they must stand up under God's Word, and they must survive under the critical glance of the modern masters of suspicion. Because these religious experiences have been tested and validated, official Catholic teaching has recognized the preferential option for the poor. Here are two texts from a pastoral statement of the Canadian Catholic bishops.[201]

> As Christians, we are called to follow Jesus by identifying with the victims of injustice, by analysing the dominant attitudes and structures that cause human suffering, and by actively supporting the poor and oppressed in their struggle to transform society.

> The option for the poor calls for economic policies which realize that the needs of the poor have priority over the wants of the rich; that the rights of workers are more important than the maximization of profits; that the participation of the marginalized groups has precedence over the preservation of the system that excludes them.

Since my joint presentation with Harold Wells in 1984, I have become persuaded that my theological justification for the option for the poor was incomplete. It seems to me now that this option also contains an inheritance from the Enlightenment. Neither the children of Israel under the direction of Moses, nor the poor on whose behalf the prophets appealed to the king and the powerful, nor the population of Palestine to whom Jesus extended his solidarity – none of these were asked to think of themselves as responsible subjects of their own history or as active agents of their liberation from injustice. The self-determination of peoples is a modern idea that emerged when the feudal order revealed its fragility and philosophers dreamt of more participatory political institutions. The religious experiences of the poor in Latin America were influenced by egalitarian ideas mediated by modern culture. This does not invalidate the faith-based character of the option for the poor. In explicating the meaning of divine revelation, Christians have learned to be critically open to Enlightenment ideas, affirming some of them and rejecting others.

Since critical theology must also be critical in regard to its own exercise, I presented in the same lecture what Protestants and Catholics regarded as the temptations of critical theology: i) Critical theology must not become exclusively concerned with earthly justice and thus become purely secular reflection, divorced from the spiritual life and worship in spirit and in truth; ii) Critical theology must not create the impression that all we need is the transformation of institutions, forgetting that we also need the conversion of the heart; iii) Critical theology must avoid the politicization of the Gospel, i.e. the reduction of the Christian message to its political implications; iv) Critical theology must protect itself from becoming a fixed ideology, forgetting that who society's victims are must be reviewed in every new historical situation; and v) Critical theology must avoid presenting the struggle for liberation as a Promethean project, thus failing to stress God's unmerited grace, which empowers people to act on behalf of justice.

Critical theology also summons forth a spirituality and forms of prayer that do not allow us to turn our backs on the poor and oppressed, but instead bind us to God's redemptive presence in history, liberating the victims of society from their multiple prisons.[202] Solidarity with people who suffer creates great sadness. We grieve when we have before our eyes the masses of people who are hungry, who cannot feed their children, who have no access to clean water, and who are excluded from education, or the masses of people who suffer when bombs are dropped on their country, who roam from place to place as refugees, or who languish in prisons and internment camps. Faced with these images, can we go on believing in a God of love? We are puzzled that the mystical authors of the past, the great women and men of prayer, did not mention the suffering of others in their description of "the dark night of the soul," the painfully felt absence of God. The option for the poor introduces us into periods of mourning when God no longer seems to exist. Some believers are so deeply hurt by the horror inflicted upon others that they find it impossible to continue to believe in a loving God: they may lose their faith altogether. A Jewish theologian has said that Auschwitz spelled the end of "untroubled theism."[203] In the face of these horrors, we have no answer. What has often rescued faith-and-justice Christians from the dark night of godlessness is the surrender to God's rescuing movement in history and beyond, revealed in Christ's death and resurrection.

Critical theology searches for a discourse on God, Christ and the Spirit that sustains the participation of believers in God's redemptive action in history through their option for society's victims and their commitment to social justice.

Critical Theology in the 1980s

It is my impression, as I indicated above, that in the 1970s Christians of the Left supported socialism of one kind or another. They regarded the master/slave relationship in the economic order as the key for understanding the oppression and alienation experienced in all of society. Yet, if I am not mistaken, in the 1980s critical theology entered a new phase. There were two reasons for this. First, the spread of a neo-liberal current in society promoted the deregulation of the economy and the privatization of publicly owned industries. This current was often called 'neo-conservative,' because it was advocated by political leaders of conservative parties: Margaret Thatcher and Ronald Reagan. This current also stirred up opposition within the churches towards the critical positions advocated by the faith-and-justice movement. In the Catholic Church, Emmett Carter, the Cardinal Archbishop of Toronto, objected to the critique of capitalism produced by the Catholic Bishops' Conference. After 1983, it must be said, this Conference published few statements on economic justice.

Yet the more important reason for the new phase of critical theology was that the economic analysis made in the '70s along with the confidence in socialism did not consider the non-economic factors of oppression. Critical reflection on these factors emerged in the '80s.

Feminist theology dealt with the subjugation of women in Church and society from the perspective of the Gospel. In Canada, important work was done by Ruth Evans, Ellen Leonard and Marilyn Legge, among others. Many feminist theologians retained the option for the poor and favoured the transformation of the present economic order. Why? Because they knew that in every historical situation, women and children constituted the great majority among the poor and oppressed. If you are for women, you must extend your solidarity to the poor.

When critical theology addressed English-speaking Canada as a whole, it overlooked that the various regions in Canada have specific problems. The west and the Maritimes, located at the margins geographically, have suffered because the centre has attracted the major share of the wealth, and politicians in Ottawa have paid little attention to the needs of these regions. Ben Smillie and Christopher Lind have produced critical theology for the prairie provinces.[204] In his work, Lind has made use of Karl Polanyi's critical economic theory to understand the problems of western farmers and outline the principles of a moral economy, an economy that respects people's humanity.[205] While we are in need of changes on the national and international level, we must also renew the local and regional conditions of economic production. The same point is made in a pastoral statement of the Catholic bishops of the Maritimes, entitled "To Establish a Kingdom of Justice."[206] The statement analyzes regional disparity in Canada; describes the economic dependency of the Maritimes on forces over which they have no control; and articulates the imperative of the Gospel in this situation, summoning people to a social struggle appropriate for their region.

A critical theology devised for Canada easily forgets the oppression of the Native peoples, the wounded state in which they find themselves, and the present renewal movement among them demanding recognition and the right of self-determination.[207] As early as 1975, the Canadian churches set up an interchurch committee called Project North to support the Native peoples in their cultural and political efforts. As more and more Christians were willing to extend their solidarity to the First Nations, the churches in consultation with Native men and women expanded Project North to become the Aboriginal Rights Commission in 1988. Its task was to work in partnership and alliance with aboriginal regional networks and political organizations.[208]

Two other areas of critical theology are Christian concern for the environment and for global peace. Douglas Hall's important book *The Steward: A Biblical Image Come of Age*[209] describes the devastation of the natural environment, develops a theological approach to ecology, and communicates a religious sense of urgency. The theology of peace from a Canadian perspective has been developed by Project Ploughshares under the brilliant direction of Ernie Regehr.[210] I also recall the dedication of Ernie Best to the cause of peace. But critical theology also deals with the problems of refugees and the discrimination experienced by immigrants. Here the interchurch committee on refugees is a competent thinker and actor.[211] Mary Jo Leddy's work and reflection at Romero House in Toronto is also well known.

Perhaps even more important than the previous fields of attention, and yet related to each of them, is critical theological reflection on Canada's relationship to the Third World. Cyril Powles's article in *Studies in Religion* [212] on the manner in which we look upon the Christian communities in the Third World demonstrates that the

Western churches participate in the ethnocentrism of the Western world. When we adopt the perspective of the Third World, we discover how deeply our own society is implicated in their plight. Lee Cormie has made the point in his work that we cannot come to an authentic understanding of our own society unless we take into account our relation to the poor countries of the South.[213] I think it was Tony Clark who first spoke of "the Canadian paradox," meaning that we are both exploited and exploiters. We are, to a large extent, controlled by American capital; at the same time, our large corporations exploit societies in the Third World. Our wealth depends to a considerable degree on natural resources and underpaid labour derived from these societies. The socialist vision of justice and equality in Canada, expressed at the Saskatoon Conference, did not consider this dimension. A socialist project for Canadian society that does not question our relationship to the Third World is in danger of being an expression of collective self-centredness: the desire for a happy Canada in an unhappy world.

What I conclude from these remarks is that in the 1980s, critical theology lost the socialist confidence it enjoyed in the '70s. What emerged was a more complex analysis of oppression, subjugation and alienation that no longer fitted into a theory that relied exclusively on economic factors. This is the message of two collections of essays published in the '80s: *Justice as Mission: An Agenda for the Church*[214] and *A Long and Faithful March.*[215] Economic inequality and exploitation do play an important role in all the justice concerns mentioned above – women's liberation, regional justice, Native self-determination, environmental protection, global peace, overcoming discrimination, and Third World justice – yet it is no longer possible to fit all of these concerns into a single social theory. These concerns, alas, do not generate a single social movement. While these issues are related to one another, they often produce conflicting policy recommendations – for instance, job creation versus protecting the environment. Inevitably the Left, both secular and religious, broke up into a series of causes, each fully justified, but lacking integration into a single social theory. This happened in all complex societies.

A common struggle for liberation, joined by all sectors of society, including men and women, only occurs when there exists one overwhelming form of oppression – occupation by a foreign power or massive poverty of the majority – making all other forms of inequality appear less important. A unified collective resistance occurred in the communist countries of Eastern Europe in 1989, when the great majority of people felt that their government had no respect for them and manipulated them as objects. In Latin America of the late '60s and '70s, economic dependency and increasing misery upheld by military governments produced an overwhelming form of oppression that prompted vast numbers of people to join the liberation movement, relativizing for the time being other forms of inequality. But this situation changed in the '80s and '90s. With the return of civilian governments and the growth of industrialization, Latin American societies have become more complex. Exploitation and exclusion now constitute an ugly reality of many facets that is no longer capable of giving rise to a single liberation movement.

The complexity of modern industrial society leads me to theological reflections that may appear meaningless to people without faith. The struggle for justice alone will not succeed in transforming society. Justice and love must go hand in hand. The movements for justice in different areas can come together only if people are willing to recognize the concerns of others; modify somewhat their own aspirations, even if this involves some sacrifice; and arrive at a workable compromise among themselves. But love also affects the manner in which Christian activists look upon the elite that defends the existing order. They will refuse to demonize these people; they will look upon them as human beings and hence bearers of human rights; they will shun the use of violence; and because they believe in the power of forgiveness, they will be ready for a social compromise, unwilling to destroy the elites altogether. Again, people of faith struggling for a more just and more friendly society will not make a religion of their politics. They will not become idolaters; they will not surrender themselves uncritically to a political ideology. In their stand against injustice, believers hold that they are sustained by a divine drift in history: the mystery of liberation revealed in Jesus Christ.

Critical Theology in the 1990s

After the collapse of communism in the Soviet bloc and the Soviet Union, neo-liberalism or the globalization of the unregulated market became the unchallenged ideology supported by the United States, now the only superpower in the world. These changes resulted in the widening of the gap between rich and poor countries and between rich and poor within each country. The new cultural indifference to justice even touched the Christian churches, reducing the influence of progressive voices. The churches became preoccupied with issues of their confessional identity, stepped back from their ecumenical commitments, fostered an abstract spirituality indifferent to political events, and resisted co-operation with secular movements struggling for social justice. The faith-and-justice Christians, even if fewer in number, tried to keep their centres and networks alive, continued to cultivate critical thinking, and waited for the arrival of a more auspicious historical moment. It would be interesting to study the critical theology in the editorials of monthly or bi-weekly newspapers such as the *United Church Observer*, the *Catalyst*, *Catholic New Times* and *Prairie Messenger*. Critical theology was becoming a theology of resistance.

At the end of the 1990s, Bill Phipps, Moderator of the United Church, was so disturbed by the contradiction between Christian faith and the unregulated market economy that he initiated a consultation throughout his Church, via Internet and e-mail, on the relationship of the Gospel to the economy.[216] While this lively exchange of ideas raised the moral awareness of many Christians, it also revealed that on this topic the Christian community is deeply divided. Bill Phipps represents a prophetic minority.

I wish to mention two creative developments in the field of critical theology that took place in the '90s. One is the Canadian Ecumenical Jubilee Initiative.[217] This imaginative undertaking fostered local and regional involvement of Christian teams in an effort to create a nationwide movement with international links, demanding the cancellation of the enormous debt that was choking many Third World countries. This movement also demanded land reform in these regions and protection for the environment.

The other creative development is the involvement of Christians in community development and, more especially, community economic development, social movements of growing importance in contemporary society. The neo-liberal economy introduced by governments in the West widens the gap between rich and poor and creates an ever-widening sector of the excluded: the unemployed and the working poor. It is in this sector that groups of disadvantaged men and women manifest socio-economic creativity and invent social and economic self-help organizations that improve the conditions of their lives, give meaning to their daily efforts and offer a service to the wider community.[218]

Christians involved in this movement or supporting it in some way have begun to think about it in theological terms. *From Corporate Greed to Common Good: Canadian Churches and Community Economic Development*[219] is a collection of essays offering theological reflections on the revitalization of communities through the co-operative efforts of their members. *Making Waves*, the Canadian review of community economic development, published its Autumn 2001 issue on the Christian support for the social economy. *The Working Centre: Experiment in Social Change*[220] describes a Christian community initiative in Waterloo, Ontario, which applies principles of the Catholic Worker Movement to community development. Since socially committed Christians in the nineteenth and 20th centuries whole-heartedly involved themselves in the co-operative movement, it is not surprising that today, socially committed Christians participate in community development and the social economy.

We have moved far away from the socialist imagination, endorsed by the Christian Left in the '70s, which in any of its forms envisaged a strong central government. Even social democracy entertained a centralizing vision of society. What has emerged in many movements of the '90s is a decentralizing imagination that encourages local engagement and the networking of local groups reaching out regionally, nationally and globally.

After September 11, 2001

With September 11, 2001, we have entered a dark phase of human history, the meaning of which is still largely hidden. What worries Christians are the reactions of governments to the terrorist attacks on the World Trade Center and the Pentagon.

Critical Christians deplore that the American government calls upon God to legitimate its war against the evil forces in the world. President Bush told the nations to make a choice: either they supported his war or they sided with the terrorists. To invoke the name of God to divide the human family into the good and the evil is an ideology at odds with Christian faith.

Critical Christians worry because the American government (and its Canadian counterpart) refuses to ask why certain groups of people in the world have such a passionate hatred of Western society and, in particular, the US. Such a question is regarded as a disloyal attempt to justify the terrorist attacks. Yet if a government does not pose this question, it may opt for policies that will further heighten the rage of these groups and magnify the insecurity of Americans and their friends.

Critical Christians are disturbed by a definition of terrorism that omits terrorism perpetrated by states.

Critical Christians deplore the military intervention in Iraq and Afghanistan, which bombs local populations, produces masses of refugees and creates conditions for civil war in these parts. The terror produced by weapons of high technology generates hatred and rage, multiplying the number of individuals willing to use their own bodies as terror-producing weapons.

Critical Christians are troubled by the role of the communications media in keeping the public in the dark about conditions in a country invaded by Western troops. Critical Christians worry about the militarization of American society; about the emphasis on security that threatens the human rights of individuals; about the promotion of an American patriotism that aims at manipulating national unanimity; about the spread of prejudice against Arabs or Muslims; about the use of the war against terror by certain governments to justify violent attacks against authentic resistance movements in their country, such as those organized by the Chechens in Russia, the Kurds in Turkey and the Palestinians in Israel. Critical Christians deplore that the reaction to terrorist attacks has made the public forget about the misery of the poor and the scandalous maldistribution of wealth and power in the world. Critical Christians deplore the spread of fundamentalism or other contempt-creating movements in the world religions.

Critical theology is becoming a theology of resistance.

Afterword

The essays collected in this book have looked at two signs of the times in the light of the Christian Gospel: religious pluralism and economic injustice. Theological reflection on significant events of the times often challenges traditional teaching and raises questions that the Church did not have to confront in the past. These essays give many examples of changes in the Church's teaching in response to signs of the times, such as the Holocaust, the horrors of World War II and the subsequent Universal Declaration of Human Rights; the collapse of colonialism after World War II; and the subsequent dialogue of civilizations. I have been so impressed by the Church's creative response, faithful to God's Word, to several significant events of modern times that I decided to summarize this doctrinal development in a book entitled *Amazing Church*.[221] Through the signs of the times, God continues to speak to the Church, disclosing the meaning and power of God's self-revelation in Jesus Christ in the conditions of the present.

I am persuaded that theological reflection on religious pluralism and economic injustice raises a question for the Church that deserves careful attention. Which of the Church's two missions has priority? Is it the mission to promote the well-being and expansion of the Catholic community, or is it the mission to promote the common good of society? The essays in this book have given prominence to the Church's commitment to social peace and economic justice and its will to respect religious pluralism and foster interreligious and intercultural reconciliation. The Church's official teaching has come to recognize that implicit in the Gospel of Jesus Christ is the social imperative to enter into solidarity with the poor and excluded and support actions on behalf of social and economic justice.

Do these new approaches neglect or even jeopardize the Church's own spiritual and social well-being? We saw that Cardinal Ratzinger was afraid that interreligious activities would encourage the error of relativism among the faithful and that the preferential option for the poor would politicize the Christian message and in doing so distort it. His critical remarks demand serious attention. Local churches, reflecting on their historical context, must carefully examine the question of which mission must be assigned priority: the service of its own expansion and flourishing, or the service of the common good of society.

Allow me to illustrate this dilemma with a number of concrete historical examples. In the Canadian province of Ontario, Catholic schools are publicly funded. The origin of the separate school system goes back to the foundation of Canada in 1867 as a Confederation of the English- and French-speaking British colonies in North America. To foster social peace and co-operation, the Confederation supported French Catholic schools for the francophone minority living in the anglophone provinces, and English Protestant schools for the anglophone minority in the province of Quebec. In Ontario, the French Catholic school system eventually became the separate Catholic school system serving francophone and anglophone Catholics. Over the past several decades, Ontario has become home to many religious communities who find it difficult to understand why Catholics have a privilege not shared by other religious groups. An organization representing the new religious communities and groups of Evangelical Christians is presently asking the government of Ontario to introduce publicly funded schools for the various religious traditions – a demand that the Catholic bishops support. But to have a multiple religious school system would be very expensive, and would divide the population and render more difficult the social integration of people coming from various cultural backgrounds. In this situation, many Catholic teachers in the Catholic school system ask themselves what attitude they should take. Should they defend the Catholic school system because it renders an important service to the Catholic community? Or should they renounce the Catholic privilege as unjust in the multi-religious society of Ontario and advocate a single school system for the sake of the common good, the social cohesion of a population? In such a situation, Catholic parishes would have to assume the responsibility for the religious education of children and young people. In the historical context of Ontario, the Church must ask itself whether to assign priority to the *bonum ecclesiae* or the *bonum commune*.

The editor of a recent book published in Europe writes in the introduction that the principal challenge of the Catholic Church is the re-evangelization of the European continent, which has become increasingly secular.[222] The North American reader is puzzled by this proposal. Reading the newspapers, we learn that European societies have serious problems with people who have emigrated from Africa and Asia: despised and excluded, many of them live apart, emphasize their difference, and make no effort to adapt to their new society. Resentment against the newcomers is widespread, and is often followed by hostile behaviour towards them. The non-integration of substantial sectors of the population is a destabilizing factor that will have serious consequences for the European societies. What is the Church's mission in this situation? Is it the re-evangelization of society, as the editor of the book suggests? Or is it promoting respect for the stranger, preaching against prejudice and demanding social justice for immigrants and refugees? Should not the Church help Europeans to understand that the culturally and ethnically homogeneous societies they have known now belong to the past, and will never exist again? European Catholics are faced with the same question: What has priority, the good of the Church or the common good of society?

To find an appropriate pastoral approach to the Muslim population, the Conference of European churches, in co-operation with the Catholic Council of European Bishops' Conferences created the Islam in Europe Committee. In 2003, this Committee published a Study Paper[223] persuading the churches to urge their members to respect their Muslim neighbours and engage in friendly dialogue with them. According to the Study Paper, Christians must not try to convert Muslims to the Christian faith; instead, they are to acquaint themselves with Islam and acquire a more profound knowledge of their own religion. The Study Paper expresses the hope that such dialogue will renew the commitment of both partners to the best of their religious traditions. Here the Church's mission to promote social peace and justice is seen as an occasion for the renewal of its own life of faith. It could even be argued that the Church's effort to increase its membership may give people the false impression that the Church is promoting itself, while its mission to demand respect for the stranger, defend the rights of minorities and serve justice and peace in society will persuade the secular population of the relevance of the Gospel and the universality of God's love, and predispose them to recover their Christian faith.

At the World Religions after 9/11 congress, held in Montreal in September 2006, a Hindu monk, Swami Dayananda Saraswati, who is well-known and greatly respected in India, gave a lecture in which he argued with passion against Christian proselytism in his country. In the West, he said, religion and culture refer to distinct spheres, and it is therefore possible to change one's religion without disturbing the culture in which one lives. In India, he continued, religion is part and parcel of people's culture, and therefore the organized effort to convert Indians to Christianity undermines the social cohesion of the country and represents an attack on the Indian identity. Swami Saraswati honoured religious freedom – the right of persons to follow their spiritual calling wherever it may lead them – but distinguished this from setting up institutions with a mission to persuade people to change their religion.

The Indian Catholic bishops have replied to similar accusations that the Church's missionary activity is protected by the Indian Constitution as an expression of people's religious liberty. This is quite correct. India has adopted a Constitution following a Western pattern that defines the government as secular, offering no public support for any religion, yet protecting the religious liberty of minorities, including their effort to attract new members. As a result, the great majority of Indians, believing Hindus attached to their religious culture and tradition, feel deserted by their government. They believe that the Constitution following a Western model does not correspond to the Indian cultural reality: it does not allow the great majority to defend its religio-cultural identity against secular and religious forces that try to dissolve it.

Some Indian Christians recognize the validity of this complaint. They therefore propose that, for the sake of the common good, the Christian Church interrupt every organized attempt to convert Indians and instead interpret its mission in India as offering pastoral services to its Christian members and as witnessing its faith in public by supporting social movements for equality, justice and peace. Here the same question emerges: Which has priority, promoting the *bonum ecclesiae* or the *bonum commune*?

Theological reflection on the two signs of the times discussed in this book offers strong arguments for the thesis that in the present historical situation, priority is to be assigned to the Church's mission to serve the common good of society. Theologians have started to speak of the Church's 'kenotic' vocation, to forget itself in the service of humanity. These theologians recall the self-emptying of Jesus, his *kenosis*, his willingness to forgo his divine status and take on the form of a servant,[224] and they argue that Christ's radical self-surrender reflects the kenosis in the life of the triune God: the total self-donation of Father, Son and Spirit to one another. There is even a kenotic dimension in God's work of creation: the omnipotent God contracts divine power out of love – to leave room for human freedom. In Protestant theology, the kenotic theme has been explored by Jürgen Moltmann[225] and, in response to him, in Catholic theology by Lucien Richard. In his *Christ: The Self-Emptying of God*,[226] Richard argues that since God, out of love, practises kenosis, and since Jesus practised kenosis in his earthly life, the Church that extends Christ's life in history must also practise kenosis. His book contains an entire chapter on the kenotic vocation of the Church. The Church, we read, does not exist for itself; the Church is for others. Its vocation is to love God and God's creation and to serve the divine Spirit that seeks to rescue creation wounded by sin from its self-destructive inclination. The self-emptying to which the Church is called makes it embrace in solidarity the entire human family and become a servant of the global common good.

The critical questions we must ask ourselves are whether this kenotic ecclesiology weakens the mystical or contemplative vocation of the Church and whether it creates indifference to the promises of eternal life. These questions deserve careful theological treatment. In this Afterword, I shall confine myself to a few brief remarks.

The commitment to universal solidarity is itself an answer to prayer and a gift of divine grace. In turn, the solidarity with humanity, deeply divided between the well-fed and the hungry, summons forth the prayer for the rescue of the victims of society and the restoration of the right order on this globe. "Thy kingdom come, thy will be done on earth… give us this day our daily bread" are prayers for the liberation of the oppressed. In turning to God in prayer, Christians do not turn their backs on suffering humanity, for the God to whom they surrender themselves is the transcendent Mystery of reconciliation, acting as Word and Spirit in the hearts of human beings, summoning forth movements of love, justice and peace. That is why the contemplative life, treasured in the Catholic tradition, can be in perfect harmony with the option for the poor and the commitment to the global common good.

The eschatological promises take on new meaning for Christians committed to universal solidarity, beginning with the poor and oppressed. For the death that preoccupies them is not their own death, but the death of the other; the death of Jesus crucified; the death of the victims of society, undernourished and marginalized, who die young. Dying as an old man or old woman after a long and interesting life is a great privilege, since the great majority of human beings do not reach old age. Most die too young, killed by famine, disease, war, revolution or revolt, by death-dealing events not unconnected to the concentration of wealth and power in the hands of the minority. Christians believe that in the resurrection of Jesus, God has rehabilitated all the victims of history. According to God's eschatological promises, the executioner shall not – in the end – triumph over the innocent victim. The persecuted, the slaughtered and the starved shall live in God.

Kenosis does not diminish the Church's spirituality of life nor make it forget God's promise of eternal life.

That the Church serves the common good of society has a special religious meaning in North America. We cannot forget that Christianity is firmly established in the White House and exercises a powerful influence in the Republican government of the United States. A recent article by Garry Wills[227] documents President Bush's policy of surrounding himself with teams of collaborators that are members of the Christian Right, or at least have sympathy for that vision of America. This Christian vision is at odds with the vision of global sharing and global peace embraced by the United Nations. The American Christian vision supports America's unilateral international policies, its military presence on other continents, the clash of civilizations, hostility to the Muslim world, Israel's occupation of Palestine, and the globalization of the unregulated market. This vision is at odds with the social teaching of the Catholic Church as well as with the social policies recommended by the major Christian churches in America. Still, the vision of America First is proposed in the name of Jesus.

According to the discourse adopted by the European Church and Pope Benedict XVI, the secularization of culture and the denial of divine transcendence have produced an ethical vacuum in European society that has made it vulnerable to personal and collective selfishness and has undermined its cultural cohesion and social solidarity. Only the return to Christian faith will rescue this society from its self-destructive orientation.

This discourse does not make sense in North America, where Christianity is entrenched in the White House. There, politicians pray together that their policies will be blessed by Jesus. To give witness to its faith in Jesus Christ, the Catholic Church – along with all Christian churches – must affirm that Jesus came as the prince of peace to bring good news to the afflicted, liberate the prisoners, free the oppressed and make the blind see (cf. Luke 4:18). Jesus, in whom the Church believes, is the servant of the common good of all nations and sustains their co-operation in support of the global common good. We invoke Jesus as *salvator mundi*, the saviour of the world.

Notes

Introduction

1   *Apostolicam actuositatem*, 14; *Dignitatis humanae*, 15; *Gravissimum educationis*, 8; *Gaudium et spes*, 4, 11, 17, 23; *Unitatis redintegratio*, 3, 4, 6.

2   John XXIII, *Pacem in terris*, 3, 9.

3   John Paul II, *Message for the World Peace Day 1990*.

I

4   http://www.dfait-maeci.gc.ca/cip-pic/ips/diplomacy-en.asp. Accessed September 18, 2006.

5   *Nostra aetate: Declaration on the Relation of the Church to Non-Christian Religions*, October 28, 1965, 3.

6   Address of John Paul II, Meeting with the Muslim Leaders at the Omayyad Great Mosque, Damascus, Sunday, May 6, 2001, 2–3 (italics added).

7   Quoted by John Paul II at a general audience held on May 5, 1999. His address at Casablanca took place on August 19, 1985.

8   Statement of H.E. Mons. Renato Raffaele Martino, to the 56th Session of the General Assembly of the United Nations on Disarmament, October 15, 2001.

9   Tariq Ramadan, *Aux sources du renouveau musulman* (Paris: Bayard, 1998).

10   Rachid Benzine, *Les nouveaux penseurs de l'islam* (Paris: Albin Michel, 2004); Alain Roussillon, *La pensée islamique contemporaine* (Paris: Téraèdre, 2003).

11   A report can be found on the website of the International Institute for the Study of Islam in the Modern World, www.isim.nl.

12   "Islam in Contemporary Turkey: the Contribution of Fethullal Gülen," *The Muslim World*, vol. 95, July 2005; M.H. Yavuz and J.L. Esposito, eds., *Turkish Islam and the Secular State: The Gülen Movement* (Syracuse: Syracuse University Press, 2003); A. Ünal and A. Williams, eds., *Advocate of Dialogue: Fethullah Gülen* (Fairfax, VA: The Fountain, 2000).

13   Lester Kurtz, "Gülen's Paradox: Combining Commitment and Tolerance," in *The Muslim World* 95/3(July 2005)375–384, 375.

14   Tariq Ramadan, *To Be a European Muslim: A Study of Islamic Sources in the European Context* (Leicester, UK: Islamic Foundation, 1999) and *Western Muslims and the Future of Islam* (Oxford: Oxford University Press, 2004).

15   For an analysis of these controversies, see Aziz Zemouri, *Faut-il faire taire Tariq Ramadan* (Paris: l'Archipel, 2005). Also Tariq Ramadan, *Peut-on vivre avec l'islam?* (Paris: Favre, 2004).

2

16   Kyoto Declaration for Peace, www.wcrp.org/files/ Kyoto%20Declaration-2006-(English).doc. Accessed June 4, 2007.

3

17   Cardinal Ratzinger, Sermon at the Mass pro eligendo summo pontifice, April 18, 2005.

18   Max Horkheimer and Theodor Adorno, *Dialectic of the Enlightenment* (New York: Herder and Herder, 1971); Martin Jay, *The Dialectical Imagination: History of the Frankfurt School* (Boston: Little, Brown, 1973).

19   John Perry, *Torture: Religious Ethics and National Security* (Ottawa: Novalis, 2005), 52–58.

20   Samuel Huntington, *The Clash of Civilizations and the Remaking of World Order* (New York: Simon & Schuster, 1996).

21   Paul Blanchard, *American Freedom and Catholic Power* (Boston: Beacon Press, 1949).

22   Alain Roussillon, *La pensée islamique contemporaine: acteurs et enjeux* (Paris: Théraèdre, 2005); Abdou Filali-Ansary, *Réformer l'islam? Une introduction aux débats contemporains* (Paris: La Découverte, 2003).

23   Jean-François Lyotard, *The Postmodern Condition* (Manchester: Manchester University Press, 1986); Gregory Baum, *Essays in Critical Theology* (Kansas City, MO: Sheed & Ward, 1994), 77–95.

24   Gregory Baum and Harold Wells, *The Reconciliation of Peoples: Challenges to the Churches* (Maryknoll, NY: Orbis Books, 1997).

25   The World Conference of Religions for Peace (WCRP): www.wcrp.org.

26   Parliament of Religions, Declaration Toward a Global Ethic (Tübingen: Foundation Global Ethic, 1993). Hans Küng was its primary author. See also Hans Küng, *A Global Ethic for Global Politics and Economics* (New York: Oxford University Press, 1998).

27   Arvind Sharma, *Are Human Rights Western?* (New York: Oxford University Press, 2006) and *Hinduism and Human Rights* (New Delhi: Oxford University Press, 2004).

28   Karl Mannheim, *Ideology and Utopia* (New York: Harcourt, Brace and World, n.d), 78–79, 85–87.

29   David Tracy, *The Analogical Imagination* (New York: Crossroad, 1981), 339–364; Gregory Baum, *Essays in Critical Theory*, 35–51.

4

30   G. Baum, "Fackenheim and Christianity," in L. Greenspan and G. Nicholson, eds., *Fackenheim: German Philosophy and Jewish Thought* (Toronto: University of Toronto Press, 1992), 176–202, 177.

31   I. Greenberg presented his theological response to the Holocaust at a Jewish-Christian symposium, held in 1974 in New York and published in E. Fleischner, ed., *Auschwitz: Beginning of a New Era* (New York: KTAV Publishing House, 1977), 7–53. See also G. Baum, "Theology after Auschwitz: A Conference Report," *The Ecumenist*, 12 (July-Aug. 1974), 65–80.

32   On J. Isaac, see the French review *Sens*, 4 (1977); on the Seelisberg Conference, see *Sens*, 10 (1998).

33   "Bearing Faithful Witness," at www.united-church.ca/bfw/finalstatement. shtm. Accessed January 23, 2007.

34   See chapter 5 below.

35   Gregory Baum, "Salvation is from the Jews: a Story of Prejudice," in *Christian Century*, 89(19 July 1978)775–7.

36   Johann-Baptist Metz, "Facing the Jews: Christian Theology after Auschwitz," in *Concilium* 173(5/1984) 26–33, 28.

37   See www.united-church.ca/bfw/home.shtm. Accessed January 23, 2007.

38   G. Baum, "The Churches, Israel and the Palestinians," *The Ecumenist*, 27 (Nov.–Dec. 1988), 1–6.

39   W. Bühlmann, *The Coming of the Third Church* (Maryknoll, NY: Orbis Books, 1977).

40   "Churches water down Mid-East policy," *Ottawa Citizen* (January 6, 2001); "Catholic Church's new Jewish initiative put to test in Mid-East statement" (January 28, 2001).

41   "Eleven Canadian Christian Leaders' Call for Peace with Justice in the Middle East (5 January 2001)," at www.ccc-cce.ca/english/justice/middleeast. htm. Accessed January 23, 2007.

42   "A church leaders' letter against anti-Semitism to the churches of Canada, the Jewish community in Canada, and to all people of good will…", at www. jcrelations.net/en/?id=2143. Accessed January 23, 2007.

43   See www.shalomctr.org.

44   See "Shalom: The Jewish Peace Letter" published by the Jewish Peace Fellowship, Box 271, Nyack, NY, 10960.

45   M. Polner and N. Goodman, eds., *The Challenge of Shalom* (Philadelphia: New Society Publishers, 1994).

46   See www.tikkun.org.

47   M. Lerner, "Atonement in the Month of Awe," on the website of *The Shalom Center*, www.shalomctr.org/comment/reply/78. Accessed March 22, 2007.

48   M. Lerner, *Healing Israel/Palestine: A Path to Peace and Reconciliation* (San Francisco: Tikkun Books, 2003).

49   The website of the Moderates is www.cemod.ca.

50   Pope John Paul II, "The Ten Commandments of Peace," March 4, 2000. See *The Ecumenist*, 39 (Summer 2002), 1.

5

51   While God is never the cause of evil, the idea of a divine "permission" for evil was acknowledged in the Decree on Justification of the Council of Trent (1547). See Denzinger/Schönmetz, eds., *Enchiridion symbolorum* (Barcelona: Herder, 1963), n. 1556, p. 378.

52   Gershom Greenberg, "Wartime American Orthodoxy and the Holocaust," *Michael* (Diaspora Research Institute, Tel-Aviv University). vol. 15, 2000, 59–94.

53   Ignaz Maybaum, *The Face of God after Auschwitz* (1965), cited in Joe Mihevc, *The Problem of Evil in Light of the Holocaust: Jewish Debates and Christian Implications* (MA Thesis, 1979, Toronto: University of St. Michael's College), 29. This substantial thesis offers an excellent analysis of the Jewish theological debate in the '60s and '70s on God and the Holocaust.

54   Richard Rubenstein, *After Auschwitz* (Indianapolis: Bobbs-Merrill Book Co., 1965). See also the more recent *The Death of God Movement and the Holocaust*, S.R. Haynes and J.K. Roth, eds. (Westport, CT: Greenwood Press, 1999).

55   Emil Fackenheim, *God's Presence in History* (New York: Harper & Row, 1970,) 14–16.

56   Elie Wiesel, *The Trial of God* (New York: Random House, 1979). For a theological analysis of this play, see W. Gross and K.J. Kuschel, *Ich schaffe Finsternis und Unheil* (Mainz: Matthias-Grünewald Verlag, 1992), 143–148.

57   Irving Greenberg, "Cloud of Hope, Pillar of Fire: Judaism, Christianity, and Modernity after the Holocaust," *Auschwitz: Beginning of a New Era?* Eva Fleischner, ed. (New York: KTAV Publishing House, 1977), 7–56, 33.

58   Hans Jonas, *Der Gottesbegriff nach Auschwitz : Eine jüdische Stimme* (Frankfurt: Suhrkamp, 1984) and "The Concept of God after Auschwitz," *Out of the Whirlwind*, Albert Friedländer, ed., revised edition (New York: UAHC Press, 1999), 465–476.

59   Walter Gross and Karl-Josef Kuschel, *Ich schaffe Finsternis und Unheil* (Mainz: Matthias-Grünewald-Verlag, 1992).

60   See Leo D. Lefebure, *Revelation, the Religions and Violence* (Maryknoll, NY: Orbis Books, 2000), 114–115.

61   L. Lefebure, 61.

62   Paul Tillich, *Systematic Theology*, Vol. I (Chicago: University of Chicago Press, 1951), 264–269.

63   P. Tillich, *Systematic Theology*, vol. I, 268.

64   P. Tillich, *Systematic Theology*, vol. I, 267.

65   P Tillich, *Systematic Theology*, vol. I, 267.

66   P. Tillich, *Systematic Theology*, vol. I, 269.

67   Paul Tillich, *Systematic Theology*, Vol. III (Chicago: Chicago University Press, 1963), 362–374.

68   P. Tillich, *Systematic Theology*, vol. III, 372.

69   P. Tillich, *Systematic Theology*, vol. III, 371.

70   P. Tillich, *Systematic Theology*, vol. III, 373.

71   Paul Tillich, *The Socialist Decision* [1932] (San Francisco: Harper & Row, 1977), 104–112.

72   Eugen Drewermann, *Der sechste Tag: Die Herkunft des Menschen und die Frage nach Gott* (Zürich/Düsseldort: Walter Verlag, 1998), 33–55.

73   E. Drewermann, 198–269.

74   E. Drewermann, 270–302.

75   See especially Jürgen Moltmann, *The Crucified God* (London: SCM, 1973) and *God in Creation* (San Francisco: Harper & Row, 1985).

76   Denzinger/Schönmetz, eds., *Enchiridion symbolorum* (Barcelona: Herder, 1963), no. 24, p. 101.

77   "God does not suffer out of deficiency of being, like created beings. But he does suffer from his love, which is the overflowing superabundance of his being. And in this sense he can suffer." Jürgen Moltmann, *Jesus Christ for Today's World* (Minneapolis: Fortress Press, 1994), 45.

78   "The dead return and the nameless will be called by their names. Ultimately the murderer will not triumph over the victim, and the torturer shall be called to account." *Jesus Christ for Today's World,* 67.

79   Maurice Zundel, *L'Évangile intérieur* (Paris: Desclée de Brouwer, 1977), 131, cited in Jean Genest, ed., *Penseurs et apôtres du XXᵉ siècle* (Montréal: Fides, 2001), 333.

80   Walter Kasper, *Der Gott Jesu Christi* (Mainz: Matthias-Grünewald Verlag, 1982), 244, cited in W.Gross and K.-J. Kuschel, *"Ich schaffe Finsternis und Unheil"* (Mainz: Matthias-Grünewald Verlag, 1991), 182.

81   Ottmar Fuchs, *"Von solcher Hoffnung kann ich leben"* (Luzern: Exodus, 1997), 139–140.

82   "The experience of freedom always springs from a coincidence of the liberating Word and the proper time, Kairos." Jürgen Moltmann, *Spirit of Life* (Minneapolis: Fortress Press,1992), 103.

83   Douglas J. Hall, *God and Human Suffering* (Minneapolis: Augsburg Publishing, 1986).

84   D. Hall, 111.

85   Gregory Baum, *Man Becoming* (New York: Herder & Herder, 1970).

86   G. Baum, *Man Becoming*, 221–232.

87   Edward Schillebeeckx, *Christ: The Experience of Jesus as Lord* (New York: Seabury Press, 1980), 728.

88   *Defectus gratiae, prima cause est ex nobis* (Summa Theologia I-II, q. 112, a. 3, ad 2).

89   A similar critique of Moltmann is made by Edward Schillebeeckx; see note 83.

90   Reinhard Voss, ed., *Versöhnungsprozesse und Gewaltfreiheit* (Idstein: Meinhardt Text and Design, 1999), 24.

91   R. Voss, 241–249.

92   See Gregory Baum, "Sickness and the Silence of God," *Concilium*, 1992, 4 (August), 23–26.

93   Emil Fackenheim, as mentioned on p. 88–89 above, had introduced the idea of God's "commanding voice" at Auschwitz.

6

94   In his *The Theory of Communicative Action*, volume 2 (Boston: Beacon Press, 1988), Habermas discusses the linguistification of the sacred in several contexts. This is his thesis: "The socially integrative and expressive functions that were at first fulfilled by ritual practice pass over to communicative action; the authority of the holy is gradually replaced by the authority of an achieved consensus. This means a freeing of communicative action from sacrally protected normative contexts.... The aura of rupture and horror that emanates from the sacred, the spell-binding power of the sacred is sublimated into the binding/bonding force of criticizable validity claims and at the same time turned into an every day occurrence." (p. 77)

95   Samuel Huntington, *The Clash of Civilizations and the New World Order* (New York: Simon & Schuster, 1996).

96   See Sharon Harper, ed., *The Temple, the Lab and the Market: Reflections on the Intersection of Science, Religion and Development* (Bloomfield, CT: Kumarian Press, 2000) and Bill Ryan, "The Lab, the Temple and the Market," *The Ecumenist*, 37 (Spring 2000), 13–15.

97   Gregory Baum, "Is It Time to Give Religion a Public Voice?" *Inroads*, 10 (2001), 77–86.

7

98   Joseph Kardinal Ratzinger, *Glaube-Wahrheit-Toleranz* (Freiburg: Herder, 2002). The book appeared in English translation two years later as *Truth and Tolerance: Christian Belief and the World Religions* (San Francisco: Ignatius Press, 2004).

99   See Gregory Baum, "The Theology of Cardinal Ratzinger: A Response to *Dominus Iesus*," *The Ecumenist*, 37 (Fall 2000), 1–3.

100   David Kendall and Gerald O'Collins, eds., *In Many and Diverse Ways: In Honour of Jacques Dupuis* (Maryknoll, NY: Orbis, 2003).

101   *Glaube–Wahrheit–Toleranz*, 87–90.

102   See John Paul II, Letter to the Heads of State, March 4, 2002.

103   The apostolic exhortation *Ecclesia in Asia* (1) of November 6, 1999. The sentence is a quotation from an earlier speech of John Paul II at Manila on January

15, 1995, addressed to the Sixth Assembly of the Federation of Asian Bishops' Conferences.

104   "Est-ce que toutes les religions se valent?" Note théologique et pastorale, Assemblées des évêques catholiques du Québec, Juin, 2005.

105   See pages 19–20 above.

106   Albert Nader, *Courants d'idées en Islam* (Montréal: Médiaspaul, 2003), 39–47, 121–129.

107   On his subsequent visit to Turkey, addressing the President of the Religious Affairs Directorate on Nov. 28, 2006, Pope Benedict XVI expressed his respect for Islam, recognized the urgency of interreligious dialogue, and even suggested that the witness of faith in the one God given jointly by Muslims and Catholics renders a significant service to today's secular world.

108   "Est-ce que toutes les religions se valent?"

109   See "Final Document," nos 1134–1165, in *Puebla and Beyond*, J. Eagelson and P. Scharper, eds. (Maryknoll, NY: Orbis, 1979), 264–267.

110   *Sollicitudo rei social* (1987), 36.

111   Gregory Baum, "Benedict XVI's First Encyclical," *The Ecumenist*, 43 (Spring 2005), 11–14.

112   According to John Paul II, this "twofold approach" was often adopted prior to Vatican Council II: "One [approach] directed to this world and this life, to which faith ought to remain extraneous; the other directed towards purely otherworldly salvation which neither enlightens nor directs existence on earth" (*Centesimus annus*, 5).

8

113   Gregory Baum and Robert Ellsberg, eds., *The Logic of Solidarity: Commentaries on Pope John Paul's Encyclical "On Social Concern"* (Maryknoll, NY: Orbis Books, 1989).

114   For the Medellín Conclusions see *The Gospel of Peace and Justice*, Joseph Gremillion, ed. (Maryknoll, NY: Orbis Books, 1976), 445–476.

115   See *Puebla and Beyond*, John Eagelson and Philip Scharper, eds. (Maryknoll, NY: Orbis Books, 1979), 264.

116   *Octogesima adveniens*, 31; *The Gospel of Peace and Justice*, 499.

117 *Justitia in mundo*, 3–5; *The Gospel of Peace and Justice*, 514.

118   Gregory Baum, "Toward a Canadian Catholic Social Theory," in *Theology and Society* (Mahwah, NJ: Paulist Press, 1987), 66–87.

119   For a history of economic theory written for non-specialists, see John Kenneth Galbraith, *The Age of Uncertainty* (Boston, 1977) and *A History of Economics* (Boston, 1987).

120   Ted Reeve, "God and the Market: Affecting Your Life and Faith," *The Ecumenist*, 38 (Winter 2001), 1–5.

121   A growing body of literature written by non-conformist economists analyzes the brave new world that is being created at this time: see Philippe Engelhard, *L'Homme mondial* (Paris: Arléa, 1996); Robert Heilbroner, *The Crisis of Vision in Modern Economic Thought* (New York: Cambridge University Press, 1995); David Korten, *When Corporations Rule the World* (West Hartford, CT: Kumarian Press, 1995); and Lester Thurow, *The Future of Capitalism* (New York: W. Morrow, 1996).

122   Maurice Blondel, *The Letter on Apologetics, and History and Dogma*, translated by A. Dru and I. Trethowan (London, 1964), 147.

123   See Gregory Baum, *Karl Polanyi on Ethics and Economics* (Montreal: McGill-Queen's University Press, 1996).

9

124   In my analysis of biblical history, I depend especially on Richard Horsley, *Jesus and Empire* (Minneapolis, MN: Fortress Press, 2003) and *Paul and Empire* (Harrisburg, PA: Trinity Press International, 1997).

125   Ivone Gebara, *Le mal au féminin. Réflexions théologiques à partir du féminisme* (Paris: L'Harmattan, 1999), 85–90.

126   In my interpretation of St. Augustine I follow Robert A. Markus, *Saeculum: History and Society in the Thought of St. Augustine* (Cambridge: Cambridge University Press, 1970).

127   See chapter 8 in this volume.

128   Richard Falk, *Religion and Humane Global Governance* (New York: Palgrave, 2001).

10

129   See *Origins*, vol. 14, September 27, 1984, no.15, 229.

130   *Redemptor hominis*, March 1979, 8 and 13. See Gerard Beigel, *Faith and Social Justice in the Teaching of Pope John Paul II* (New York: Peter Lang, 1997), 83–88 and John Saward, *Christ Is the Answer: The Christ-centred Theology of John Paul II* (New York: Alba House, 1995), 55–62.

131   Arista Maria Cirtautas, *The Polish Solidarity Movement* (London: Routledge, 1997).

132   Cirtautas, 166.

133   Cirtautas, 169–174.

134   Cirtautas, 174–179.

135   See, for instance, John Paul II's remarks on this topic in his *Crossing the Threshold of Hope* (New York: Knopf, 1994), 69–70 and in his interview with Jas Gawronski, *Actualités religieuses dans le monde*, no.116, November 15, 1993, 8.

136   See E.F. Sheridan, SJ, ed., *Do Justice! The Social Teaching of the Canadian Bishops [1945–1986]* (Montreal: Éditions Paulines, 1987), 399–410.

137   *Jean-Paul II au Canada. 1. Messages au peuple de Dieu* (Montréal: Fides, 1984), 83.

138   Gregory Baum, "Faith and Liberation: Development Since Vatican II," *Theology and Society* (New York: Paulist Press, 1987), 3–31.

139   See, for instance, the speech given by the Pope at Bacolad, the Philippines, on February 20, 1981 [*Origins*, vol. 10, no. 39, March 12, 1989, 61–63, 62] and the Pope's encyclical of November 10, 1994, *Tertio Millenio adveniente,* 51.

140   *Origins*, vol. 8, no. 34, February 8, 1979, 544.

141   *Origins*, vol. 8, no. 34. February 8, 1979, 529–538.

142   *Origins*, vol. 14, no. 13, September 13, 1984, 193–204 and vol. 15, no. 44, April 17,1986, 713–728.

143   *Origins*, vol. 15, no. 42, April 3, 1986, 681–685, 684.

144   See Constance Colonna-Cesari, *Urbi et Orbi: enquête sur la géopolitique vaticane* (Paris: La Découverte, 1992); Ugo Colombo Sacco, *John Paul II and World Politics* (Belgium: Peeters, 1999); Tad Szulc, *Pope John Paul II* (New York:

Scribner, 1995), 378–381; Alain Vircondelet, *Jean-Paul II* (Paris: Julliard, 1994), 445–446; Michael Walsh, *John Paul II* (London: HarperCollins, 1994), 102.

145   In the first sentence of paragraph 22 in *Sollicitudo rei socialis*, John Paul II speaks of the "unexpected" events of the year 1989. "Who could have expected this only a few years ago?" he said in a speech given in 1993 at the University of Riga in Latvia, *Documentation catholique* vol. 75, September 8, 1993, 873.

146   See note 145.

147   *Documentation catholique*, vol. 73, July 21, 1991, 692 (my translation from the French).

148   *Documentation catholique*, vol. 73, June 20, 1991, 672–674, 673 (my translation from the French).

149   *Documentation catholique*, vol. 73, June 20, 1991, 668 (my translation from the French).

150   *Documentation catholique*, vol. 75, September 8, 1993, 872–874, 873 (my translation from the French).

151   Ibid.

152   *Documentation catholique*, vol. 79, June 10, 1997, 658 (my translation from the French).

153   Alain Vircondelet, *Jean-Paul II* (Paris: Julliard, 1994), 530 (my translation from the French).

154   See, for instance, the Quebec bishops [Yvonne Bergeron, "Paroles d'évêques à contre-courant, Les message du 1er mai," in Michel Beaudin et al., dir. *Intervenir à contre-courant* (Montréal: Fides, 1998), 63–92] and the German bishops [*Für eine Zukunft in Solidarität und Gerechtigkeit*, Message of the Protestant Church in Germany and the German Conference of Catholic Bishops, 1997].

11

155   Best known among the pastoral statements of the CCCB is "Ethical Reflections on the Economic Crisis" (December 22, 1982). See E.F. Sheridan, ed., *Do Justice! The Social Teaching of the Canadian Catholic Bishops* (Montréal: Éditions Paulines, 1987), 399–410.

156   "Politisés chrétiens: A Christian-Marxist Network in Quebec" in Gregory Baum, *The Church in Quebec* (Ottawa: Novalis, 1991), 167–189.

157   E.F. Sheridan, 332.

158   E.F. Sheridan, 427.

159   E.F. Sheridan, 492.

160   Benoît Lévesque and William A. Ninacs, "The Social Economy in Canada: The Quebec Experience," in Eric Shragge and Jean-Marc Fontan, eds., *Social Economy: International Debates and Perspectives* (Montreal: Black Rose, 2000), 112–129. Also Louis Favreau and Benoît Lévesque, eds., *Développement économique communautaire* (Québec: Presses de l'Université du Québec, 1996) and Jack Quarter, *Canada's Social Economy* (Toronto: James Lorimer, 1992).

161   William A. Ninacs, "A Review of the Theory and Practice of Social Economy in Quebec" (2001), 17–18, published by SRSA (Société de recherche sociale appliquée), Ottawa, and available on the SRSA web site (www.srdc.org). The success of the social economy and the spread of 'le mouvement communautaire' in Quebec belong to the factors that made possible the creation of a new left-wing, community-oriented political party, *Québec Solidaire*, in February 2006.

162   L. Boivin and M. Fortier, eds., *L'économie sociale: l'avenir d'une illusion* (Montréal; Fides, 1998).

163   "Economic Justice for All," no. 200, in David O'Brien and Thomas Shannon, eds., *Catholic Social Thought* (Maryknoll, NY: Orbis, 1992), 623.

164   *Mater et magistra*, 85–90; *Catholic Social Thought*, 98.

165   See the CCCB's 1961 Labour Day Message and 1976 statement "On Decent Housing for All," in E.F. Sheridan, ed., *Do Justice!*, 89 and 311.

166   See the pastoral statement of the CCCB, "Ethical Reflections on Canada's Socio-Economic Order" (1983), 50, in *Do Justice!*, 430; and the 1982 pastoral letter of Bishop Bertrand Blanchet, "Le mouvement coopératif," in Gérard Rocher, ed., *La justice sociale: Messages sociaux, économiques et politiques des évêques du Québec* (Montréal: Bellarmin, 1984), 325–326.

167   Moses Coady, *Masters of Their Own Destiny* (New York: Harper & Row, 1939).

168   See Gregory Baum, *Catholics and Canadian Socialism* (Toronto: James Lorimer, 1980), 194–195.

169   In *Sollicitudo rei socialis*, 15 (*Catholic Social Thought*, 403) John Paul II speaks of "the creative subjectivity of the citizens," a concept he repeatedly applies to defend initiative and responsibility in the economic and political order.

170   Proudhon adopted this term to honour a co-operative community in Lyon called 'the Mutualists.' See George Woodcock, *Pierre-Joseph Proudhon* (Montreal: Black Rose, 1987), 74.

171   Woodcock, 203.

172   Karl Polanyi, *The Great Transformation* [1944] (Boston: Beacon Press, 1957). See Gregory Baum, *Karl Polanyi: On Ethics and Economics* (Montreal: McGill-Queens University Press, 1996).

173   Tariq Ramadan, *Western Muslims and the Future of Islam* (New York: Oxford University Press, 2004), 199.

12

174   Jacques Maritain, *Primauté du spirituel* (Paris: Plon, 1927).

175   Maritain, *Primauté du spirituel*, 106.

176   Jacques Maritain, *Du régime temporel et de la liberté* (Paris: Desclée de Brouwer, 1933).

177   Jacques Maritain, *Christianisme et démocratie* (New York: Éditions de la Maison Française, 1943).

178   John Paul II, Homily at the Eucharist at Edmonton Airport, September 17, 1984, 4.

179   Karol Wojtyla (John Paul II), *The Acting Person* (Boston: Reidel Publishing, 1979).

180   For 'man as subject' and 'human subjectivity,' see *Laborem exercens* (1981), 6 and 12 and *Sollicitudo rei socialis* (1987), 15.

181   Daniel Tanguay, *Léo Strauss: Une biographie intellectuelle* (Paris: B. Grasset, 2003) and Shadia Drury, *The Political Ideas of Leo Strauss* (New York: PalgraveMacmillan, 2005). A vigorous debate about the ideas and influence of Leo Strauss is easily accessible on the Internet.

182   Alan Wolfe, "A Fascist Philosopher Helps Us Understand Contemporary Politics," *The Chronicle Review* (The Chronicle of Higher Education), April 2, 2004; Heinrich Meier, *Carl Schmitt and Leo Strauss: The Hidden Dialogue* (Chicago: University of Chicago Press, 1995).

13

183   *New Delhi to Uppsala, 1961–1968: Report of the Central Committee* (Geneva: WCC, 1968), 59–65.

184   Joseph Gremillion, ed., *The Gospel of Peace and Justice* (Maryknoll, NY: Orbis, 1976), 455–463.

185   Leonardo Boff and Gustavo Gutierrez (Catholic), José Miguez Bonino and Rubem Alves (Protestant).

186   Johann-Baptist Metz, Jürgen Moltmann and Dorothee Soelle.

187   Kari Levitt, *Silent Surrender* (Toronto: Macmillan, 1970).

188   It deserves to be remembered that by the 1960s, Leslie Dewart had published his radical theological reflections in *Christianity and Revolution: The Lesson of Cuba* (1962) and *The Future of Belief: Theism in a World Come of Age* (1966), and Donald Evans had offered his critical ideas in *Communist Faith and Christian Faith* (1964) and several essays.

189   A Brief to the Special Senate Committee on Poverty (June 1970), Development Demands Justice (March 1973), A Statement of Concern to the Prime Minister and Cabinet (March 1976): see E.F. Sheridan, ed., *Do Justice!* (Toronto: Jesuit Centre for Social Faith and Justice, 1987), 182–196, 239–249 and 295–306.

190   Christopher Lind and Joe Mihevc, eds., *Coalition for Justice* (Ottawa: Novalis, 1994).

191   My essay deals only with critical theology in English-speaking Canada; *Intersecting Voices* also contains essays by Carolyn Sharp on critical theology in Quebec (67–82), Cristina Vanin on feminist theology in English-speaking Canada (96–118), Monique Dumais on feminist theology in Quebec (83–95), Heather Eaton on ecologically concerned theology (246–265), and Harold Cardinal and Daryold Winkler on the emancipatory struggle of the Native peoples (192–222).

192   Martin Rumscheidt, ed., *Footnote to a Theology: The Karl Barth Colloquium of 1972* (Waterloo: Studies in Religion Supplement), 1974.

193   For the proceedings, see Benjamin Smillie, ed., *Political Theology in the Canadian Context* (Waterloo: Studies in Religion Supplement, 1982). For a report on the conference, see Gregory Baum, "Political Theology in Canada," *The Ecumenist*, 15 (Mar.-Apr., 1977), 33–46.

194   Gregory Baum, *The Church in Quebec* (Ottawa: Novalis, 1991), ch. 3, "Politisés chrétiens," 67–90.

195   Gregory Baum, *Theology and Society* (New York: Paulist Press, 1987): "Faith and Liberation: Development after Vatican II," 3–31 and "Towards a Canadian Catholic Social Theory," 66–87.

196   Patrick Kerans, *Sinful Social Structures* (New York: Paulist Press, 1974).

197   Gregory Baum, *Religion and Alienation,* 2nd ed. (Ottawa: Novalis, 2006), 168–171.

198   Juan Segundo, *The Liberation of Theology* (Maryknoll, NY: Orbis, 1976); Joe Holland, *Social Analysis: Linking Faith and Justice* (Maryknoll, NY: Orbis, 1984). See also the hermeneutical circle spelled out in the Canadian Catholic Bishops' statement, "Ethical Reflections on Canada's Socio-Economic Order" (1983), *Do Justice!*, E.F. Sheridan, ed., 411–434, 412.

199   Johann-Baptist Metz, *Theology of the World* (New York: Herder & Herder, 1969).

200   Gregory Baum and Harold Wells, "Political Theology in Conflict," *The Ecumenist*, 22 (Sept.–Oct., 1984), 81–87.

201   "Ethical Reflections on the Economic Crisis" (1982), *Do Justice!*, 399–410, 400.

202   Gregory Baum, *Compassion and Solidarity* (Toronto: Anansi, 1992), 76–80.

203   See note 53.

204   Ben Smillie, *Beyond the Social Gospel: Church Protest in the Prairies* (Saskatoon: Fifth House, 1991); Christopher Lind, *Something's Wrong Somewhere* (Halifax: Fernwood Publishing, 1995).

205   *Something's Wrong Somewhere*, 52–66.

206   "To Establish a Kingdom of Justice," *Catholic New Times*, June 17, 1979.

207   See note 191.

208   Peter Hamel, "The Aboriginal Rights Coalition," in Christoper Lind and Joe Mihevc, eds., *Coalitions for Justice,* 16–36.

209   Douglas Hall, *The Steward: A Biblical Image Come of Age* (Grand Rapids, MI: Eerdmans, 1991). His book was translated into French for the Quebec readership.

210   Ernie Regehr, "Project Ploughshares," in *Coalitions for Justice*, 185–202.

211   Henriette Thompson, "The Inter-Church Committee on Refugees," in *Coalitions for Justice*, 203–218.

212   Cyril Powles, "Christianity and the Third World," *Studies in Religion*, 13 (1984), 131–144.

213   Lee Cormie, "The Hermeneutical Privilege of the Oppressed," *Proceedings of the Catholic Theological Society of America,* vol. 33 (1978), 155–181; "Liberation and Salvation: A First World View," in B. Mahan and L.D. Richesin, eds., *The Challenge of Liberation Theology: A First World Response* (Maryknoll, NY: Orbis, 1981), 21–47.

214   Terry Brown and Christopher Lind, eds., *Justice as Mission: An Agenda for the Church* (Burlington, ON: Trinity Press, 1985).

215   Harold Wells and Roger Hutchinson, eds., *A Long and Faithful March* (The United Church Publishing House, 1989).

216   Ted Reeve, "God and the Market: The United Church of Canada Moderator's Consultation on Faith and the Economy," *The Ecumenist* 38 (Winter 2001), 1–5.

217   See Lee Cormie's essay on the Canadian Ecumenical Jubilee Initiative in *Intersecting Voices: Critical Theologies in a Land of Diversity*.

218   Chapter 11 in this book examines community development and the social economy in the light of Catholic social teaching.

219   Murray MacAdam, ed., *From Corporate Greed to Common Good: Canadian Churches and Community Economic Development* (Ottawa: Novalis, 1998).

220   Kenneth Westhues, *The Working Centre: Experiment in Social Change* (Waterloo, ON: Working Centre Publication, 1995).

Afterword

221   Gregory Baum, *Amazing Church* (Ottawa: Novalis and Maryknoll, NY: Orbis, 2005).

222   Gabriel Flynn, ed., *Yves Congar: Theologian of the Church* (Louvain: Peeters Press and Grand Rapids, MI: Eerdmans, 2005), 1.

223   www.ccee.ch/english/fields/islamcommittee.htm. Accessed October 31, 2006.

224   See Philippians 2:7.

225   Jürgen Moltmann, *God in Creation* (San Francisco: Harper and Row, 1985); John Polkinghorne, ed., *The Work of Love: Creation as Kenosis* (Grand Rapids, MI: Eerdmans, 2001).

226   Lucien Richard, *Christ: The Self-Emptying of God* (New York : Paulist Press, 1997).

227   *The New York Review of Books*, vol. 53, no. 18, November 16, 2006.

Author's Note

An earlier version of "Muslim-Christian Dialogue after 9/11" was given as a lecture at the Centre for Catholic Experience at St. Jerome's University in Waterloo, Ontario, on January 20, 2006. It was recorded by CBC Radio One for future broadcast and subsequently published in *The Ecumenist*, 43 (Winter 2006), 1–8.

An earlier version of "Interreligious Dialogue Attentive to Western Enlightenment" was given as a paper at the Global Congress of the World's Religions after September 11, Montreal, September 11–15, 2006, organized by Prof. Arvind Sharma of McGill University's Faculty of Religious Studies.

"Relativism No, Pluralism Yes" also appears in *Love and Freedom: Essays in Honour of Harold G. Wells* (Toronto: *Toronto Journal of Theology*, 2007).

An earlier version of "Jewish-Christian Dialogue under the Shadow of the Israeli-Palestinian Conflict" first appeared in *Juifs et chrétiens: Théologiques* (Université de Montréal), vol. 11 (2003), 205–220.

An earlier version of "Jewish and Christian Reflections on Divine Providence" appeared in *The Ecumenist*, 39 (Winter 2002), 6–13.

An earlier version of The Post-Secular Society: A Proposal of Jürgen Habermas appeared in Marc Dumas et al., eds., *Théologie et Culture* (Québec: Les presses de l'Université Laval, 2004), 7–20.

"Contrasting Interpretations of Religious Pluralism and Modernity" is based on two articles of mine: "The Cardinal and the Pope (I)" *The Ecumenist*, 42 (Summer 2005), 1–5 and "The Cardinal and the Pope (II)" *The Ecumenist*, 42 (Fall 2005), 16–19.

An earlier version of "Social Injustice in Today's World" appeared in K. Arsenault et al., eds., *Stone Soup: Reflections on Economic Injustice* (Montréal: Éditions Paulines, 1997).

An earlier version of "Resisting Empire" was presented in French at the Congrès de l'Entraide missionnaire of September 2004 and later published in English in *The Ecumenist*, 42 (Spring 2005), 9–12.

"Pope John Paul II's Social Teaching" was published in *The New Catholic Encyclopedia: Jubilee Volume – The Wojtyla Years* (Washington, D.C.: The Catholic University of America, 2001), 43–51.

A version of "Alternative Models of Economic Development" appears in *Journal of Catholic Social Thought*, Winter 2007.

An earlier version of "The Common Good in a Pluralistic Society" was delivered as a lecture to the Ontario English Catholic Teachers Association (OECTA) in August 2006.

An earlier version of "Critical Theology in Canada" was published in D. Simon and D. Schweitzer, eds., *Intersecting Voices: Critical Theologies in a Land of Diversity* (Ottawa: Novalis, 2005), 49–66